Ashley Hay writes journalism and short fiction and has published one previous book, *The Secret*. She has worked for *The Independent Monthly*, the University of London, and *The Bulletin*. She lives in Sydney.

Also by Ashley Hay

The Secret: the strange marriage of Annabella Milbanke and Lord Byron

gum

ashley hay

Duffy & Snellgrove
Sydney

Published by Duffy & Snellgrove in 2002
PO Box 177 Potts Point NSW 1335 Australia
info@duffyandsnellgrove.com.au

Distributed by Pan Macmillan

The writing of this book was assisted by the
Commonwealth Government through the Arts Council,
its arts funding and advisory body.

Cover design by Alex Snellgrove
Cover image by Robyn Stacey
With thanks to the Royal Botanic Gardens Sydney

Typeset by Cooper Graphics
Printed by Griffin Press

ISBN 1 876631 26 0

visit our website: www.duffyandsnellgrove.com.au

for Steve Offner

This old slow battlefield: parings of armour,
cracked collars, elbows, scattered on the ground.

New trees step out of old: lemon and ochre
splitting out of grey everywhere …

you can never reach the heart of the gum forest.

Les Murray, from 'The Gum Forest'

contents

the seven peacekeepers

It's a tall and elegant gum, and it leans back into the bush at an angle that makes space for it among the geebungs and the banksias, the red gums and the bloodwoods nearby. I'm halfway along a track that runs from the inland shore of Botany Bay's south head across to the coast when I see it. The space around it makes it look like it's standing in a pool of light.

gum

Its trunk, from a distance, is clear and pale, and if I mimic its angle, I can take in its full length. To look at a big tree, you have to tilt your head back, right back – it's a reverential way to stand. I follow its stretch, from the roots spreading under the ground, past the rough dark bark where its trunk breaches the earth and on to its stripped smooth skin, through the elbows and armpits where its branches – some dark and bare, some pale with light leaves at their ends – push out. The leaves are sparse, and the blue-grey of their green makes them look like part of the sky as much as part of the tree. Covered with thousands of tiny mouths, they breathe in carbon dioxide and breathe out oxygen, while their surfaces turn with the path of the sun.

It's hard to avoid eucalypts in Australia: divide the continent into portions of one degree latitude and longitude and you'd have 808 squares with these trees in all but 35 of them. Over 700 species make up the genus and, with a dozen exceptions, this is the only place where they grow naturally – from shaggy-barked blackbutts on the east coast's dunes, to the bright bark of snow gums up at the alpine treeline, to silky-white ghost gums in the centre. There are scrubby mallees that won't pass shoulder-height, and pillars of mountain ash that shoot a hundred metres into the sky: in Western Australia there are dark-leaved jarrahs that can grow to either of these heights. Site-specific, they carve the country into distinct ribbons and patches: one species grows up a hill and stops where another suddenly starts and grows down the other side.

Most Australians know a bit about eucalypts (it's easier, though botanically dubious, to roll them all down to the vernacular of 'gum trees'), even if it's just something they learnt at school. Something about huge root systems perhaps, or the lignotubers that sprout new life after a bushfire, or maybe something more poetic. The way sunlight breaks through their leaves and makes them look molten. The smell of those leaves crushed – the smell of the whole country, some say. Sailors used to call to their passengers as they approached Australia's edge: 'Come up on deck, you can smell the eucalypts.' Or the sound their leaves makes in the wind – it's different from the noise a breeze draws from other trees. A French soldier looking for a way through the Blue Mountains in 1802 described it as 'surges'. It's like the sound you hear when you push your fingers through your hair – a sound that you hear inside yourself as well as outside.

People walk past gum trees every day. Sometimes they see them in another country and think how far both they and the tree are from home; sometimes they pass the same gum again and again, and don't even register it. And sometimes some people begin to look at a gum and find that they can never completely get their gaze away from this group of trees again. They might be scientists or explorers, foresters or conservationists, artists or writers, but they all become eucalyptographers, caught up with work that is inextricably eucalyptic. They take the trees on; they champion them.

Walking along this track at Botany Bay, I know how these obsessions work. Like anything, the more you know about eucalypts, the more you want to know – and the more you know, the more impossible it becomes to walk past a gum tree without stopping, and looking, and seeing what it is.

This one, between the coast and the bay, is a scribbly gum. That trunk, which is a clear, light and solid colour from a distance, becomes close-up a pattern of ochres and golds, oranges and tans, rosy-reds, all overlapping in whorls and shadings and stains. These are the colours of the rocks in the cliffs and the shore nearby, but this tree trunk doesn't feel like stone. It's warm, and sort of like velvet. The bark gives a bit under your hand when you press it, like a cushion with words embroidered on its surface – even though the sepia ink of its distinctive squiggles is larvae left by some kind of moth. The scribbles make it easy to believe that there are stories hidden in the trees: if you could turn at the right moment or hold your head at the right angle, you'd catch their calligraphy resolving into words.

Looking up through the scribbly gum's leaves, at the distance and space always visible through their gaps, I wonder what sort of story you'd get if you ran the eucalyptographers together. If you joined up the different things they had noticed in their different lifetimes, perhaps you could see through what people had done to these trees to how the trees had affected them in return – the way you could see the land, the light, through the trees' leaves. No other landscape in the world is so dominated by one genus – and just as 'gum' became shorthand for the trees, the trees became shorthand for the place.

People have always wanted stories about Australia's trees. Even before Europeans were certain that these antipodes existed, they predicted that its trees would be loaded – not with gum but with *balf*, a reddish-brown fruit, something like an olive. Eat four, and you'd be drunk. Eat six, and you'd sleep for a day. Eat any more than that, and you'd die – but in such a state of ecstasy. Trees of exotic potential.

And before Europeans were certain the antipodes existed, the D'harawal people – who lived on the land where this scribbly gum grows – had their own story for its trees. It was the story of a leader, the Yandel'bana, and his seven warriors who tried to establish peace between all the country's clans. Faced by a particularly malevolent bunch of spirits, the Wiree, the seven warriors were turned into seven kinds of eucalypt. Disguised, they would lure the Wiree in, then reveal themselves as men, then trap them.

The warrior Mai'andowi, who knew medicines, became a gum with young leaves that could be steamed to a vapour for almost any sickness. Bai'yali, the firemaker, became a tree whose inner bark was good for tinder. Boo'angi, Terri'yergro and Kai'yeroo – who made or wielded the best weapons – became three trees that could be used to make weapons themselves. Bourrounj, the warrior who found food, became a gum with smoke that could push evil spirits out of men. And Mugga'go, good at finding places for the warriors to sleep and rest, became a tall hard gum that was good for shelters itself.

The Yandel'bana remained as himself, putting down his weapons, washing his body, and piling up a large fire that he coaxed with tinder from each of his warriors' trees. He took some bark from the trunk of one of his men, he took some sap from another. He took their leaves, branches, gumnuts, and the nectar of their blossoms. And from the dirt under the place where the trunk of his seventh warrior stood, he took a root. He added it all to the pyre in the centre of the circle made by the seven trees, his transformed peacekeepers.

The air filled with a million sparks like fireflies shooting up to multiply the stars. And the Yandel'bana lay down by its warmth and pretended to sleep as the Wiree moved towards his beacon.

In the middle of the night's darkness, they planned, they'd steal his spirit. His, and the other seven. But they saw only one man, the Yandel'bana, lying by himself next to a fire. They disguised themselves as the Yandel'bana's mother – all concern, all compassion. 'My son,' the Wiree said, 'you have returned safely – but where are your friends?' And they shook the Yandel'bana's shoulder while he stretched and lolled and seemed to be just waking up, tired after a long day's walk.

He smiled at the Wiree as if he did see his mother, and he said, 'My friends are safe,' as the bark and leaves fell away from his warrior-trees. The Wiree, panicking as they found they were suddenly surrounded, turned themselves into the malevolent unpredictability of a Williwilli and tried to escape in its chaos. But the seven treemen, their hands held to make a fast circle, walked slowly towards the whirling sorcerers, crowding their evil into the fire where its dark powers slid away.

Recovered from trunks and bark, each warrior found a single wound. One was missing a tooth; another was missing some skin from his leg; there was blood on another's arm. The warrior who had given a whole branch to the fire was missing his little finger – the warrior who had lost one of his roots was missing a toe. One stood with wet, swollen eyes, and another with a bald patch of missing hair.

But the Wiree's evil was gone.

The Yandel'bana and his seven warriors lived the rest of their lives in the land where they defeated the Wiree, and when they died, they were transformed again into the trees they had become that night. Their names became the gums' names: Mai'andowi, the smooth-barked gum; Bai'yali, the stringy-bark; Boo'angi, spotted; Terri'yergro, scaly-barked; Kai'yeroo, the ribbon gum; Bourrounj, the peppermint; and Mugga'go, the ironbark. The Yandel'bana was given the round, sculpted shape of an angophora – a tree that thrives near gums – and they grew together, towards the sky, the seven peacekeepers and their leader.

On the edge of the coast in the D'harawal place where the story of the seven warriors comes from, where the Yandel'bana's gums had stood, protective, for thousands of years, and where the scribbly gum grows tall and elegant now, a creaking wooden ship appeared one day in April 1770. The D'harawal people watched it come in – such a small thing from such a large ocean.

This was the beginning of *Eucalyptus*.

becoming eucalyptus

The tents look pretty amongst the trees ...

—Lt Ralph Clark of the First Fleet, 1788

The creaking ship was the *Endeavour*, a converted collier making her way around the south seas under the captaincy of James Cook. She was a floating outpost of the British Empire and all that it represented. She had left Plymouth more than a year and a half earlier, dispatched by the British Admiralty to observe the transit of Venus from Tahiti, with an additional set of secret instructions for Cook to sail his ship west, and west again, to search for the mythical Great Southern Continent – the true Antipodes, the place where the trees of *Balf* grew.

She carried two things which would make a world of difference to the Yandel'bana's trees – not to mention the people who lived beneath them. One was the flag required to claim land for the King of England. The other was a wealthy and enthusiastic young botanist called Joseph Banks. Just 25 years old, Banks had set sail kitted out for botanising, with a band of artists, naturalists, servants and dogs – plus his library and his guitar – crammed into what was usually the captain's cabin. Born with a curiosity about the natural world and a private fortune big enough to indulge it handsomely, he had talked his way onto the *Endeavour* through personal access to the First Lord of the Admiralty. 'Every blockhead,' he remarked, undertook a Grand Tour through the cultural highlights and fleshpots of Europe. 'My Grand Tour,' he said, 'shall be one around the whole globe.'

He had spent more than £10,000 equipping himself and his party: everything from boxes and barrels and an underwater telescope to special wax – both beeswax and Myrica – for storing seeds. As one observer commented, watching the laden mob set sail, 'no people ever went to sea better fitted out for the purpose of Natural History'. Banks and his team had trawled plantlife from Brazil (sneaking ashore at night because the viceroy refused them permission to collect), Tierra del Fuego, Tahiti, the waters of the Pacific, and New Zealand.

Completing the map of New Zealand's coastline, the *Endeavour* had paused. The Great Southern Continent had failed to materialise in the middle of the Pacific Ocean.

Cook considered his options, and chose to head further west, 'till we fall in with the East Coast of New Holland', which he would chart to its northernmost point. He would take home another new map for the Admiralty.

Other European and Asian ships had touched at New Holland, or passed by it, for centuries. One Dutch captain even acknowledged that its west coast had 'many fine smelling trees and out of their wood is to be drawne oyl smelling as a rose'. However 'for the rest,' the Dutchman shrugged, the trees were 'small and miserable' and the place, as a whole, was summarily dismissed as 'nothing but a barren, dry wasteland.' Different sailors had seen different trees, dismissing them as other things that grew in other parts of the world. No one had dropped anchor long enough or gone inland far enough to get any but the sketchiest idea of the place. No one had claimed it for their kings or countries.

James Cook's crew sighted the eastern edge of its land on April 19, 1770, and Joseph Banks was ambivalent about what he could see. One day the country 'rose in gentle sloping hills which had the appearance of the highest fertility'; half a week along it resembled 'the back of a lean cow, covered in general with long hairs, but, nevertheless, where her scraggy hipbones have stuck out further than they ought, accidental rubs and knocks have entirely bared them of their share of covering.'

For nine days the *Endeavour* sailed up the continent's east coast, watching the plumes of smoke that indicated inhabitants and looking for somewhere to land. Finally, seeing the mouth of a great open bay, they sailed in, past the sandstone cliffs, past the trees, and they dropped anchor. Stingray Harbour, Cook wrote carefully on his map.

The next day, they lowered a boat and headed for the shore. Cook, Banks, a South Sea Islander (whom Cook had requisitioned in Tahiti, hoping he would speak the language of other native people the *Endeavour* might meet), and men with muskets. The shore, the land beyond it, was sandy and barren. Further in, there were trees.

Cook and his men saw huts made from sheets of bark and canoes made of the same stuff, curled and tied at the ends. They saw the people who lived in these huts. The English fired their muskets; the men on shore threw a stone. 'Emmidiatly after this,' Cook wrote, 'we landed, which we had no sooner done than they throw'd two darts at us.'

They stood on the shore of this unknown place, scratching in the sand for fresh water and peering through the trees. The D'harawal people peered back. Cook left some strings of beads and ribbons in the bark huts on the beach, taking away with him the pile of fish-bone darts he found on the floor. Then the white men rowed back to their ship, and the black families – 'blacker than any we have seen in the Voyage tho by no means negro,' commented Banks – went back to their huts, ignoring the bright, shiny gifts.

While the *Endeavour*'s men filled cask after cask with fresh water, hauled in net after net of fish, cut swathes through the soft patches of grass for the long-suffering stock still on board the boat, and didn't get much further in communicating with the locals, Banks began to collect. His party of helpers had dwindled: two of his servants had stolen rum, drunk it outside, and frozen to death in South America; an artist had died of dysentery in Tahiti. But he still had his companion naturalist, Daniel Solander, and one artist – Sydney Parkinson – to single-handedly draw all that he and Solander could collect.

They ranged around the water's edge, and as far into this new land as they could go in a day. They stripped leaves, nipped blossoms, picked flowers. Sometimes there were just the two naturalists, their servants and the dogs; sometimes there were as many as ten men, including Cook, all armed, walking into the country 'until we compleatly tired ourselves'. They walked around the south arm of the bay, and down the southern coast. They walked three or four miles up the coast from the bay's northern head, sampling the plants they passed.

Every day, they brought more and more of this 'non-descript' stuff (meaning that no European eyes had seen it before or, more importantly, had named it) back to the ship. Then Banks and Solander and Parkinson holed up in their one room, reeking of salt and men and months at sea and brimming with specimens, and the two naturalists explained to the artist what he should capture of each plant while he drew things he had never seen before.

'We sat till dark at the great table with the draughtsman opposite and showed him in what way to make his drawings,' Banks wrote: 'ourselves made rapid descriptions of all the details … while the specimen was still fresh.' (They had so much stuff that Banks gave up a whole day on the seashore with the plants spread out around him in drying paper, held down by rocks.) And as the specimens wilted and faded, Parkinson sketched faster and faster: sharp black lines to outline the leaf and flower, and notes to himself on the colours to be washed in later, building up his own code, while the botanists pressed and dried and stored their twigs and leaves.

There was one kind of tree that caught every eye. It was the biggest they could see, and it was the most ubiquitous. Most noticeably, it oozed a thick, sticky resin. *Sanguis draconis*, Banks suggested: the tree oozed Dragon's Blood, like trees in Madeira and the Canary Islands. Rough brownish-grey bark fractured over its trunk and branches like a mosaic; its long leaves were glossy green on the top, lighter underneath. It was a comforting thing to find because it corresponded with the accounts of two earlier European sailors who had sailed to the underside of the world and published journals from their voyages. Abel Tasman, passing by what he called Van Diemen's Land in 1642, had commented on the gum oozing out of trees, and the piratical William Dampier, making for the west coast of New Holland several decades later, had compared the gum he saw trickling from trees there to Dragon's Blood. 'The gum distils out of the knots or cracks that are in the bodies of the trees,' Banks could read from the copy of Dampier's book that he had with him. 'We compared it with some of the Gum-Dragon or Dragon's Blood that was aboard, and it was of the same colour and taste.'

There was no doubt that it was the plants – the trees – that made an impression on the visitors. So much so that Cook rubbed out 'Stingray Harbour' on his map, and changed it altogether: 'The great quantity of plants Mr Banks and Dr Solander have found in this place occasioned my giving it the name of Botany Bay,' he wrote, before summarising the timber available as 'in great plenty, yet there is very little variety; the biggest trees are as large or larger than our Oaks in England, and grows a good deal like them, and yields a reddish gum; the wood itself is heavy, hard and black.'

As Cook made this entry, the *Endeavour* had already left its marks on Botany Bay. A sailor, dead from tuberculosis, had been buried with a packet of seeds from his sweetheart's garden in his pocket. The trunk of one of the trees closest to the British landing point had been carved with the ship's name and the date of its arrival. The English colours had been raised on the shore.

The ship weighed anchor, sailed back out through the bay's heads, turned left, and continued north along the coast. Within a week, Banks, Solander and Parkinson had completed 'drawing the plants got in the last harbour, which had been kept fresh till this time by means of tin chests and wet cloths. In 14 days just,' Banks boasted to his journal, 'one draughtsman has made 94 sketch drawings, so quick a hand has he acquired by use.'

They didn't have a single drawing of those numerous gum-oozing trees at Botany Bay, although they had taken a specimen from one of the branches. There was a proper way of doing everything in 1770, and the rules of botany demanded that floral specimens be drawn with blossoms. The gum trees had not been in flower.

They landed at Bustard Bay, more than two weeks up the coast, and saw 'many of the trees yielding gum like *sanguis draconis*: they differed, however, from those seen in the last harbour in having their leaves longer and hanging down like those of a weeping willow,' Banks observed, 'tho notwithstanding that I believe they were of the same species.' Another week on, they made land at Thirsty Sound, by which time this gum stuff was so familiar that Banks wrote simply: 'Most of the trees were gum trees.'

He called them gum trees for the first time, and the name slipped into common usage. When the *Endeavour* ran aground on the Great Barrier Reef, the trees were finally found in blossom, and Parkinson sketched a narrow-leaved red ironbark and a smooth white-barked gum. Like the trees oozing their gum in Botany Bay, these seemed to Solander to resemble trees he had seen and designated 'Metrosideros' in Tahiti and New Zealand. These trees, he thought, were the same kind of thing: it made sense that a tree in New Holland would be the same as a tree growing just across the ocean in New Zealand. The undrawn plant from Botany Bay, for example, Solander would call *Metrosideros gummifera*.

As the repaired ship cleared the northernmost point of the New Welsh coast (Cook named it New Wales, claiming its entire length for King George III), 'gum trees' was the accepted way of referring to this ubiquitous timber. They had found it at each of the landfalls they made, and Cook, summarising his knowledge of this 670 leagues of land (3200 kilometres) said flatly that 'The Woods do not produce any great variety of trees. There are only two or three sorts that can be called timber; the largest is the Gum Tree, which growes all over the Countrey, the wood of this tree is too hard and ponderous for the most common uses.'

Still, snuggled in among the 30,382 plant specimens which Joseph Banks carried back to London, the gum trees were making their first trip to the other side of the world.

What should have happened was simple: natural science expected its practitioners to sail to new parts of the world, collect previously unknown things, and return them all to the centres of European learning. Most importantly, the names and descriptions attached to these new things were then published as quickly as possible, allowing everyone who didn't have the opportunity of sailing around the world to know what they would find if they could.

According to this scheme of things, the *Endeavour* would sail back into London where Joseph Banks would be hailed by the scientific establishment. Honours would be conferred, and Banks and Solander would begin to work their way through their collection. Botanical names – like Solander's 'Metrosideros' – would be published and pass into general usage. Then, as they looked at the 'Metrosideros' and the New Welsh 'gum trees', Banks and Solander would realise that these weren't the same as each other at all. They would recognise the gum tree as its own genus, its own type, and give it a new name. After a short and industrious stretch of time, Banks would publish a stunningly engraved and staggeringly comprehensive account of everything he had brought home. Botanists and natural historians from one end of the kingdom to the other would thus have access to this exotic new resource, making the flora of a place 12,000 miles away – gums, acacias, banksias, casuarinas – familiar to scholars who would never go further than their sitting rooms.

But what actually happened was this: Joseph Banks

arrived home with his 3600 different species of plant, and he committed the botanical equivalent of stuffing them all under the bed. It was true that he was feted from one end of polite society to the next: he was presented to the King ahead of Cook and he was hailed by Europe's greatest botanists for his efforts on the expedition as the 'immortal Banks'. His house, already bursting with collections (Banks hoarded everything from important specimens down to visiting cards and lists of how much his friends weighed), teemed with leaves and seeds and flowers and bits of bark, preserved in jars, pressed into papers, sketched from Parkinson's original drawings by the finest botanical draughtsmen. Any gentleman could wander in as if it were some vast exhibition, and it became known as 'a perfect museum; every room,' one visitor enthused, 'contains an inestimable treasure ... What raptures they must have felt,' the visitor supposed, 'to land upon country where everything was new to them! Whole forests of nondescript trees clothed with the most beautiful flowers and foliage.'

In one room sat a representative selection of all the *Endeavour* specimens – including the 1400 or so new species that had never been seen in Europe before. But plant matter sitting in a room was not a contribution to science: it was just a repository of the exotic – a slightly larger cabinet of curiosities than other noblemen might gather. Banks could have everything arranged and catalogued and even named in his maze of cupboards and collections, but if he didn't publish anything, it counted for nothing. You could give a plant any name you liked, but a name wasn't a name until it was published. In the later decades of the 18th century, natural historians were taken up with one pursuit above all others – the mission to classify and name the whole world.

This grand quest had sprung from the systematic bosom of Carl von Linné ('Linnaeus', in the Latin he wrote in), a Swedish taxonomist who had devised a nomenclature for animals, vegetables and minerals which would clearly mark out which was related to which, and where the boundaries stood between different families, different genera, different species. His system was based, in the case of flora, on the gender of plants – which did give rise to some ribald remarks among naturalists and other intellectuals. But it had caught on as a way of trying to make sense of the world. It was Linnaeus who had taught Banks' Dr Solander all he knew, and it was Linnaeus who called Banks immortal. So great was Banks' contribution to knowledge, he said, that he hoped this whole new continent of New Holland would be renamed 'Banksia' in his honour. He wrote more than once asking about the progress of the great project to publish the *Endeavour*'s floral collections.

There were several problems. First, 30,000 was an immense number of specimens for anyone to get through. Second, coming back from the South Seas made Joseph Banks famous – and being famous took up a lot of his time. Third, it became clear that what he enjoyed in the project of natural history was the collecting – the travel, the adventure – not the tedious comparing and contrasting, describing and transcribing, needed to turn sheets of plant specimens into a scholarly volume. While Dr Solander began to work his way painstakingly through the plants, Banks spent his time being painted by one of London's leading portraitists. He looked suave, wearing the feathered cloak of a Maori chief, surrounded by artefacts from the voyage, and he leaned forward, looking as if the excitement and the potential of the whole world was within his reach.

While scientific and botanical Europe waited to read Banks' account of the marvellous things he had brought home, he became busy with other things, one of which was a plan to travel back to the south seas with Cook on his second voyage of discovery. A bigger, better expedition, Banks envisaged: if the Royal Society had thought the £10,000 spent on the *Endeavour* was substantial, they would be astonished by what he had planned for his return. An entire portion of one of the ships under Cook's command would be modified. He would take a party of sixteen, including a celebrated painter. He would even, sneakily, pick up a mistress in Madeira, having sent her on ahead of himself, disguised as a 'Mr Burnett' and ready to be brought on board to complete his extravagant party. He wanted more dogs. He wanted more space. And he wanted, at the other end of the journey, many, many more plants. Linnaeus wrote sternly that it did not do for one to go off again when work on the first load of plants one had brought home was still unfinished … Banks and Solander ignored him.

But by the time Cook tried to sail, the *Resolution* – after Banks had finished designing and installing his modifications to its structure at a personal cost of £5000 – was so cumbersome and top-heavy that it lolled and listed and could hardly make any headway. The modifications, the Admiralty told Banks stiffly, would have to go. They would not, said Banks: he would rather withdraw from the whole expedition. Which he did – and took his party (without the unfortunate 'Mr Burnett', whose presence in Madeira was reported to the British Admiralty several months later by a rather bemused Captain Cook) off on an expedition to Iceland instead.

Cook sailed, with the *Resolution* and the *Discovery*, back into the Pacific, back across those huge blue waters that held no sign of the Great Southern Continent, with two new naturalists on one of the ships, and no plans to revisit any of the land that had been rechristened from New Wales to New South Wales. But in dreadful weather somewhere below Van Diemen's Land in 1774, the two vessels lost sight of each other. Heading for a safe anchorage, the *Resolution* reached Adventure Bay on Bruny Island, and the gum trees got their second chance to attract the attention of British botany. The only problem was, Cook's two botanists were on the *Discovery*, on the other side of the Tasman Sea. Still, the captain of the *Resolution*, Tobias Furneaux, understood the new obligations His Majesty's mariners had to natural history in the wake of Joseph Banks' mighty undertaking. While his ship took water and wood, he described the country around the bay, paying particular attention to its forests.

'The sides of the hills are covered with large trees,' he saw, 'and very thick, growing to a great height before they branch off. They are, all of them, of the evergreen kind, and different to any I ever saw: the wood is very brittle and easily split; there is very little variety of sorts, having seen but two.' Describing these he said, 'the leaves of one are long and narrow, and the seed (of which I got a few) is in the shape of a button and has a very agreeable smell. The leaves of the other are like the bay, and it has a seed like the whitehorn with an agreeable spicy taste and smell. Out of the trees we cut down for firewood, there issued some gum, which the surgeon called gumlac.'

Furneaux pocketed his handful of seeds, and carried them back to England and the King's Botanic Gardens at Kew, now under the directorship of Banks. They were pressed into a pot of soil and sprouted in next to no time. 'Metrosideros', Banks pronounced, like those trees in Tahiti, New Zealand, and Botany Bay – and soon enough they were being sold under that name by London's nurserymen.

Just under three years after Furneaux's harvest, Cook's third and final voyage sailed into the same bay on Bruny Island. This time, proper botanical specimens were collected from the trees by 'my surgeon, with his usual diligence', wrote Cook. And where Cook had dismissed what he saw of New South Wales in 1770 as entirely without 'any one thing that can become an article in trade to invite Europeans to fix a settlement upon it,' he conceded that these tall, new gum trees were 'fit for spars, oars, and many other uses; and would, on occasion, make good masts (perhaps none better), if a method could be found to lighten' the timber.

William Anderson, Cook's surgeon, took great botanical care with his description. The trees, he reported, grew 'to a great height, and in general quite straight, branching but little till towards the top.' He described the bark: 'white, which makes them appear, at a distance, as if they had been peeled.' The gum that was often trapped beneath it had an astringent taste. He examined the leaves, the clusters of white flowers, and the fruit. Of these buds, he saw that there were two types, some smaller, some larger, and he thought that this made it 'somewhat probable that there are two *species* of this tree'. He ate the gum, he ate the bark from the smaller branches, he ate the fruit and the leaves, and he found them to have 'an agreeable pungent taste, and an aromatic smell, not unlike the peppermint. And in its nature,' he suggested, the tree had 'some affinity with the *myrtus*' – the myrtaceae family.

The first person to pay a gum tree such particular and botanical attention, Anderson wrote his suggestion for a name for the species – *Aromadendrum* – onto the specimen sheet that he carried home, carefully pressed into lush paper, to be presented to Joseph Banks, director of the King's Botanic Gardens and recognised expert on Pacific flora.

It was 1778. The gums struck from Tobias Furneaux's seeds were propagating happily in fashionable hothouses around England. The gums brought home in the *Endeavour* were still waiting to be published and made known to the world – and William Anderson's Aromadendrums were sent to join them. With his description of them merely published in an account of exploration, and *Aromadendrum* only written in pencil on a specimen sheet that was swallowed up by Banks' capacious repository, the trees remained unnamed and 'nondescript'.

It took the arrival in London in 1786 of a tree-obsessed Frenchman, looking to avoid the turmoil of French politics at the time, to get the gums named. Eucalypts were classified by neither Joseph Banks nor anyone who had ever seen them growing in their natural state. They were named by Charles Louis L'Héritier de Brutelle, an amateur botanist, magistrate by profession, and an aristocratic supporter of the theory of revolution. As any botanist visiting London would have, he wanted to see Joseph Banks' expansive herbarium.

L'Héritier liked trees: 'they are the part that is most neglected by all botanists,' he said, and his contemporaries acknowledged his lack of interest in the smaller plants, saying that he did 'nothing with herbs'. His overall botanical mission, while in London, was 'to publish new plants, not illustrated or badly known.' Banks' unexamined repositories were exactly the place for him. In the library of Banks' grand house on Soho Square, L'Héritier took out the dried piece of tree collected on Cook's third voyage. The fruit was barrel- or egg-shaped, a wooden bud with lips closing around a hollow centre. He thought, as Anderson had, that it belonged to the same family as a myrtle, or a peppermint. There was a smooth casing – an operculum – around the developing flowers. He turned it, and thought not of anything Latin (the language Linnaeans usually went for), but rather Greek: *eu*, meaning 'well', and *klyptus*, meaning covered. *Eucalyptus*. Its leaves – quite asymmetrical, quite unbalanced in the way they grew – suggested *obliqua*.

Eucalyptus obliqua, he wrote carefully, naming the specimen, naming the species, starting a new genus.

He arranged to have it drawn by one of the leading botanical illustrators of the day, planning to include it in a book, his *Sertum Anglicum*, literally an 'English wreath', a token of gratitude to English botanists after his fifteen months in London. It would be, he hoped, 'a special work [on] the rarest plants of which I had drawings made.' The book was a rather haphazard collection, with thirteen new genera (out of the 35 he had studied) and 65 new species (from 124). L'Héritier had wanted to call all the new genera after English botanists, but could only come up with seven names (Banks, for instance, was already given to the *Banksia*) – and the gum tree was one of the ones that missed out.

His book finally appeared in late 1788, giving the trees their Western botanical name as the British convicts bivouacked beneath them on the shore of European Australia for the first time.

For the disturbance of their landscape as the English moved in, the eucalypts, their continent, and the people who lived among them had Joseph Banks to thank. He might have thought that strips of the coastline resembled nothing so much as the back end of a scraggy bovine – with possibly enough resources to support anyone unlucky enough to find themselves shipwrecked on it – but when it came to recommending a place where several prison-hulks' worth of convicts might be offloaded, he could think of no finer destination than Botany Bay. On the basis of just over a week there, Banks advocated its good climate, its arable soil, its 'cowardly' natives, its abundant fresh fish, its plentiful wood, water and pasture, and rounded off by saying he expected any colony established there would be self-sufficient within a year.

Off sailed eleven ships and a thousand or so people, of whom 750 were convicts and the rest were the people required to administer them and guard them and heal them and pray for them and bury them if they died. The white settlement of Australia was a fast-tracked and hellish enterprise. The governor, Arthur Phillip, had argued hard for an advance party – well provisioned – to be sent off to plant crops, erect shelter, and establish a British foothold on the continent for their arrival. But the government dithered so long about its decision to send anyone anywhere that there was suddenly not enough time.

They sailed towards the blank map Cook had named, with Banks' voice assuring them regarding the indigenous population: 'I am inclined to believe that they would speedily abandon the country to the newcomers.'

Phillip took one look at the botanist's playground and declared it uninhabitable. Thousands of miles from supplies – from anywhere – there was nothing much waiting for them but that grave of Cook's sailor, sprouting roses on the wrong side of the world. In the height of summer, Phillip couldn't even find a decent fresh water source.

In the first month of 1788, the D'harawal people watched from the edge of the trees as the eleven ships which had arrived in Botany Bay sailed off again five days later. About twenty kilometres up the coast they went, into the land of another language, another people, through a deep and glorious harbour and onto a shore running with fresh water and covered with tall, elegant gums. Their silvery trunks, with edges of blue and rose-pink in their bark and slender grey-green leaves, were so thick that 'each man stepped from the boat literally into a wood'.

Phillip ordered the first of them to be cut down on January 27, 1788 – the day after he had hoisted the flag and announced the place as Sydney (not in honour of Sydney Parkinson, but after the Home and Colonial Secretary who had dispatched him and his fleet) – and this soon became 'the principal business' of the convicts, 'clearing the land, cutting, grubbing and burning down trees, sawing timber and plank.'

Assuming that the trees around Port Jackson would be the same species Cook had written about down the coast in Botany Bay (which wasn't necessarily the case), Phillip acknowledged that 'The timber of the site is well described in Captain Cook's voyage, but unfortunately,' he went on, 'it has one very bad quality which puts us to very great inconvenience: I mean the large gumtree, which splits and warps in such a manner when used green, to which necessity obliges us.' There was a better option, he said, 'the timber which in its growth resembles a fir tree.' But although it warped less, 'we are obliged to fetch it from some distance and it will not float.'

And there were other problems. The trees blunted every axe the settlers had brought with them and, if anyone did manage to chop one down, left a huge hostile stump which was almost impossible to shift. As they tried to build shelters, they found the wood was 'of universally so bad a grain as almost to preclude a possibility of using it: the increase of labour occasioned by this in our buildings,' said one officer, 'has been such as nearly to exceed belief.' And in their attempts to find a new mast, more than 40 of 'the choicest young trees' had to be felled to find enough wood, 'the trees being either rotten at the heart or riven by the gum, which abounds in them.'

They were branded 'of little use but firewood'. It may have been true, the commander of the marines commented, that the 'whole face' of the place was 'covered with trees, but not one bit of timber have we yet found that is fit for any other purpose than to make the pot boil.' They were nothing but a useless menace. It became increasingly obvious that the British had landed on what was truly the Antipodes – that place where everything was upside down and back to front: some of the trees, as autumn turned towards winter, began to lose not their leaves but their bark. Great messy strips of it dangled down and blew in the breeze. 'We *have* and *shall* have all through the Winter green Trees in abundance to look at,' one surgeon wrote home happily, 'that is more than you can say in your Winter.'

But in this strange new place, trying to establish crops with the seeds and plants he'd brought, trying to find food for his charges, trying to meet London's expectation that the colony would swiftly be self-sufficient, the governor had no one with any botanical knowledge to give him any advice – not so much as a gardener. He was sure, he said, that Joseph Banks had discovered everything that there was to discover in the eight days the *Endeavour* had moored in Botany Bay, but that didn't help when he kept losing swathes of potential food crops by planting seeds and seedlings at the wrong time of year in the wrong sort of soil. In the face of this, he politely observed to London, he thought it may have been helpful to have had someone who knew about these things.

Joseph Banks' interest in New South Welsh botany had been rekindled by the time the First Fleet set sail. Hungry for more specimens, he had instructed a good number of the Fleet's officers, from the governor down, to collect as much as they could for him and send it back to London – like a greedy child, wanting more and more treats for itself. But while they had sailed with a pianoforte and a printing press, Banks had not thought to pack them a gardener. (Among London's gardeners, gum trees were so popular that two companies of nurserymen thought of sending collectors halfway round the world to speed up supply – which would have seemed the height of flippancy and irrelevance to the people starving in Sydney.)

As for Banks' own long-past visit to that coast, people asked less frequently when its collections might be published. When Dr Solander died in 1782, it was understandable that the work would lag. Yet only two years later, Banks was assuring correspondents that the project 'was drawing near to its end', claiming that, as all the descriptions of the specimens had been 'made while the plants were fresh, nothing remains to do than complete the drawings which have still not been altogether finished and to add synonyms from books that we did not have with us or have been published since.' Two months, he said. But it was never done, and a decade on, with the work still unpublished, he said simply that it was 'retarded' by his other concerns. Sometimes other botanists, like L'Héritier, worked on the specimens – one named nine eucalypts between 1791 and 1797 – but the great bulk of them simply sat.

Banks did send Phillip his gardeners. After a shipwreck killed the first two, the next lot managed to get through and Sydney's future began to brighten. 'You are to send to me a specimen of every sort of plant you meet with,' Banks had charged everyone who sailed for Sydney, 'furnished likewise with flowers and fruits.' This they did, sending also the first useful products they turned up in their strange new home: warm, malleable clay which Josiah Wedgwood thought was ideal for making pottery, and several small phials of oil taken from the tree they called the peppermint gum. It had proved 'serviceable in medicine,' the colony's chief surgeon reported back to Banks, 'particularly in dysentric complaints where it has sometimes succeeded where all preparations have failed. To blunt its acrid qualities,' he revealed, 'it is usual to combine it with opiates.'

As the century turned, Banks also sent a government-endorsed collector, George Caley, to live in Sydney, and a government-endorsed botanist, Robert Brown, to circumnavigate the entire continent with Matthew Flinders. He kept talking about going back to Botany Bay himself – or to the new settlement in Van Diemen's Land, or maybe even to Norfolk Island. But he was getting bigger, and older, and both his influence and his gout (which was making his handwriting more and more illegible) were increasing. In the end it was just as easy to convince the government to hire these two men to go and do the work for him. Banks stayed fast in London, receiving his packets of plants.

Neither Brown nor Caley went to Australia to focus specifically on gum trees: in fact, Brown reported back to Banks, Caley didn't seem to have done any work on any trees at all in his first years in the colony, still pegging his interest on plants that reminded him of something familiarly English. But you couldn't botanise in Australia without going into the gum forest at some stage, and both took sprig after sprig of eucalypts for Joseph Banks in London.

By the end of his time in Sydney a decade later, Caley had collected specimens and made observations of more than 50 eucalypts around Sydney alone. He had indigenous information on 24 of them, having asked the people who had lived there far longer than him about the trees he was collecting. Working the country to the west of Sydney with his assistant Moowat'tin (so useful, he said, for climbing up to fetch him specimens of nuts and blossoms, where other collectors had to resort to chopping entire trees down to get at these things), Caley was the first white man to realise that the trees could hybridise. He had noticed a tree that resembled both the Sydney peppermint and the blackbutt, and wrote to Banks, 'This is neither Weraboyne [*E. piperita*] nor Tarundea [*E. pilularis*]. I only know of a single tree of it. Nor do the natives know of any other.'

And Brown, sailing anticlockwise around Australia with Matthew Flinders (while the French, always suspected of wanting a slice of this continent for themselves, sailed threateningly clockwise), had descriptions of roughly a hundred eucalypts copied out in manuscript by the time he completed his survey. All of which disappeared into the vast jaws of Banks' collections.

Robert Brown wanted to publish his discoveries, incorporating both Caley's work and Banks' own *Endeavour* specimens in a newly popular system, more workable than Linnaeus'. But the first volume of this large undertaking (Brown envisaged it comprising 3400 species) was met with a terrible silence: of 250 copies printed in 1810 – at a cost of £93, which Brown footed – he gave 25 or so to Europe's leading botanists and botanical societies, and only 26 copies were sold. The subsequent volumes (which would have covered the eucalypts' family) remained unpublished, and the only other mention he made of gums was in his appendix for Flinders' record of circumnavigating Terra Australis. 'Of *Eucalyptus* alone,' Brown wrote in this essay, 'nearly 100 species have already been observed; most of these are trees, many of them of great and some of enormous dimensions.' He was the first person to see that 'although so generally spread over the whole of Terra Australis,' gum trees were 'hardly found beyond this country.' He was the first person to see them growing, in all their variety, at more than two or three isolated spots on the massive continent. But he published no more about them.

Around the gum trees, in the spaces being hacked out among them, the new colony may have been feeding itself, and settlements may have been pushing out from Sydney along the east coast – even down into Van Diemen's Land – but these were still small and isolated places. After twenty years, it was still confined, unable to see what lay inland, its view and its passage blocked by the sandstone plateau that rose up from Sydney's coastal plain. Some of the 50 different sorts of gum trees already teased out from the plain's flora grew up onto its elevation; others – unknown – came from the country beyond to meet them. Between them, the emanations of the oil in their leaves turned the air a purple-blue, tinging the trees and their space a colour like indigo. The barrier became known as the Blue Mountains.

It had been one of George Caley's missions to cross that barrier and see what the country's interior held – he had made more than one attempt on it before he left in 1810. It was another three years before an Aboriginal guide led three white men along a track he knew, and they found themselves looking at a wealth of pasture beyond the sandstone. Water, wood and grass: the requirements of a settlement were much the same as those of a harbouring ship. Travelling through such an abundance, 'through forest land, remarkably well watered, and with several open meadows, clear of trees, and covered with high good grass,' they saw nothing less than 'forest or grassland, sufficient in extent ... to support the stock of the colony for the next thirty years.' A road was put in; descriptions and specimens were sent back to the ageing Joseph Banks, and the governor rode out to admire and commemorate the progress and the fecundity and the possibilities of this expanding Australia. He took an artist, John Lewin, with him to paint this conquered landscape.

The only free professional artist to have settled in Australia – and the first to use oils in Sydney (he once suffered such a shortage of carmine that he had to put an ad in the local paper, asking if anyone could spare some) – Lewin sketched and drew his way out to these Blue Mountains, across them, and back again. Past the red forest gums and river red gums that peppered Sydney's plain, up through the stands of ash and mountain grey gum and scribbly gum and peppermints across the ridges, down into all that beautiful grass. Back in Sydney, he painted the commemorative *Evans Peak, Blue Mountains*. And along the ridge that sliced the painting, he painted sparse trees topped accurately with eucalypt leaves so spare that you could see the light coming through them, the blue sky behind them, rather than making them one solid mass. But the governor was only concerned with painting as a means of expanding the quantity of land he governed. He didn't care about the accuracy of the trees that were painted for him. What he cared about was that they should make people back in Britain want to sail around the globe for six months and set themselves up in Australia. The nexus of art and exploration, as he saw it, was public relations – whether the trees were accurate or not.

He commissioned *Views of Australia* from a convict appropriately transported for forgery – all Arcadian images and pretty parklands. 'Behold,' the advertisement for these images trumpeted, 'the gloomy grandeur of the solitary woods and forests exchanged for the noise and bustle of thronged marts of commerce.' The trees could be painted any-which-way as far as the governor was concerned: the important thing was that they were going to make way for entrepreneurial productivity. Australia needed to be sold again, as successfully as Banks had sold it to the House of Commons' committee as an infinite prison.

In 1820, 50 years after he had frolicked in the botanical playground of Australia's east coast, Joseph Banks – botanist, president of the Royal Society for more than 40 years, progenitor of the English settlement in Sydney in so many ways – died without having published a line about any of the things he had seen or collected. He died, too, holding in that mammoth collection a number of manuscripts which were lodged with him in trust, the work of several of Australia's first collectors and botanists.

Robert Brown's work had disappeared, as had Caley's: it would take almost a century for someone to find his carefully recorded list of Aboriginal names for 24 Sydney gums. Even L'Héritier's publication of the genus name *Eucalyptus* was so unremarked that London kept calling the trees 'Metrosideros' – Solander's old, inaccurate name – on into the 19th century. (His *Metrosideros gummifera*, published posthumously, stood incorrectly until 1925 for the tree that should have been *Eucalyptus gummifera*, although his examination of eucalyptus buds, made before they even had the name 'eucalypt', has been hailed as one of the most astute studies of them made.)

The whole lot slithered into the basements of museums and other people's collections, untouched for years, while the place Cook had recorded as 'in a pure state of nature,' full of 'all such things as nature hath bestow'd upon it in a flourishing state,' became a busy quagmire of convicts and settlers and migrants and entrepreneurs.

The trees' old Aboriginal names faded while their shiny new European ones waited in the background.

the explorers' trees

The yarra tree was here before
The white man came among us,
The water is ours, and not enough
For these large thirsty monsters …

Then preach no more the white man's faith
Nor tell of Eve and Adam.
No trees of knowledge e'er grew here,
We'd burn them if we had 'em …

—Major Thomas Livingston Mitchell,
'Reply of the Aboriginal Native to the White Man'
(freely translated), 1846

The British government, so capably advised by Sir Joseph Banks for so many years, hadn't given the potential of the new colony much thought beyond its role as a sizeable and distant gaol. It hadn't been part of the plan for Botany Bay that free settlers would want to build houses there and live among the gum trees. Australia was for imprisoning felons. The 'free' people who would farm its soil would be the convicts who'd won their ticket-of-leave. Having done their time, most of them would stay in this new, isolated country. They would tame it and make it productive. The only other people offered any of the land at first were the ordinary soldiers and the non-commissioned officers.

Accordingly, while no one had packed a gardener for the First Fleet, a surveyor had been sent to carve up the landscape. Military men could expect 150 acres after three years service, while the convicts stood to receive 30 acres if they were single, 50 if married. Unfortunately the gentleman appointed had little practical experience of the job. What was more, as Sydney grew and prospered, it became clear that free settlers did want to come to seek their fortune, and that they expected fair portions of land too. Settlers and sheep arrived to live in the land presumed to be up for claim in the moment the continent was declared *terra nullius*.

The new people found gums they could build with, although they still found their axes ineffectual against the hard wood. From the smallness of the first settlements, pushing further and further in to the country, they began to disrupt the old cycles of growing and burning that had kept the place clear. The landscape that arriving Englishmen since Cook had remarked on as a 'gentleman's park', where hardly a tree needed to be felled for grazing and planting, began to change. As more people arrived, more land was required, the pace of that change increased, and New South Wales took the idea of itself as a permanent, potential establishment a bit more seriously.

Waves of exploration pushed into the countryside. Some groups disappeared through the lines of trees into the vast mystery of whatever was beyond the settlements, never to be heard from again. Others went off and found rivers and coasts and lakes and grass for the newly imported and hoofed livestock that were filling up a landscape used to soft-padded animal feet. And just as the semantics of the 18th-century British Empire allowed Captain Cook to have 'discovered' Australia and allowed European botanists to 'name' its plants, so the men who set out from the coast and hacked their way in through various directions were allowed to be 'explorers' and 'discoverers' too.

Quite frequently their expeditions were short and direct, accompanied by Aboriginal guides who led them straight to the thing they wanted to 'discover' along tracks that had been established for aeons – like the path across the Blue Mountains. Another two men walked from Sydney to what would become Melbourne, along a track that was well-worn then and has since been bitumened into the Hume Highway. Another walked across the desert to King George's Sound in Western Australia, led by his indigenous guide who was simply walking home, and not only knew the way but – helpfully – where to find water as he went.

The explorers kept journals and diaries to describe the places they saw and thus satisfy the various demands of an interested readership in London. This comprised not only a public hungry for adventure, and a government that wanted to know whether those pesky French had run up a *tricolore* anywhere, but also potential settlers wanting to know which land sounded good for farming, and which they should avoid. The trees themselves tended to give way to all this. 'I could leave no mark here more than cutting trees,' one explorer-surveyor had said of the Lachlan River, due west of Sydney, in 1815. He mentioned, for interested prospectors, that 'the country continues good, and better than ever I expected to discover.'

Two years later another observed, 'these flats are certainly not adapted for cattle,' as he travelled further along the Lachlan again. 'The grass is too swampy, and the bushes, swamps and lagoons are too thickly intermingled with the better portions, to render it either a safe or desirable grazing country. The timber is universally bad and small; a few large misshapen gum trees on the immediate banks of the river may be considered as exceptions.' Explorers were required to bring home not just descriptions of what they had seen and how to get there, but also real estate information – some brought home the downsides; others, the puff.

In the new white mythology of the place, too, single eucalypts sometimes came to stand for the success or failure of whole expeditions. A solid eucalypt growing out at an angle towards that increasingly busy road between Sydney and its newly found and bountiful grazing country beyond the Blue Mountains was tagged 'the Explorers' Tree' to commemorate the three white men who had crossed the sandstone plateau. There was the old river red gum (*Eucalyptus camaldulensis*) carved to celebrate the claiming of the huge Murray River, the tree marked to celebrate exploration of the Lachlan and – much later, in 1861 – the 'Dig tree' coolibah (*E. microtheca*) in far north Queensland, which marked the end of Burke and Wills.

More usually, though, trees were lopped or removed, not memorialised. Axes were only one option when you couldn't pick out an obvious path: you could always burn your way through. The journals and diaries explorers published, describing how things looked in these new spaces, featured gum trees that may not have been left standing shortly after they had been 'discovered', and views just created with axes and flames. At least some of the explorers were aware of the mess they made. As Charles Sturt described it later, heading towards the centre of the continent: 'our animals had laid the ground bare for miles around the camp, and never came towards it but to drink. The axe had made a broad gap in the line of gum trees which ornamented the creek, and had destroyed its appearance.'

While exploration cut paths into the continent of Australia, it was not a precise science. The accounts of what somewhere looked like might have been reliable, but exactly where it was often proved harder to pinpoint. Beyond how to get to a certain place, and then back again, explorers' maps were more broad-brush sketches – often inaccurate – than the precise surveys potential settlers wanted to satisfy their more particular curiosities about clearings and reliable fresh water sources and where land was available.

Only three years after Joseph Banks' death, the regular report of the colonial commissioner recommended that a systematic survey of New South Wales was urgently needed. Getting land apportioned to settlers in a position to purchase it – and thus, as he pointed out, inject much-needed capital into the settlement – was a most important consideration. The man who would unravel this mess arrived in Sydney on September 9, 1827 with his surveyor's chain (100 links each precisely 7.92 inches long, making a total length of 66 feet), his theodolite, his wife, and three children. This was Major Thomas Livingston Mitchell. Denied a Scottish inheritance he believed was his right, Mitchell had spent his life thus far (he was 35) pursuing promotions and commissions. He had gone into the army, where he became a surveyor – out in front of the troops on Wellington's Peninsula campaign, providing information about land and resources for his generals. And then he had undertaken five years alone in Spain and Portugal, revisiting every battleground and completing accurate maps of each. The task was vast, methodical and fairly thankless: Mitchell put his head down and got on with it, filling his evenings with the completion of a detailed daily journal and the composition of some 55 poems extolling the glory of nature.

Returning to England, he spent eight years working on those maps, writing a small, useful volume – *Outlines of a System of Surveying for Geographical and Military Purposes comprising the principles on which the surface of the earth may be represented on plans* – and lobbying for his next position. The offer of £500 a year as assistant-surveyor-general in a new colony – with succession to the top job guaranteed on retirement or death of the incumbent, John Oxley – seemed pretty good, even though it meant leaving the Peninsula maps unpublished. His mother, on the other hand, was both 'astonished and distressed' that he would think about going to such an antipodean hell. 'I have always looked upon this place with horror,' she said, 'and pitied the families that went there.'

But Major Mitchell had a more optimistic view of what might be possible in this 'land of the gum-trees'. And he was the sort of man who researched things: he followed his acceptance of the appointment with a book-buying spree, wangled an introduction to the Geological Society of London, and another to the author of *An Account of Some*

Geological Specimens from the Coast of Australia. He parlayed this into breakfast with the president of the Royal Astronomical Society and a meeting with Banks' botanist Robert Brown, now the caretaker of his collections. He even took advice on the skinning and stuffing of birds. Drawing lessons and the rudiments of landscape painting were already under his belt, thanks to several months of private tutelage from a landscape artist who exhibited in the Royal Academy and had published useful books like *Sketches of Trees* and *Progressive Lessons Sketched from Nature.* Mitchell also noted the given aesthetic position that 'among all the beauties of nature nothing is so transient as a tree, which is liable to so many accidents. A scene therefore which depends merely on a few trees,' he transcribed into his notebook, 'is not worth recording.'

All of this meant that Major Mitchell arrived to observe Australia with an encyclopaedic interest in his surroundings – geographical, geological, astronomical, artistic and botanical. His first concern became the preparation of a map on a scale never before contemplated in the colony. It had been requested in the King's Instructions two years earlier that 'a Commission should issue under the Great Seal of New South Wales … a survey of the whole colony', but little progress was made until Governor Darling of New South Wales asked Mitchell to prepare a memorandum on such a task, less than six months after his arrival in Sydney.

The project of undertaking a trigonometric survey of the colony had been one of Mitchell's first suggestions for his own occupation. Detailed and all-encompassing, it would be a way of getting to know the country. But Oxley 'denied the possibility of surveying the country' in such a way. 'I begged to be allowed to attempt it,' Mitchell recalled years later. 'Mr Oxley said he would not allow anyone to try it.'

Nevertheless, at the governor's express request, Mitchell was able to begin – although as he reported straight up, what would make such an enterprise difficult was all those trees. It was one thing to map relatively clear country, but marking out wooded land was a different undertaking altogether. Take the case of Ireland, he said: 'In the Trigonometrical Survey of that Country now in progress, the Surveyors employed by Contract' – and these were a 'considerable number' – 'survey annually 150 square miles. At this rate, were this Country to be free from Woods like Ireland, and no Grants to be measured, it might be calculated that the Survey should be accomplished by the present hands in 24 years.' Not only was this country annoyingly sylvan, and much larger than Ireland, it had a survey department that hadn't even managed to finish surveying people's farms. All of which was frustrating for would-be emigrants in London.

But where preceding surveyors like Oxley had faltered, Mitchell was eager to begin. The governor recommended that a few more men be appointed, that the plan be advanced, and Mitchell (having measured a standard baseline on the sand at Botany Bay, where he came 'accidentally on a brass plate fixed in the rock marking the first spot where Captain Cook landed on these shores') headed south-west to Mt Jellore, a peak that was visible from the top of the Sydney lighthouse.

It was a marvellous view. From the mountain's summit, he could see all the way up past the lighthouse to Mt Warra-wolong (near the place you call 'Newcastle', his native guide said helpfully) a hundred miles north, and out to Mt Hay, Mt Tomah and the Blue Mountains in the north-west. He could see, with his naked eye, the new gaol walls in Sydney, and through the theodolite he could watch the sails of the town's two new windmills swinging their arcs.

It was May 1828. As he watched the settlement shimmer on the horizon, as he took the initial bearings and measurements for the first general trigonometrical survey of the colony and a more careful, particular survey of its land, Oxley died, and Mitchell succeeded to the top job. He was all ambition: this place would be opened up, would be possessed for the Empire in the very precise, bureaucratic kind of way that surveying represented. During which it would also be cleared of a sizeable number of eucalypts. The first thing a surveyor needed to do was to climb to the top of the highest available position and open up a clear line of sight. Which meant chopping down trees. 'Yesterday evening,' Major Mitchell reported, 'the men had cut down most of the trees on the summit; and this morning they succeeded in clearing the whole top of the hill.' A few trees should be left, he directed, as his marker, his beacon, visible from any other vantage point. On Mt Jellore, this first hill, 'we left seven trees standing on the summit … and on one of these, a man carved my name, and nailed a copper penny piece to it, shewing the head of His Majesty K. Geo. IV.' It had been a pleasant first excursion, although there'd been the usual trouble with axes blunted by the hard eucalyptic wood, and nobody had remembered to pack candles. It was fortunate, then, that 'the full moon shone brightly every night.'

Having begun, Mitchell formed his plan:

> 1. To extend across the Colony a series of triangles, by measuring the angles with a good theodolite, at the various elevated stations to be cleared of trees for this purpose; measuring also a base as accurately as possible
> 2. To intersect from such stations, all other prominent points (whether accessible or otherwise) which might be visible from each
> 3. To fill up the detail by measuring with the chain and circumferentor (the usual method of proceeding in woody countries) all principal features, such as rivers and mountain ranges, conducting the work so that the triangles should be referable to two or more of the fixed points, that they might thus be adapted to these points independently of the scale or plotting …

It would be a painstaking catalogue of the country, each major point measured with reference to others, and the shapes made up by these points overlaid and fitted together, all on the one scale. Compared to the glancing topographies made by ships skirting the coast, or the strange perspective of early attempts to draw the settlements, Mitchell's was an exercise of overwhelming precision.

His teams, spilling out through the colony's forests with

their chains and their axes, would not only be responsible for measuring the land. They would, to a large extent, have the naming of it. And here, said Mitchell, he would like to retain the native names. He would one day be credited with the reform of 'colonial nomenclature' for pointing out to his men that 'the natives can furnish you with names for every flat and almost every hill' – although he later developed a habit of celebrating anyone he could think of from the war in Spain.

On transcription, Mitchell was clear: listing specific examples, he concluded that 'by avoiding ... unnecessary consonants and diphthongs, names to which some have given fourteen letters may be written in nine as Gulangula for Ghoolanghoolah, Brulee for Bhroulhee ... and many other words in which there are letters as superfluous as gum trees on hills.'

Arriving at Mt Warrawolong – whose peak he had seen from Jellore – just over a year later, in July 1829, Mitchell found it 'broad and covered in enormous trees'. He calculated he would need '20 men and axes with provisions for ten days to clear the hill.' He had six men and axes with him, and 'a very large tree took the whole day to cut – however its fall made a considerable breach in the wood on the summit – opening Jellore to view from the centre of the summit.' The government-issue axes, he noted, 'supplied from the Lumber Yard were of such bad quality that they soon became useless – the steel being either wanting – or not welded into the iron so that it came off.'

To accurately capture the shape of the land, you had to change it. Mitchell looked south-west to Jellore – to the seven trees jutting up – and then turned away, taking in the ranges and valleys around him. He sent for more axes.

For three and a half years, Mitchell and his team trawled New South Wales' nineteen counties, compiling growing lists of reference points, features and information – clearing some trees, measuring around others. In November 1831 he was 'happy to say that our survey of the principal ranges of the colony is well advanced.' The backbone of the map had already been assembled by February of that year, and no new farms were being issued or gazetted without their details and dimensions being added to the capacious chart. Now, he said, the instructions he would give his surveyors would 'comprise all that will be necessary to complete a map of the principal features.'

Against his prediction that the map would take around a quarter of a century, getting the bulk of the work done in three years was almost miraculous. He had approached the work as he approached all his tasks – methodically and relentlessly – expecting of his team of men as much as he expected of himself. Delegating the more detailed feature work to his team, Mitchell had travelled south, north and west, marking the colony out in triangles. He had, he boasted, 'written my name in the rocks and on the mountains of this country,' and the country seemed somehow to have begun to write itself in him. Like the night he climbed into the Bungonia caves and emerged to find himself dazzled by brilliant moonlight flooding across the landscape, which gave 'a more romantic effect to the scene' of 'fallen trees with white stems lying across from cliff to cliff.' Or the impact that a corroboree out near Bathurst made on him, the dancers imitating the wind moving through the huge tree boughs they held so that the breeze itself seemed to be keeping time with their music. This was, thought Mitchell, a greater treat than any ballet he'd seen at Covent Garden.

What he wanted to do now was head out beyond the limits of the nineteen counties altogether, beyond the limitations of his own job as surveyor-general. He had always understood that there was another, greater mission which he could undertake: with the framework for the map in place, he was ready to begin. Major Mitchell was heading off to the unwritten spaces on the map – the voids that men could still fill with dreams as exotic as the idea of the *Balf* trees and their nuts of ecstasy. More exciting than going to war, he thought, was this opportunity 'to spread the light of civilisation over a portion of the globe yet unknown ... [where] intelligent man would find a region teeming with useful vegetation.' Leaving his surveyors their tasks, he prepared himself, this practical civil servant who exalted measurement and accuracy above all things, for one of the most fantastic explorations the colony had mounted.

It was Sir Joseph Banks, at the end of the 18th century, who had got everyone supposing that there must be a system of great rivers in the middle of a great piece of land like Australia. It was, he had declared, 'impossible to believe that such a body of land as large as all Europe does not produce vast rivers capable of being navigated into the heart of the interior.' Accordingly, when an escaped convict called George Clarke – also known as 'The Barber' – came back into captivity with stories of 'a noble river to the northward', which 'takes a north-westerly course' and, he claimed, dumped straight into what is now the Gulf of Carpentaria, almost directly opposite Timor, the upper echelons of government were willing to pay a great deal of attention. How useful it would be if there was a river that led straight up the globe towards India. How useful it would be if Major Mitchell could find it.

In theory, he already knew it was there. In the report he prepared on its existence, his logic was splendid. Consider the east coast of the country, he said, and the way the only range of mountains then discovered ran parallel to it. The arc formed by this, concave towards the land's interior regions, 'may therefore be supposed' to hold a concentration of water. Look to the basin that holds the Amazon, he said; and look at the beginning of the Ganges in a similarly curved range. What further evidence did you need? Mitchell named his river the Kindur.

As for Mitchell's own qualifications for the job, whether or not he managed to bring home a great river for the colony and its governors, they knew he would return with an absolutely detailed, accurate and comprehensible map. For whenever Mitchell explored, he had 'a surveyor constantly chaining the whole day's journey. I then took the latitude of my camp in the evening, by several stars and the bearing from one camp to another, as given by each day's journey, always plotted and filled in, was intersected and checked by parallel line of the latitude of each camp.'

On November 24, 1831, feeling 'the ardour of my early youth, when I first sought distinction in the crowded camp and battlefield, revive,' Mitchell rode out to join his exploration party, to lead them up past Mt Warrawolong, and on into the unknown.

He made an inauspicious start: four days later, setting out from a station in the Hunter Valley and still two weeks short of the known limits of the colony, he and his assistant surveyor 'lost ourselves and, consequently, a good portion of the day from having rode too carelessly through the forest country, while engaged in conversation respecting the intended journey.' He began marking nicks in the trees he passed, the established method of tracking a new road in the colony.

It seemed similarly inauspicious that he was leading his party straight out into summer bushfires. 'During the last three days of our journey, the woods were burning before us,' he reported in the expedition's third week, 'but fortunately' – making the best of it – 'the fire was one day's march in advance of our party, and thus the flames had cleared every thing away before our arrival so that our camp was not exposed to danger.' His men, his horses, his bullocks walked on: 'trees lay smoking as we passed.'

As they left the last settlers' homes, near Tamworth, and Mitchell saw what he called 'terra incognita' before him, a man had been sent back for more flour and sugar, instructed simply 'to follow along my line of marked trees with all possible speed.' With his mind on the great Kindur River

Mitchell was dismissing the trees he passed in his 'terra incognita' in one or two perfunctory lines – 'forests of box' or plains 'wooded rather thickly with a broad-leaf eucalyptus.'

His men, horses and bullocks moved north towards the hotter, drier places. From Tamworth they followed the Peel River (aggravatingly flowing in the wrong direction to join the Kindur) before striking out across the countryside. There, at the centre of a plain, he saw a meandering line of trees, which his local guide told him 'marked the course of the Namoi.' It was some of those 'superfluous' eucalypts, Mitchell now discovered, that could show him the way to his great watercourse.

Following George Caley's example and paying attention to indigenous knowledge about certain gums, Mitchell learnnt that the sleek white trunks of the river red gum (*E. camaldulensis*) usually grew along riverbanks. Useful for spotting the Namoi in the middle of a plain and more useful, two or so weeks later, for simply finding water that the men and animals could drink. 'When almost in despair,' Mitchell wrote on January 3, 1832, 'I observed a small hollow, with an unusually large gum-tree hanging over it; and my delight in such circumstances may be imagined when I perceived on going forward the goodly white trunk of the tree reflected in a large pond.'

Two days later, with two men so parched they couldn't walk and the temperature above a hundred, Mitchell again headed for a line of trees, assuring his party that they 'should meet with water,' and sent back a kettleful to prove it. The next day, he used the same method to find a creek. 'I again remarked,' he noted, that 'the eucalyptus, so common in the colony, was only to be seen near water; so that its white shining bark and gnarled branches, while they reminded us of home at Sydney, also marked out the spots for fixing our nightly home in the bush.' He may have paused on his way out of Sydney to swoon and sniff rosebuds in a very English garden, but a man who thought of 'home at Sydney' when he saw a gum personified the changing gaze of a colony that was finding itself occasionally fond of its eucalypts and its landscape. That 'home' was Sydney, rather than 12,000 miles away somewhere in the British Isles, marked a turning point in the way people living under gum trees thought about where they were – and how long they might be there.

In the land beyond Nandewar Range, river after river proved not to be the Kindur. Mitchell travelled up to Mugindi, where one of the upper streams of the huge Darling River – the Barwon – now marks the Queensland/New South Wales border, then out to Collarenebri where the Darling meets the Gwydir. Finally, in February 1832, he turned back.

The colony was so hungry for new land, whether or not it led to the Kindur, that settlers were clearing the trees and building their homes along the route Mitchell had taken out of the colony on that first expedition even before he'd completed the return journey.

Back in Sydney, through 1832 and 1833, Major Mitchell seemed settled: he had a new governor to work with, whom he liked; he was being praised for the line of road he had found down Mt Victoria, the steep pass at the back of the Blue Mountains; he was appointed Colonial Architect, and was all in all so busy that he had little time to either write up the journal of his first expedition or get on with finishing the colony's big map, whose progress was 'also retarded', he confessed a year after returning from the Namoi and beyond, although he was 'happy to say that the drawing and compilation is now almost complete'.

He was happy, too, at home. He had four more children, and for the first time in years he seemed fond of his wife, and to miss her when he was away. Mitchell had been an enthusiastic suitor, serenading his 17-year-old English sweetheart through her window in Portugal at two in the morning ('accompanied by Señor Vigo Rabaglio on guitar') and, newly married, gazing at sunsets off the Portuguese coast with her. But through the first years of their marriage he had called her 'totally unfit for any domestic charge, and her negligence in dress, house etc, is incredible.'

In 1826, after the death of their fourth child, Mitchell could only complain that his work was 'often interrupted', and remark that dealing with croup and taxes were fitting ways to celebrate 'the anniversary of my unhappy marriage', while his wife worried that two more of their children were perilously ill. But from the time they landed in Sydney, he was proud of her and even loved her. In Australia, he saw her as a loving wife and competent mother of their final count of eleven children. And he saw a countryside he could be fond of and belong in.

The same sense of belonging lay underneath the surprising answer Charles Darwin received in 1835 when he suggested to a group of girls he met in Parramatta that they were English. They laughed at him and said they'd never seen England: how could they possibly be anything other than Australian? It was there, too, in the similarly surprising suggestion by one horticulturalist at about the same time that eucalypts should be left standing for aesthetic reasons, and in a poem by one 'Native Minstrel' bemoaning the 'rude invasions of the falling axe' cutting swathes through the gums. Both of which were a long way from some of the first aesthetic responses the trees had endured. While they had had fans among early white arrivals (one said they exceeded the 'tallest and most stately trees I ever saw in any nobleman's grounds in England'), there were those who flatly rejected the land and the eucalypts as ugly and downright unacceptable. Not so much 'evergreens', someone punned, as 'nevergreens'.

And their uselessness as timber was nothing compared to how bad they were for composing pictures. Declaring that artists would 'in vain seek here for that beauty which arises' from richly varied vistas, one early convict painter had said that, if pressed, he might 'select and combine' different bits and pieces of the landscape to 'avoid that sameness and find engaging employment' – and paint an entirely made-up, but palatable, picture.

Others were even less optimistic: Barron Field, a Supreme Court judge and poet who arrived in New South Wales in 1816, made the requisite crossing of the Blue Mountains six years later, despairing at the sight of the gums. What, he asked glumly, 'can a painter do with one cold olive-green?' He suspected, too, that their leaves, hanging vertically, were 'partly the cause of their unpicturesqueness – of the monotony of their leaf.' There was 'a dry harshness about the perennial leaf,' he said, 'that does not savour of humanity in my eyes. There is no flesh and blood in it: it is not of us, and is nothing to us.' In the whole of the colony, he asserted, there was 'not a single scene of which a painter could make a landscape, without greatly disguising the true character of the trees.'

Yet in the early 19th century, definitions of what was beautiful were undergoing a change. And monotony – or, to be more polite, those bristling singular stands of gums – should have been at the top of the list. Aesthetic arbiters as high up the chain as Wordsworth had looked at uniform trees of native forests and given their approval. 'It is indeed true,' Wordsworth had declared, 'that in countries where the larch is a native, and where, without interruption, it may sweep from valley to valley, and from hill to hill, a sublime image may be produced by such a forest, in the same manner as by one composed of any other single tree.'

The eucalypts should have had people swooning at their matchless beauty. Instead of which, people kept looking at them and recoiling. 'Forests of tall gum trees covered from base to peak,' commented one traveller crossing the Blue Mountains (and obviously less sympathetic than the precise John Lewin), 'but instead of a beauty in the landscape, these were a deformity.'

It was fortunate for the trees that people eventually turned from the Blue Mountains and Sydney as their sole possibilities for scenery, and branched out to Van Diemen's Land – Tasmania – as well. There they found gum trees that they actually liked the look of, and gum trees that 'composed a most noble forest'. While one newly arrived bureaucrat had found nothing positive to say about the 'stunted ragged and frightful appearance' of Sydney's trees, he swooned over 'forms that till lately I thought were to be found nowhere but in the imagination of the painter' when he reached Van Diemen's Land.

It was there, too, that eucalypts captured the imagination of one painter, and found their first dedicated portraitist. John Glover had arrived on the island's east coast, well north of the bay where Tobias Furneaux and William Anderson had collected *Eucalyptus obliqua*, and had taken the gum trees at face value. Like L'Héritier, he was a tree man – his sketchbooks were full of English varieties – and he saw the eucalypts for what they were.

As he arrived at the Tamar River on the *Thomas Lawrie* in 1831, he hardly looked the catalyst for great change in anything much. He wasn't young: he was 64, overweight and suffered from gout. He had two clubfeet, and his sight was failing. Having sailed half a year around the world to join his sons, he stood with a book held out in front of him, his eyes shuttling from the blankness of its page to the trees that made up the scenery outside Launceston. There were blackwoods and other wattles. There were eucalypts. This first sketch, on the inside cover of a book bristling with Durham and English coasts and heavy dark-green deciduous trees, was his beginning.

Glover's lines were heavy, traced over and corrected. But the shading around those lines indicated clearly the elegant, curvaceous lines of the gum trees' trunks – trunks that turned and intertwined and weaved. Then there were the leaves, rubbed back to nothing more than a smudge in some places, as tenuous as the trunks were solid. He looked, and he saw that, through the foliage, no matter how many trees there were, there were hints and glimmers of what was beyond: light, land, more and more leaves – just as John Lewin had noticed almost twenty years earlier, painting the newly crossed Blue Mountains. 'There is a remarkable peculiarity in the trees in this country,' Glover wrote carefully about the painting that grew from this first sketch. 'However numerous, they rarely prevent your tracing through them the whole distant country.'

Back in London, he had been celebrated as one of a group of artists who 'dared to paint nature as they see her, with greens, and blues, and greys, and warm and cool tints, as arranged by her skilful hand, instead of making their pictures like Claude or Poussin or Ruysdael or anyone else'. He had brought that daring with him.

Glover arrived like just about every other person with plans for setting up little Britain on the far edge of the Pacific – he had boxes of English seeds and trays of English plants. A little more extreme, he had also packed cages of English birds. Unfortunately his plants had died during the voyage, but the seeds (and the songbirds) survived to be unleashed on the two and a half thousand acres of land he was given to settle, twelve months after he arrived, on a rivulet ambitiously named the Nile, in a valley thick with *Eucalyptus viminalis* and, more curvaceously, *E. pauciflora* – the manna and the snow gums. He built a handsome and airy studio with skylights, planted his English garden, and began to look around.

He carved his sketchbook pages into rectangles, and in each one he drew a careful, painstaking study of a eucalypt, practising their shapes and lines. In his studio, he painted them into heroic landscapes. After that first drawing from the banks of the Tamar, he finished 300 sketches in his first six months alone, and people out riding passed him on the side of the road, 'buried in a painting'. The contradiction of it: he had his English plants, his fine studio, and all Glover wanted to do was be outside working on these first portraits of the gum trees. These he boxed up and sent to England to be viewed and critiqued, taking care to spell out which trees appeared in which painting: she-oaks, wattles, gums. He sent a few pictures in 1832, followed by 68 canvases for a one-man exhibition in Old Bond Street in 1835. A moment of eucalyptic glory: a bursting into the world of aesthetics and critical opinion.

Unfortunately for the gums, London looked under and over its glasses and found itself much less rapturous than Glover about their artistic possibilities. The *Morning Post* took his point about the transparent tracery of the leaves, admiring the way they gave 'to the artist the enviable privilege ... of viewing the distant landscape on every side through their bare serpent-like branches and delicate foliage'. But the *Times* still felt that the eucalypts were 'neither so delicate nor so umbrageous as the trees of Europe: they are not so well adapted to the beauties of landscape as the oak, the elm, the beech, and the poplar of this country; there is, moreover, a sameness of appearance about them, which deprives their representation of interest'.

In Tasmania, whether they liked the paintings or not, there was one thing the locals couldn't disagree with: Glover painted the trees to look the way they really looked, whether you thought that was elegantly designed or, as one viewer stridently put it, 'with hideous fidelity to Nature'. People's eyes were changing: they came, glanced at the gum trees, and then started to look again. 'On near examination,' one traveller noticed, the 'unvaried mantle of olive-green' actually had 'much gracefulness in form, both of species and of individual trees, and many delicate or minute shades of verdure which, combined with the ever changing ash-grey colour of the shedding bark of the *Eucalyptae*, the undulating and often broken surface upon which it thrives, and the resplendent sky above, present a world of interest and attraction.'

While London considered the notion of leaves that let the country and its sky be seen among their shapes, and Charles Darwin considered the notion of young ladies who spoke the King's English but identified themselves as 'Australian', Major Mitchell finally completed his 'Survey of Nineteen Counties'. It had taken just over six years – rather than the 24 he had estimated using Ireland as his example – and, from July 1835, was available for £1 a copy.

His team had come through mutiny, tent conflagrations, men stabbing other men with forks, drownings, lost bullocks, and theodolite legs being dropped down ravines. Through this, he had made New South Wales specific, marking it out into assignable portions and identifiable landmarks, from the Manning River in the north, along the Liverpool Range and down to Molong, Orange, Cowra and Yass, and beyond Bateman's Bay in the south. Mitchell had conquered more than 24 million acres in 66-foot lengths: he had quantified it and made it available. On a scale of eight and three-quarter miles to the inch, he thought that, 'as a piece of constructive planning and drawing of mountain ranges, and true lines of rivers ... it is the most accurate map ever made of any country to such an extent.' As assiduous as ever, he had completed it, he said, 'chiefly on

Sundays when I ought to have been at Church with my family.'

In 1835, as Glover's gums hung for judgment in London and the first copies of the map were made ready for publication, Mitchell launched off on his second mission in search of the Great River Kindur, which he hoped to find this time by proving that the Darling did *not* join the Murray, as some thought, but kept flowing west, or possibly north-west.

He set out along the Great Western Road that he himself had helped to plot, out past Bathurst to Boree where his men, his animals and his provisions were waiting '"in the merry greene wood",' he quipped poetically, with his tent 'already pitched on the sweet-scented turf.' He rode ahead of them each morning, notching the trees to mark the route they should follow. It was the autumn of 1835, but the team again found itself tramping through recently burnt country, where the 'new grass … presented a shining verdure in the rays of the descending sun' and the natives 'were fine looking men, enjoying contentment and happiness, within the precincts of their native wood. Their enjoyment seemed derived so directly from nature,' Mitchell commented, 'that it almost excited a feeling of regret that civilised men, enervated by luxury and all its concomitant diseases, should ever disturb the haunts of these rude but happy people.' By May, they were in bushfires again, out near the Bogan River. Entering 'almost immediately the burning forest,' Mitchell wrote, 'huge trees fell now and then with a crashing sound, loud as thunder, while others hung just ready to fall, and as the country was chiefly open forest, the smoke, at times, added much sublimity to the scene.'

This time, surveying all the way with those painstaking

66-foot chainlengths, they found that rather than having to chop trees down to make trig points on peaks, the trees could be climbed and used as trig points themselves when no other summit rose up from a flat plain. To Mitchell, 'the picturesque grouping and character of the trees' could make a view 'finer … than any we had hitherto seen.' Adding to their understanding of what a gum could be used for, the party found that a green bough carried in front of you was a gesture of peace towards the native populations – while to take a bough, 'spit upon it, and then thrust it into the fire' was a declaration of hostility. Mitchell learnt the local names of those helpful water-marking gums he had used on his first expedition: they might have been river red gums to the white explorers, but they were 'yarra' to the people in the language of this place.

In opening up the landscape and its trees for the rest of the colony, Mitchell found that they opened him up too. On two occasions the size and sunlight of the place he was trying to annotate blinded him into transient ophthalmia: it was an occupational hazard of big sky, bright light and horizons that ran away across the flat. Yet he took in the smallest details of lush colour, like the green foliage of shrubs 'contrasting beautifully with the more prevailing light grey tinge and with white stems and branches' of the trees, or 'blades of green grass among the yellow stalks' on a plain recently ablaze. While measuring angles for his survey, keeping an eye on his team, watching for somewhere to camp, Mitchell could still notice the detail of 'soil changing, becoming red and firm' and timber he 'had never seen before'. The middle of Australia remained as unlike the Amazon basin as ever, and Mitchell rode back into Sydney six months later, proving himself very good at searching for things that didn't exist – and very good at describing landscapes for people to dream about.

Finally, on his third expedition, he found a great prize to bring home and celebrate, even if it wasn't that perpetually elusive River Kindur. Mitchell had struck out west again in March 1836, ostensibly to return to Menindee and complete the survey of the Darling. Instead, he made a looping trip out of Sydney to the south-west, tracing the courses and junctions of the Lachlan River with the Murrumbidgee, the Murrumbidgee with the Murray and the Murray with the Darling, though he didn't travel as far north as Menindee. Then he headed down towards the continent's south coast, following the water and the line of the river red gums that marked out its course.

The smooth white yarra, he learnt during this expedition, were very different from the rough-barked eucalypts called 'dwarf box' (by a previous explorer) and 'goborro' (by his guide). Where he had previously assumed that any gum tree marked a source of water, the differences between species was 'ascertained only after examining many a hopeless hollow where grew the "goborro" by itself.' He slowly realised that he might see his 'sable guides eagerly scanning the "yarra" from afar, when in search of water, and condemning any distant view of "goborro" trees as hopeless, during that dry season.'

The yarra were not only functional trees but, to Major Mitchell's eye, beautiful ones, growing 'to a gigantic size, the height sometimes exceeding 100 feet.' Their 'huge gnarled trunks, wild romantic formed branches often twisting in coils, shining white or light red bark, and dark masses of foliage, with consequent streaks of shadow below, frequently produced effects fully equal to the wildest forest scenery of Ruysdael or Waterloo. Often as I hurried along,' he confessed one night beside the Lachlan, 'did I take my last look with reluctance of scenes forming the most captivating studies.'

Crossing the Loddon at its junction with the Murray, and then turning south to cross it again in early July, he found, not a large river, but the spectacularly grassed and relatively treeless plains he tagged 'Australia Felix', under the shadow of the Grampians in what would become western Victoria. It was a landscape that moved him to poetic heights: 'We had at length discovered a country ready for the immediate reception of civilised man, and fit to become eventually one of the great nations on the earth. Unencumbered with too much wood, yet possessing enough for all purposes; with an exuberant soil under a temperate climate; bounded by the sea-coast and mighty rivers ... this highly interesting region lay before me with all its features new and untouched as they fell from the hand of the Creator!

'Of this Eden,' he gushed on July 13, 'it seemed that I was the only Adam; and it was indeed a sort of paradise to me, permitted thus to be the first to explore its mountains and streams – to behold its scenery – to investigate its geological character – and, finally, by my survey, to develop those natural advantages all still unknown to the civilised world, but yet certain to become, at no distant date, of vast importance to a new people.'

It was captivating. It was Eden. One of his men was

confident, too, that 'nothing can surpass the excellence, picturesque beauty of this undulating forest country, thickly timbered with forest-oak, blue gum and box trees.' And it was a landscape in which Major Mitchell was completely comfortable. In fact, it was so familiar that he complained of entering woods and finding 'instead of rare things, the black-butted gum and casuarinae,' common elsewhere. 'The woolly gum also grew there,' he recorded, noting particularly that it was 'a tree much resembling the box in the bark on its trunk, although that on the branches, unlike the box, is smooth and shining.'

On his first expedition, almost five years earlier, the trees had been dealt with on the whole as *eucalyptus* – few distinguishing marks, few common names. Now, Mitchell recorded their differences. He had become a man who noticed the shape of their leaves, who could look at a gum and realise it was one he had never come across before.

Climbing to the top of Mt William, and caught there for a cold night without shelter, wood or provisions, Major Mitchell noticed 'a new species of eucalyptus with short broad viscid leaves, and rough-warted branches.' He took it home to be named and classified as *Eucalyptus alpina*.

Robert Brown would have been proud of him.

As Mitchell made his way back up towards Sydney, he was in complete possession of the countryside. It was October 1836: he had been away six months, and the jewel of Australia Felix was his to deliver to the colony. He was back in country where he need not give 'the slightest thought about where I should pass the night, quite sure that some friendly hut or house would receive me, and afford snugger shelter and better fare than I had seen for many a day.' He was tired. He wanted to be home. He had travelled more than 2400 miles. Yet, coming along towards the Yass Plains, he was gripped again and again by 'the scenery,' which 'at various points of the river seen this day, was very beautiful.'

In the lengthening afternoon, he marked 'the gigantic and luxuriant growth of the yarra eucalyptus [which] everywhere produced fine effects. And one tree, in particular, pleased me so much that I was tempted to draw it, although the shades of evening would scarcely permit; but while thus engaged, I sent my servant forward to look for some hut or station, that I might remain the longer to complete my drawing. I arrived long after dark.'

The published account of Major Mitchell's three expeditions into unsurveyed space sold out in a few weeks.

Back in England after a decade away, everyone in London wanted to ask him about the places he'd seen, the places he'd said were so beautiful, so lush, so full of potential. He was feted by people who wanted his first-hand account of that place he'd described as 'another Eden'. He had given them more than a map to follow, an adventure to read or a description of somewhere they could dream about: he had given them a place where they could imagine settling among the trees, making new lives. Hailed as 'the Cook of Australian inland discovery', Mitchell had carried the trees far beyond the unfriendly, inhospitable first impression Cook had given of them from his brief days on three slivers of the coast.

For Mitchell, there were more surveys, more roads plotted – his work from the Peninsula campaigns was even finally published. Back in Australia in 1845 and 1846, he undertook another trek to look for the Kindur – and this time he claimed to have found it. At last, the great river that would run up the middle of Australia, pouring into the ocean from the East Kimberleys, and opening up a direct trade route with India. (He had wanted so badly to find it that he'd once described, ten years before, the pleasure of sleeping on 'a snug bit of turf … within two feet of the stream, so that the welcome murmur of its rippling waters assisted my dreams of undiscovered rivers.') In fact what he'd found were the headwaters of the Barcoo, which ended in the frequently parched Lake Eyre.

Writing up his public account of this fourth expedition, he made sure it contained the popular ingredients of the first three. Not only was there the apparent revelation of this long-sought piece of water, there was another place people could picture themselves in, as they had done with Australia Felix. This time, it was a place Mitchell called Lake Salvator – a lake every subsequent explorer said was non-existent – surrounded by countryside Mitchell declared 'surpassed any I had ever seen in picturesque outline.' In its hills he could discern the shapes of gothic cathedrals, ruins and forts 'in contrast with the flowing outlines of evergreen woods.'

It wasn't only Lake Salvator that didn't exist. The Kindur was a sputtering creek. Even Australia Felix looked less lush to other eyes that arrived in it. But Mitchell had his success: he had written the landscape more and more as a place he felt at home in, and he had persuaded people they could make it their own as well. For him, the undeniable achievement of painstakingly mapping the colony was never enough. He could see the size of what he'd done: 'a survey connecting a surface extending across 17 degrees of latitude by chain measurements, tied together and verified by triangulation, exists nowhere else, that I am aware of, on the globe,' he claimed in 1852, a few years before the end of his life.

He appreciated the treacherous conditions his men had endured: 'the fate of the surveyors employed has been in general unfortunate. Some have died miserably, amongst them two of my own sons; madness has deprived the service of others; and premature old age, brought on by constant exposure in the field, is but too apparent.' But he had always wanted to be an explorer, though his success lay more in the methodical way he went about exploring than in the reality of any mighty rivers he brought home. By his fourth journey, he was establishing depot camps with fully-fledged vegetable patches along the way to grow melons, cucumbers, radishes and lettuce, while other explorers still made reckless and under-supplied dashes into the unknown.

In his career, Major Thomas Livingston Mitchell drove himself to an end point that other people would have said was too far away. But he knew how much his own progress between the trees, with his chain and his theodolite, would change their land forever. Just as his Aboriginal guides showed him how trees marked the way to water, he left his own marks in their trunks. And settlers followed those marks out to the forests and plains he promised them were full of potential.

He watched Aboriginal fires and the environment they managed, confident that, without this control and regulation, the Australian bush would have been as dense a jungle as the forests of New Zealand and America, so difficult for settlers and stock to navigate. White men, he thought, weren't much interested in noticing these things.

It was beauty, in the end, that he found in the forests he walked through. His stories were popular in London for their optimism, for their depiction of adventure in isolated tracts of unknown landscape. As one magazine said simply of his descriptions of the places he had seen, 'we were not prepared for the beauty exhibited by the Australian landscape'. His descriptions had made the trees more desirable, and they had made the country those trees grew in both more familiar and more accessible. He knew that every inch of his explorations took him through land with 'many interesting plants … not previously seen,' as he had described it all the way back in the early days of his second expedition. What the eucalypts needed now was the person who would concentrate on what 'interesting plants' they were.

baron blue gum

Give them a fair showing of place and climate, and they will thrive and enrich their environment. This tree has the hardiness of the ancient; it also has virtues which will enlarge the comforts and lengthen the days of men …

—Samuel Lockwood, 1878

It was the beginning of summer, December 1847, when a small German ship, the *Hermann von Beckerath*, sailed towards the Spencer Gulf, heading for the place that was becoming Adelaide. On board was a pharmacist, Ferdinand Müller, 22 years old, travelling with his two sisters. A bushfire surged along the shoreline, and he watched the trees spark and flare while he trawled nets over the side of the ship: he was collecting algae and weed, collecting Australian plants, before he'd even set foot on its soil.

Müller had a passion for botany – it was a requirement of the doctorate of pharmacy he'd received that students assemble a large personal herbarium, and pharmacy was always his means to the end of botany. He'd seen eucalypt specimens before too, in conservatoriums and herbariums. He'd even seen one growing in a botanic garden in northern Germany. But it wasn't specifically botany that had brought him to Australia. It was his sisters, whose consumptive health was going to be improved by the country's air. It was his own nervous suspicion that he would succumb to consumption if he kept breathing dank north German air. He had plans to set up a little pharmacy: his family's neighbours and friends had already made the journey to Australia and sent back good reports about this new place and its possibilities. One had written from Western Australia that botanising was possible on a vast scale.

Once ashore, Müller found work in a chemist's shop on Adelaide's main street and began, almost immediately, to study the plants around him, struggling home 'loaded up' with specimens for his sisters to press and dry. From the first, he later recalled, his attention was caught by the eucalypts. The genus lodged inside him, but Adelaide did not. He bought some land in the Bugle Ranges and tried his hand at farming. It was a failure. He wrote to his uncles about the possibility of returning to Germany, which they discouraged. So he went back to his pharmacy job, determined to try again, and had himself naturalised, anglicising his name as 'Mueller'.

In his collecting forays he pushed out, further and further from Adelaide, to the lush softness of the Mt Lofty

Ranges, the salty mud-flats of Lake Torrens, and all the way up to the Flinders Ranges, where he climbed the mountain Flinders had named for Robert Brown. He went further east, to the Murray River, and explored its mallee eucalypts. He began to publish short botanical papers.

Mueller seemed to be settling into this new life when two friends appeared at his door, on their way to Victoria's recently discovered goldfields to find their fortunes. They asked him to join them and, early in 1852, he decided that he would – gold meant quick money, he reasoned, and quick money meant more leisure for collecting. He travelled to Melbourne, but before he could get up to the diggings, he was introduced to the governor, Charles La Trobe, himself an ardent amateur natural historian who lamented the lack of scientific men in the colony. It was about all he had to lament: apart from that, his colony was thriving. All that gold kept the governmental coffers nicely full. What better to spend it on than the encouragement of science in the now-flourishing town of Melbourne? Scientists from the US and beyond already suspected that the number of Australian species rivalled that of Brazil, renowned for its diversity – those species just needed people to study them.

La Trobe had money for employment, and there were plenty of people who wanted to make the most of that. One was a man from Liverpool called William Swainson who, some months before, had assured La Trobe he could take the gums on single-handed. Find them, classify them, name them – in their entirety. He was an optimistic and slightly brazen collector who had spent much of his life soliciting short-term botanical commissions. He saw that the new antipodean colonies needed to understand their timber. He saw that lots of that timber was eucalypt. He tailored his services accordingly.

Swainson had begun collecting when Sir Joseph Banks still presided over the vegetation of the British Empire. Returning home from military service in Sicily and Malta, Swainson had sent packets of seeds to him (which was enterprising and commendable), had asked him for letters of introduction to the governor of Brazil (which was slightly inappropriate, but achievable) and then sent him Brazilian collections (which was very acceptable). He had then asked Sir Joseph to solicit the British government for financial support on his behalf. Which, as Sir Joseph pointed out, wasn't a possibility.

By the time Swainson reached Australia, 30 years after his last request of Banks, he was 62 and in poor health. He travelled along the coast south of Sydney and began to study its eucalypts, applying simultaneously to the New South Wales and Victorian governments for official employment in this task. Two horses, a manservant and £450 he asked, in return for twelve months of his studies, his collections and his drawings. After all, he said to La Trobe, 'it is well known that the "Gum-trees" remain a *chaos*' – even, he pointed out, after the attention of some of Europe and England's finest botanical minds. He presented himself as the man for the job, although he was entirely incorrect in saying that only 40 species of eucalypt had been identified across the whole continent. There had been claims made for more than 160 different species of eucalypt by 1852 (some of which conflicted with others; some of which doubled up names for species), more than 50 of which were listed in one volume. But Swainson wasn't one to look at the numbers too closely.

La Trobe, considering that Swainson would 'add to our knowledge of what we are and what we have in many ways', offered him £350 plus expenses, a house in the Dandenongs to the east of Melbourne, and a starting date of September 1852. Swainson accepted – and then failed to appear. Four months after his starting date he hadn't even reached Victoria and the trees he was supposed to be classifying: laid up sick in country New South Wales, he said – although he had managed to pop out and discover 42 new sorts of gum trees while he was convalescing. At last, in the middle of January 1853, he made his way into Sydney and set sail for Melbourne.

He arrived just in time to hear of another botanical appointment La Trobe had made. Ferdinand Mueller had been employed as Victoria's first government botanist starting on January 26, 1853, with a salary of £400 a year. 'There is an honest looking German here, who as far as I can judge seems to be more of a botanist than any man I have hitherto met in the colony,' was the way La Trobe introduced Mueller. 'I shall give him every encouragement.'

Technically speaking, Mueller would report to the Victorian government. But it was Sir William Hooker – director of the Royal Botanic Gardens at Kew on the other side of the world, and consequently the arbiter of all matters botanical throughout the British Empire – who would effectively be his superior. Mueller – verbosely polite, slightly obsequious, grandly visionary – fired off his first letters seeking Sir William's approval by outlining his own plans for Australian botany. It was his heart's desire, he said in early February (after just over a week in the job), to describe the whole Australian flora, which he had estimated at roughly 10,000 species. 'No doubt, Sir William, you will consider my scheme bold and premature, and perhaps myself ambitious, still I can assure you that neither egoism nor overestimation of my own powers, but only my ardent desire to promote our favourite science, is the impulse to the task, so laborious, so trying and so perilous.'

And he spent a paragraph complimenting La Trobe's other recent botanical employee. 'Your venerable friend, Mr W. Swainson, devotes himself since a year attentively and entirely to the examination of the intricate genus *Eucalyptus*,' he enthused inaccurately to Kew, 'and in his advanced age, I think, the youthful ardour cannot be enough acknowledged, with which he perseveres in this difficult undertaking.'

Mr Swainson, for his part, held no such high opinion of Mueller, however high his opinion of himself (the rest of the world might regard him as a collector for hire, but Swainson saw himself as a knowledgeable botanist). 'It appears to me repugnant to justice or equity,' he complained to the Victorian legislature in March 1853, 'that a young gentleman, who has just entered the walks of science (more as a collector than a demonstrator of Botany) should have his services more heavily remunerated than one who, having laboured in science for *half a century*, is now about to terminate his career.' He complained about a lack of resources. He complained that his house leaked. And he complained, too, about the impossibility of travel. He was in such a bad state of health, he found himself 'left without funds to defray the enormous expense of travelling', and as he had 'nearly lost my life by being benighted in the Dandenong forests,' he 'must be excused from making such excursions in the future.'

It was an odd request to come from a professional collector, and much at odds with Mueller's approach. That first letter to Sir William Hooker had been written from a camp in the Victorian alps, where he had gone to collect specimens to compare with plants taken from the lesser and, as he put it, 'merely alpestrious' mountains such as the Grampians, by Major Mitchell and others. Swainson, living in the middle of the forests he had been employed to collect from, didn't want to go out his front door for more than a day trip.

'A grumbler of the first water,' commented La Trobe.

Still, in October 1853 Swainson filed his report. 'Without taking too much credit to myself,' he said in the accompanying statement, 'I feel satisfied that these discoveries will be regarded with as much surprise and almost incredulity among the botanists, as was that of gold in Australia among the geologists of Britain.' He had found, he said matter-of-factly, no less than 1520 species or varieties of eucalypts – not to mention 400-odd casuarinas and pines. This from a man who had arrived months late to take up his position and, two months later, said he wouldn't be able to get out much to look for more specimens. Yet he emerged from the wilderness claiming to have identified one and a half thousand different gums. There might be a lot of trees in Australia, and a lot of them might be many different species of eucalypt. But to have found 1500 different species in one piece of Victoria in well under a year seemed extreme.

And there was more. That reference to British amazement about the discovery of gold was not merely Swainson's attempt to give his report the flavour of the moment. He had observed, he said, something very interesting about the way Australia and its gums worked. 'I have now materials also for asserting,' he assured La Trobe, 'that in very many instances [eucalypts] are in *veins above* the earth, as regularly and definitely as veins or earths or metals are *beneath* the surface.' It was all so simple: 'We are justified in concluding the whole of Australia will exhibit the same, and that consequently a time will come when the Auriferous districts hitherto undiscovered will be at once made known by the particular genera of *Eucalypti* that, I doubt not, will be found upon their surface.' He promised eucalypts that could divine gold.

The 'surprise' and 'incredulity' Swainson had predicted didn't even begin to describe the response to his report. Mueller said diplomatically that it was only because his and Swainson's 'views with regard to the limits of the species diverge so widely that we could not cooperate, as I otherwise would have sincerely desired,' in working on the gums. 'The intricate genus *Eucalyptus* requires great attention yet,' he told Hooker.

Sir William himself summarily dismissed Swainson's claims. On the subject of botany, he announced, Swainson was 'as ignorant as a goose'. Then he said simply that in all his life, 'I think I never read such a series of trash and nonsense'. He wished he could be more positive about Mr Swainson's report, 'of which the Governor himself speaks doubtfully'. But in the end, it was 'a matter of congratulation that the term of Mr Swainson's engagement with the Colony had expired'.

Readers of Swainson's report said that they had 'never read before such childish "*bosh*"' signed by a Friend of the Royal Society. 'He makes out over 1500 species of these!! ... all *discovered* in five months!!!' If you took off the noughts, someone suggested, it would be 'much nearer the truth – yet this man is now employed at a high remuneration doing similar work in Van Diemen's land ...'

Swainson left Victoria – hateful place, he spat – and went to Tasmania to collect seeds and arrange the colony's shell collection, never working out which eucalypt was the X that marked Australia's gold. Still, he kept an eye out for other gums and announced his 'discovery' of *Eucalyptus globulus* – the blue gum – which he had apparently missed during his time in Victoria.

La Trobe and Kew conceded an error of judgment in employing Swainson, but they had nothing but the highest praise for Mueller. 'My clever little botanist has returned,' La Trobe enthused after one of Mueller's collection trips, 'having done quite as much as I expected and more than any but a German, drunk with the love of his science – and careless of ease – and regardless of difficulty in whatever form it might present itself.' And from Kew, Sir William concurred that 'not one has done so much in so short a space of time, combining the science with the economical and commercial uses of plants.'

Mueller would cover thousands of miles on horseback, in South Australia, in Victoria and up into New South Wales, in Western Australia and Tasmania, and – most lengthily – as a member of Augustus Gregory's massive North Australian Exploring Expedition from the Victoria River and Arnhem Land to Brisbane in 1855–56, where he distinguished himself by once getting lost until four in the afternoon while completely absorbed in his plants, and – another time – by differentiating 30 different eucalypts 'on the spot'.

The energy that La Trobe and Hooker had remarked on seemed to gain momentum and push him into perpetual motion. His work never stopped: there were books to read, school textbooks to write, exams to set, clubs to address, reports to file, specimens to request, specimens to classify, and pounds and pounds of seed parcels to weigh up and send around the world to any country that asked. He wrote 3000 letters a year, pouring every waking hour into botany. Pushing through sixteen-hour days, with no weekends, a rough woollen muffler wrapped around his neck, clumpy wooden clogs on his feet, and a diet of coffee and black bread, he worked in isolation. It took two months for a steamer to carry a letter to England, and two months to carry the reply back again: that was the timeframe for his professional correspondence.

Then, on top of his post as government botanist, he was made director of the Royal Botanic Gardens in Melbourne in 1857, and discovered that of the 6000 varieties of plants growing there, only four were eucalypts. He was working hard as the champion of one particular tree: *Euca-*

lyptus globulus, the blue gum that Swainson had not even seen in Victoria. It was, to Mueller, the most definitive and majestic of gums. As he recalled, his obsession had begun when he noticed the species on one of his first excursions out from Melbourne and became, he said, 'fully aware of the unparalleled forestral importance of the Blue Gum-tree, and obtained full information on its great utilitarian value.' The speed and ease of their growth he found superior not only to other eucalypts, but to any other hardwood; its strength was equal to an oak, and it was 'one of our best timbers for joists, studs, rafters or any other heavy scantlings' in house-building. Invaluable for everything from ship- and carriage-building down to planking and poles, it was also cheaper to plant forests of blue gums than almost any other tree – and when those forests were planted on sterile land, 'unless it is absolute sand, [it] will soon be transformed into a verdant and salubrious grove.'

Since he had landed in Adelaide, eucalypts had absorbed him. 'I have a great desire of preparing a monographia of this genus,' he had confessed to Sir William Hooker as early as October 1853, 'could I only get authentic specimens.' This work of classifying and untangling the eucalypts would, he pointed out, be best done by a botanist working in Australia, as it would be 'almost impossible to discriminate many species well without studying them in this country.' He was proposing something revolutionary.

Here was the strangeness of colonial botany. Living in the middle of Melbourne, Mueller was surrounded by gum trees, both live ones and the specimens he'd collected. But to identify his specimens he needed to compare them with the first specimen used to classify and name their species – the type specimens – most of which were dried, labelled, and stored in London, in Kew, in Paris, in Geneva. Everywhere but in Australia itself. The last concerted burst of eucalypt naming (apart from Swainson's, which no one seemed to pay much attention to) had been done by Nikolai Turczaninow, a Russian botanist in Kharkov who bought a stack of local specimens from West Australian collectors and worked his way through them. If Mueller wanted to check if something he had found was something Turczaninow had named – *E. falcata*, for instance – the 'original' was in Russia.

At first he seemed willing to combine his fieldwork with Kew's insistence that he complete his work among their old collections: come to Kew, Sir William Hooker and his son and deputy, Joseph, encouraged him, and bring all these new, northern eucalypts with you. And Mueller agreed. When the Gregory expedition finished, and he travelled down to Sydney, he began to arrange all that he had brought home. His first letter about these specimens ran for pages – and, sitting among all his tropical specimens, he saw that eucalypts clearly formed 'the most important part of my herbarium. After watching the Eucalypti of tropical Australia day after day for nearly 16 months, I can confidently hope that in my interpretation of the species I have not much aberred from the truth.'

But in Sydney, and then back in Melbourne, he began to hesitate about making the trip to London, finding excuses for staying where he was. Which wasn't hard – the directorship of Melbourne's botanic gardens alone represented a huge increase in his workload (although none in salary). 'I do not think my essay on tropical Eucalypti needs to be postponed until I arrive in England,' he suggested in 1857, 'although I may have failed in recognising a *few* old species of that intricate genus.'

He had a new plan for dealing with the problem that Kew and its original collections were 12,000 miles away: he would write up his paper and send it – and the specimens he had used – to England, and *Kew*'s botanists could wade through them, and their own type specimens, to check and verify his work.

He'd come up with two new ways of classifying eucalypts: group them together by studying the way the valves at the top of each bud burst open when the blossoms bloomed and the gumnuts these left, or group them together according to their bark. 'For the use of the colonists,' he said, 'the bark will always afford the best mark of distinction.' And in support of this system he pointed out that 'I should from my herbarium spricks alone unhesitatingly pronounce the silver-leaved Ironbark, the silver-leaved Box tree and one of the Bathurst Stringybark Trees as identical! or rather as insignificant varieties of the same species. And yet nothing can be more striking than the difference in texture and structure of the bark of these three species.' Here was another revolution in botanical method: systematic botany used fruit and flowers to classify anything from a tiny plant up to an enormous forest tree – even the leaves were less important than buds and blooms. Collectors did not as a matter of course collect bark.

He worked these outlandish notions into a paper that remained true to the strict, systematic form of botanical writing. 'Conspectus Eucalyptorum Australiae intertropicae et subtropicae' was its rather catchy heading – short descriptions, in Latin, and an explanation of his two suggested systems for reducing such a large number of trees to more manageable groups. Like the D'harawal people and their story of the seven peacekeepers, he set up seven categories of his own for the gums.

And then he posted it to England, asking – since he wasn't going there himself to check his statements about which euclaypt was what against all the original specimens that Kew had stored – that the Hookers check everything themselves. It was hardly a workable arrangement. It took 'upwards of a week's hard work,' Joseph Hooker scolded, for them to revise his paper: 'comparing your specimens and descriptions and confirming synonymy and reference with proper care is much slower work than you are aware of ... You have no conception,' he said, 'of the amount of trouble and time it takes to correct an error of identification.' The paper, with its two simple lists of categories, was delivered in Mueller's absence to the botanical coterie of London in the winter of 1858, without much comment.

It had established one thing: Kew was adamant that, next time, Mueller would come and do his own checking. 'We do look with the greatest anxiety to your visiting England and throwing your magnificent materials into a collected whole,' they assured him. If he wanted the top task Australian botany had on offer – the authorship of the great *Flora Australiensis*, which would do what Robert Brown had wanted to do in 1810 and set out every known plant in the country, and which Mueller had nominated himself for in his first days as Victoria's botanist – he would have to go to London.

But his work in Victoria was expanding and expanding. By the end of the fifties, he was on the Board of Science, the Board of Agriculture, was a member of the colony's Horticultural Society, had begun his own journal to publish new species and genera, and had even arranged an honorary doctorate of medicine for himself to improve his chances of a position at the newly established University of Melbourne. He was active, too, in the Acclimatisation Society, which wanted to introduce exotic plants and animals to improve the look of Australia, even considering monkeys 'for the amusement of the wayfarer whom their gambols would delight as he lay under some gum tree in the forest on a sultry day'. His network of collectors and correspondents expanded too, sending more and more pieces of Australia's flora to Melbourne. If he left the colony at such a time of expansion and change, he argued, he might find someone else in his position when he returned.

As it became more obvious that he wouldn't – or couldn't – travel to London, Kew appointed George Bentham as the *Flora*'s author. Bentham was the botanist who had had the unenviable task of checking Mueller's work on the tropical eucalypts, and he was a man who had never been anywhere near Australia in his life.

Mueller argued the decision – and the point that an Australian *Flora* should be written, or at least researched, in Australia – until the end of 1859 before he finally began posting off specimens he thought Bentham would need. What he would do instead, he thought, was begin his own monograph on all Australia's eucalypts – the other task he had always craved – so that Bentham could quote from it in the *Flora*. Informing Kew that he had 'a foundation for a monographic labour', he wrote to Bentham early in 1862 that, 'if no unforeseen hindrances arise, I shall employ our artist for the next two years principally in furnishing the plates (in large folio) of the Eucalypti for my monograph, probably,' he estimated, 'a hundred plates.'

He applied to Victoria's Chief Secretary for authority to publish his monograph on the eucalypts of Australia in

July that year, and his request was approved eleven days later. Before the month was out, he had already printed the first of 'the large folio plates of the Eucalypti for my monograph. They may, therefore, be quoted in the Flora already.'

It would have been a smooth process, but for an extraordinary combination of those 'unforeseen hindrances'. For all his work, for all his enthusiasm, Ferdinand Mueller's *Eucalyptographia* would not be published for another seventeen years. And not even the most gifted of fortune-tellers could have predicted the great range of hindrances Mueller would face.

In 1863, it was finance. Those gold-rich colonial coffers were no longer quite so full, and with publications Mueller already had underway – including a complete census of the colony's indigenous plants – put on hold, the likelihood of getting something new off the ground (and Mueller expected his 'Eucalyptography', as he casually called it, would need ten volumes) was small. In 1864, he blamed the *Flora* itself for causing his own works to be 'temporarily deferred, in order that precedence of publication may be given to the corresponding volumes on the universal empire of plants in Australia emanating in London.' The next year was taken up with all the preparations his department was expected to make for the great Intercolonial Exhibition of Australasia which would be held in Melbourne in 1866–67. Agricultural, botanical and scientific displays had to be assembled, programs written, notes prepared, submissions judged. The monograph was shelved while he designed complex diagrams of a faux-tree to be built hundreds of feet high from the wood of two eucalypts (*E. stuartiana* and *E. goniocalyx*) to show city-dwellers the magnificent dimensions these trees grew to in the forests they had never seen. (It looked a bit like a Mayan pyramid, with 'slaps' of wood 'cemented together with some adhesive substance and the fissures painted in imitation of bark'.)

In 1866, Mueller was still suffering the effects of reduced funding, but Bentham was nearing completion of *his* volume dealing with eucalypts for the *Flora*. Surrounded by sheets and sheets of dried specimens in London, he admitted to Mueller that he was 'perfectly confused' by the eucalypts, although Mueller wrote to assure him that 'your investigations into the specific characters of the Eucalypti will render your work most famous'.

In the earliest days of their collaboration, Bentham had written to Mueller about the impossibility of getting even 'the most acute and right-judging botanists' to agree on how different plants could – or should – be separated into different species of the same genera, 'without even taking into account,' he commented, 'that all men tend to attach undue importance to evidence discovered by themselves over that which others have brought forward.' As far as the gums went, this was a particularly good description of Mueller's attitude. And while he assured Bentham it would be the work on gums that would elevate the *Flora* as a whole, he made sure other botanists knew his own claims on the genus.

When Bentham finally finished the *Flora*'s eucalypts (at Christmas, 1866) and published this volume, the *Flora*'s third, the following year, Mueller sent congratulations. Bentham had listed 134 different sorts of eucalypt, with an additional twenty which he thought were subspecies, or specimens he'd seen without fruit or flowers, or names from garden catalogues without proper classification. Mueller approved.

Bentham knew, though, that his work on eucalypts was merely a stopgap, the best that could be done to unravel the work that had preceded his on the genus. It wasn't new, and he knew it wasn't definitive. 'I had been in hopes,' he had said to Mueller more than once, 'that you would have monographised this genus before I came to it, and now I must leave it to you to prepare a complete monograph with proper illustrations, which can only be properly done in the country' – as Mueller had always insisted – 'with your means and talents and which you might make a lasting monument to your memory.'

As the decade passed and Bentham continued writing Australia's *Flora* in London, Mueller kept lending him material – 'about 70 large crates, filled with 90,000 completely arranged specimens,' he estimated over the course of the project – lamenting at the same time how long Bentham was taking. 'Circumstances are driving me relentlessly in this turbulent country,' he wrote to Germany, complaining that he could have been getting on with his own work 'if the continuation of Bentham's work did not force me to meet my obligations honourably as co-worker, or rather assistant.'

No closer to publishing his own monograph, and ill for periods of the late sixties, his interest in eucalypts – particularly his search for useful byproducts – was undiminished. His efforts ranged from experiments to demonstrate that asphalt would dissolve in eucalyptus oil, to the invention of cigars and snuff from gum leaves. He also tried to invent some easily portable food, 'mixed with the powder of dried eucalyptus leaves', that could be fed to koalas, allowing them to be sent back to London alive. (If this proved tricky, he wrote to the British Museum, he 'could most easily send you specimens in Alcohol, and perhaps, if you deem them desirable ... you would be so friendly to cause a caske of spirits mixed with some oil of turpentine to be sent for the purpose of preserving such animals.') In his first years in Melbourne, Mueller had hosted a young French physician who, standing beneath the botanic gardens' blue gums, suggested that they might 'cure' malaria (these were the days before anyone knew it was mosquitoes that were responsible for transmitting the disease). Taking up the idea, Mueller sent blue gums to the monks at Tre Fontane in Italy to drain the Pontine Marshes outside Rome of all the malarial fevers that lurked there, and their success prompted the Italian government to 'gratuitously distribute' 5000 blue gum plants to another particularly malarial site. He also helped an English immigrant, Joseph Bosisto, set up a eucalyptus oil factory, whose business boomed.

It was little wonder the eucalyptus oil trade was so successful – floods of miraculous 'cures' were attributed to it. A Mr Mercer from Bendigo said it had 'cured' his cancer of the tongue, and another gentleman's gonorrhoea was 'cured' with injections of gum arabic and eucalyptus extract. The leaves themselves were so popular as cures for malaria that they were sold in London shops for sixpence each, while Mueller advocated placing 'fresh branchlets' of mountain ash under hospital beds as they were 'not only antiseptic, but also sedative and to some extent hypnotic'. Eucalyptus leaves, he claimed, 'generate ozone largely for the purification of the air; the volatile oil is very antiseptic.' The last part was true at least and, beyond the extremity of its claims to cure cancer and gonorrhoea – which it couldn't – the oil got on with making a more realistic name for itself as a popular disinfectant.

Mueller's packets of seeds whizzed across the oceans to places as far-flung as Mauritius, Turkmenistan and Gambia, with detailed instructions on how to strike them, and transplant them, so that the seeds would be most productive and bring forth 'several thousand trees'. The British consulate asked Kew what sorts of plants might improve the vegetation of Jerusalem, and Kew, forwarding that request to Melbourne, received the reply that, of course, the best things to plant were eucalypts, and the prophecy that 'the time would come when Australian vegetation would spread over dry sunbaked deserts and mitigate the effects of drought'. One Algerian resident watched the imported saplings flourishing in sandy soil and imagined nothing less than reclaiming the entire Sahara with the spreading roots of this colonising tree.

But for all these successful promotions, Mueller's eucalyptic monograph was still not written – and the unforeseen hindrances that had held it up during the 1860s were nothing compared to the circumstances his turbulent country would throw at him during the 1870s. The decade started badly. There was mounting criticism of his management of Melbourne's botanic gardens, and a dubiously titled 'inspector of forests' was appointed. He began his own work in the gardens and chopped down several of Mueller's trees. Then Mueller was awarded a German baronetcy (Baron von Mueller, he became, designing a coat of arms to feature 'a shield with a golden field, within two erect branches of *Eucalyptus globulus* intertwined at their base'). 'Baron Blue Gum', the papers began to call him. Not as a term of endearment.

He placed letters in the *West Australian*, asking its citizens to collect for him. As well as flowers and fruit, he wanted bark, and the newspaper commented on how appropriate this occupation would be for the 'many ladies living in these far distant parts of the colony, bereft, to a great extent, of those intellectual resources to which many of them have been accustomed'. In foreign journals he was praised as a 'most indefatigable and industrious botanist' and a 'monument of self-devotion, zeal, industry and talent'. 'What director of a botanic garden,' the same article asked, 'ever fulfilled his duties more efficiently than Ferdinand von Mueller, or who has sacrificed health, fortune, personal convenience to a greater extent in the discharge of his duties – many of them self-imposed – than he?' (It was a good thing, other botanists muttered, that Mueller never married: he 'could not possibly have found time for his wife's company, and it would not have been fair to put her into competition with, say, a new Eucalypt.' Yet he had had as many as four engagements – to a woman several years his senior whom he jilted either because she was too old to have children or he was impotent, to a 19-year-old girl, to a lady in Italy, and to one of Sydney's few female scientists.)

Mueller's sacrifices and achievements, the article continued, were 'well enough known in Europe, but we have been pained for a long time past to perceive signs that a very different estimate is placed on the Baron's services by a section of his fellow colonists'. The public muttered that it wasn't the role of their *Victorian* botanist to go around publishing things that weren't strictly to do with Victoria. They muttered that Mueller spent too much time on other colonies – and it was true that he had always regarded all of Australia as his botanical domain. The newspapers even accused him of introducing the rampant and noxious Capeweed. Mueller pointed out testily that it had been reported as 'inexterminable' a full fourteen years before he arrived from Germany.

Then there was the question of aesthetics. For Mueller a garden, particularly a botanic one, was a scientific resource. For the citizens of Melbourne, it was a pretty place where one could promenade. They weren't interested in how quickly the Baron's newly planted pines would grow, and what this might mean for a fledgling softwood forestry industry. They wanted green grass, pathways and grottoes.

And there was no doubt that Mueller's passion for forests was at odds with the British approach of the Victorian parliament. The Germany of Mueller's time was already advancing the art and science of forestry, while England, unlike the rest of Europe, retained a more laissez-faire approach. If one wanted timber, one simply colonised a place with lots of it, and began to chop it down.

'No city,' Mueller had said, trying to attract people's attention to the forest-scape they were eating with their developments and suburbs, 'however great its splendour ... can arouse those sentiments of veneration which, among all the grand works of nature, an undisturbed forest region is apt to call forth.' They shrugged while he argued for controls on felling, on ringbarking, on clearing – for some attention to be paid to the rapid rate of deforestation.

As the complaints about and criticisms of his work

grew louder, the number of political enemies he had in Victoria's changeable parliament increased (he had seen nine governors and thirteen premiers in the two decades since he arrived in Melbourne). Suddenly it wasn't only the funding for Mueller's publications that was debated and cut. Account after account was delayed and questioned over, causing him on one occasion to write to the colony's under-secretary with some exasperation that 'the poor man who provided so many weeks ago the Eucalyptus seeds for India writes again to me from Sandhurst in great *distress* on Saturday, urging pay … Surely it is not right to keep poor men's just claim in this way for so long a time.'

Finally, in May 1873, Mueller was dismissed as director of Melbourne's botanic gardens, and William Guilfoyle – a man he had encouraged as a collector, who he now dismissed as a mere 'landscape gardener', and a man with 'a taste for growing daffodils for the dandies, and for constructing lean-tos for the lovers' – was given charge. With, to Mueller's outrage, a vastly increased budget. It was all very well for this upstart to be praised for his green grass and his pretty flowers, he exploded, but would no one remember that he had *never* been given funding for irrigation – had had to water *everything* by hand – and that, even with 'no money to grow flowers on a more extensive scale than I did … all bazaars and church-festivals and tea-meetings had baskets or even cartloads full.'

The Victorian Colonial Department of Botany – of which he, the government botanist, was head – was slashed to a staff of one. Ferdinand Mueller. He lost the house he had lived and worked in for twenty years. He lost his laboratory, which was subsequently dismantled. He had nowhere to unpack his library. He lost access to an office, to assistants, to a budget – he wrote, somewhat melodramatically, that he expected he would have to take on the role of his messenger and his horse and cart, since he'd lost access to those too. He was reduced to one salary out of which he had to rent somewhere to live, somewhere to work and pay anyone who worked for him. And, as 'point de honneur', as he put it, he never entered the gardens again. He referred to it as 'being driven out of the garden', and it was no less dramatic and terrible than the expulsion of Adam and Eve.

For four years he fought the decision, railing that a botanist without a garden was like a general without an army, and exhorting everyone he could think of to put in a good word for him. He complained that Kew didn't support him. He complained that colleagues around the world abandoned him. It was a good thing, he blustered, that he had never married: he could go to ruin now without involving anyone else. He suspected a nepotistic plot to install the cousin of a member of parliament. He suspected that he was being targeted by Masons. He also said, more than once, that he thought it was all because he was foreign. Meanwhile Melbourne revelled in the lush grasses and ornamental ponds that appeared in Mueller's 'scientific' garden: 'Baron von Mueller is not there any longer,' it sniffed, 'manufacturing his blue gum tea and his blue gum cigars.'

Mueller became more and more isolated, living for some of the time in nothing larger than a hotel room, working out of a rented office, skirting the edge of his lost gardens each day to go from one to the other. He kept writing, kept publishing, through one crisis of funding to another. And he still claimed that any new specimens of gums, collected from anywhere, 'would and could be to no one in the whole world of more interest than to myself.' They still mattered more to him than any other genus.

Finally, in 1877, with yet another premier appointed – and one at least occasionally more sympathetic to Mueller – the government began to talk again of Mueller's work on eucalypts, and when it might be published. With the idea approved in theory, Mueller began to assemble his text, writing to England and France for duplicates of the eucalypt specimens their botanists had assigned names from. A professor at Kew, in a snub that ignored the 90,000 specimens Bentham had borrowed from Mueller, wrote curtly that none of Kew's specimens could be spared as a loan.

He plodded on, sending illustrations he had already prepared to Algeria to help them identify their eucalypts, and even offering – in the absence of funds for his own publication – to write the section on Myrtaceae (the family that includes gum trees) for a massive *Flora* of the whole world that was being planned in Europe. To the new premier he spoke of 'the long-contemplated and now forthcoming descriptive Eucalyptus Atlas, approved by you, Sir,' providing as evidence of the project's existence 'proof plates appended herewith.'

Writing to Bentham in 1878, he referred to 'more than five years "struggle for existence"' – after which time, he confessed, he had 'got not even so far as to obtain an office building again.' It gave him, he said, 'a most bitter feeling, and were I not a Christian, it would have long ago driven me to desperation.' Enormous quantities of money were being found for the botanic gardens' new director, while his

'Eucalyptus Atlas makes very slow progress, simply because I have no departmental means.'

In July 1879 the book's lithographer died, and the time when the project would see the light of day seemed as far off as ever. Then, in September that year, the premier approved the requisition for Baron von Mueller's Eucalyptus Atlas, and its first four volumes – the material prepared for so long – were printed at last, ready to be sent around the world. 'The issue of this Atlas,' he wrote with uncharacteristic understatement in its introduction, 'has been for a long time under contemplation.'

It was a grand concept, his *Eucalyptographia*. A 'Descriptive Atlas', he called it, planning to publish at least ten volumes – or 'decades' – with essays on ten different species in each. The format was a long way from Bentham's succinct entries in the *Flora*. This was celebration on a vast scale – at least a folio page for each species, plus a full-page lithograph of the leaves, fruit and buds. The detail, he said, was justified because 'of all generic groups of Australian plants that of *Eucalyptus* is the most difficult for elaboration.'

It was not all he had envisaged it would be – and he wanted people to remember how his grandest ambitions, and the subsequent scope of his work, had been thwarted. 'In any review,' he wrote to Harvard's Professor of Botany, 'kindly remember that I have been cruelly excluded out of my botanic garden for more than six years, where I had about 60 species of Eucalyptus under culture, many of them since lost.' In addition, 'you will also kindly consider that many of the experimental tests of the woods ... could not be carried out, since in 1873 even my laboratory was pulled down by mere malice, and I even was deprived of my apparatus.'

Still, he knew it went further than any eucalyptic work had gone before – and he was as confident as ever of just how far that was. 'On this genus, which prevails over the whole continent of Australia,' he wrote to Switzerland, 'observations will have yet to be made for many years, though perhaps not much will be added to the species hereafter.'

Such a guide to the trees. The percentages of water in their air-dried wood. How much oil each leaf would yield. Anatomical plates of their cork-cells and crystal-cells. Some he had measured and claimed were the tallest trees in Her Majesty's Empire. With particular species, he went further and claimed them as 'one of the most remarkable and important of all plants in the whole creation!' Beyond the gums' often-cited capacity to cure malaria, reclaim deserts, produce marvellous oil and make cigars, three different parts of the blue gum alone could be used for three different ship parts. Forests of this species, Mueller added, 'can be accomplished more cheaply and more easily than that of almost any other tree, while the return is twice or three-times earlier than that of the most productive Pine- or Oak-tree.'

He included a beginner's guide to collecting: 'observant rural colonists as well as travellers in any portion of Australia could much advance a thorough knowledge of the Eucalypts by securing for the writer of these pages some leafy branchlets with flowerbuds, expanded flowers and ripe fruits of any species of Eucalypt,' he said. And preferably, he added, 'accompanied whenever it can be done by notes on the geologic formation of the places of growth, the aboriginal vernacular, the height of the trees, the peculiarities of the bark and timber of each species, the time of flowering and such other data as may seem of interest.' He didn't think it was much to ask.

It took Mueller five years to publish ten volumes of his Atlas: the first four appeared in 1879, and by the end of 1880 he had issued parts five, six (which included *E. globulus* – 'the ordinary Blue Gum-tree of Victoria and Tasmania,' as he, who thought it the most extraordinary tree in the world, introduced it offhandedly), and seven. As he had mused in his introduction to the first volume, if it was a question of 'the limits to be assigned to a work such as an Eucalyptography, supposed to serve industrial and forestral as well as scientific purposes,' there may be 'no limit to a work of this kind.' His discussion of *E. globulus* took up eighteen pages, including a two and a half page list of articles, reports and descriptions written about them. 'Perhaps not even to the Royal Oak of England has such an extensive literature been devoted,' he suggested, and offered too that 'it is not too much to assert that among rather more than one thousand different species of tree, indigenous in Australia, *E. globulus* takes the first position in importance.'

Volume eight was published in April 1882 with Mueller confident that, when he was done, 'there will not then be left much to be done in Eucalyptus, as Bentham and myself overrated the species from imperfect material in 1866 in the *Flora*.' But the last two volumes took another two years to appear, as he continued to complain of melancholy and insomnia. There were more international exhibitions to occupy his time. Then the government printery burnt down, and he spent the months running up to 1884 unwell with what he feared was that consumptive chest he'd come to Australia to avoid. He was given the slimmest of budgets as government botanist, expected to pay for himself and all his work out of it – and then asked if he could make any savings. He still chewed over the circumstances of his dismissal.

Finally, in late October 1884, the tenth part of the monograph was printed and ready to be bound. The government printer assured the premier that this completed the work, but Mueller thought it needed at least two more instalments. He was confident, though, that of the twenty or thirty species of eucalypt which he hadn't dealt with, none showed any likelihood 'of becoming of superior technic importance.' It was even possible, he speculated, that it might take longer than 'the remaining years of this century' for these last eucalypt species to be understood and analysed. European settlement and its system of botanical classification was less than 100 years old in Australia, but Mueller believed that he had found every important species of gum (he'd brought them down to 100 in the ten volumes of his Atlas), that there was nothing important left to find, and that it would take years for anyone to locate such minor species of trees.

When one review of the Eucalyptography suggested that his removal as the botanic gardens' director could only have been a positive thing, because of the 'valuable time he saves for the true botanical work by his riddance from the multifarious cares, which garden-superintendence involves,'

Mueller exploded. He had been 'driven out of house and home, away from *my* thousands of kinds of living plants, from the staff trained by me, from my laboratory and seed magazine, and indeed all I had.' As he saw it, it was a 'senseless and cruel measure, dictated by envy and nepotism,' and it had 'had a *most disastrous effect* ... My God!' he flourished at the end of his reply, 'what could I have done to advance science in Australia and give it a practical and useful bearing in new colonies, had I been left with only slender means in my creation.'

In 1892, when he was 67 years old, there were rumours that the government wanted to retire Mueller as government botanist after 39 years and put him on a pension. Some of the newspapers who had supported his removal from the gardens in 1873 now wrote outraged editorials in support of him. One ventured that 'during the many years that Baron von Mueller has held the position, it has been a matter of congratulation that a scientist of such distinguished and worldwide reputation should be in the service of the Victorian government' and that 'it was known that while he breathed he would continue the performance of duties which have ever been of absorbing interest to him.'

'It is but fair,' another editorial commented, 'that some of the many misconceptions about the range of the Baron's work and the value of his labours should be publicly corrected.' There was not a single man, it said, 'whose tendencies and plans have been more practical than his,' citing his 'largely illustrated work' on the eucalypts as 'one for continued reference regarding our native timber resources.'

But Mueller knew that he could have done much, much more. 'Even the Eucalyptus Atlas,' he wrote in letter after letter, 'how far more useful could I have made it had I remained amidst my cultivated trees at the Garden.' He kept working on it, writing in 1895 – a year before he died – that he had 'most plates ready for another decade,' though it was never published. One of his last contributions to an Australian pharmaceutical journal that same year was called simply 'A New Eucalyptus'.

The newspapers' supposition that he would work as long as he breathed proved correct: Baron Ferdinand von Mueller kept moving forward. His last letters were full of requests of and instructions for collectors – send me anything, he wrote, from a moss up to a eucalypt – and offers to send gum tree seeds to new places in the world.

Even as he died on October 10, 1896, there wasn't much peace. Huge parcels and packages of his letters and specimens were passed out his back window during his last hours – his knowledge dispersed, stolen, fragmented. If people were looking for some private fortune, it was long spent, contributed with his salary to running his department. If they were looking for the title deeds to lush land he was supposed to own, it had been sold years before to fund his research, his collections, his writing. And if they were looking for some grand piece of knowledge, an amazing new gum, an amazing cure or eucalyptic invention – well, he was one of the most assiduous publishers in the business: 800 books and major articles, and 1500 publications overall in 110 different periodicals. Everything he knew about eucalypts was already out there for anyone to see.

He had made botany a study that belonged to the country the plants grew in, and with all his work, all his knowledge, he should have been the person who could get to the end of the eucalypts' story. Name them and claim them. But even he had known the job couldn't be finished: 'the subject is so large and surrounded by so many perplexities,' he had written in his Eucalyptography, 'that even now [the author] can offer his observations only fragmentary.'

Afterwards, people started questioning how many eucalypts Mueller had reclassified, how many plants he had peremptorily renamed, how many species he had identified from the most spurious specimens. They started looking for well-accepted names in his publications to discover that – for no apparent reason – he'd called them something else. His work, previously hailed as the work of Australia's great systematic botanist, came under more and more scrutiny, and the director of Sydney's botanic gardens, J. H. Maiden, had an entire revision of the genus *Eucalyptus* underway by the first years of the new century.

When World War I broke out, the memory of Mueller dimmed further. 'Most of us were more or less hypnotised in regard to the Germans before the war,' wrote Maiden, who had formerly revered Mueller as his 'master'. 'But I simply don't want to have anything to do with them,' he said. 'They are made of a different kind of clay to ordinary human beings.'

Mueller had arrived in a scattered and sparse place, and seen it to the brink of Federation. Ahead of his time, he had followed the trees across the borders colonies had imposed on them – it was one of the criticisms he had to deal with most often, that he was the Victorian botanist but that he paid vast attention to the rest of the continent's plants and treated them equally as his to work with. In combining all that he could discover about all of the eucalypts, he had made them national too – an Australian tree – just as Australia was about to see itself as a nation. What the gums would do next was more about the imagination of that new country than anything to do with botany.

snug and cud inc

The Australian landscape generally lacks colour … but as one's eye grows accustomed to the light, the exquisite tones of the Australian landscape appear. The bush, at first a drab monotony of brown and dull grey-green, has its own iridescence…

—Paul McGuire, *Australian Journey*, 1939

May Gibbs was only four years old when the steamer deposited her, her mother, a big brother and a baby one, on the edge of South Australia's Franklin Harbour in the middle of the summer that spanned 1881–82. They'd sailed from England to join her father on the farm he was trying to create there. It was wretchedly hot, and presently her mother was looking at the middle-of-nowhere place she had expected would be a jolly English sort of farm. Through the afternoon, waiting for her father to appear, May watched her mother try to be optimistic in the face of her bewilderment, and when Herbert Gibbs came out of the bush to find them at dusk – a wild turkey in one hand and a huge bunch of wildflowers in the other – May took the bouquet from her father's hand while her mother smiled. That armful of flowers was unlike anything that grew in Surrey.

She said later that she could draw before she could walk. She remembered herself always finding stories about things, spinning them together with lengths of narrative to entertain herself, her siblings, her cousins. By the time she was nine, her family had sailed back around to Western Australia to another farm, which had meant saying goodbye to all the friends, all the personalities that she'd found in South Australia – and that included the plants. She had a page of drawings published in the Perth *Bulletin* when she was twelve, and requisitioned a horse so that she could ride further afield and get to know more about her bush. She went walking, too, with her father – himself an artist – and he taught her how to sketch the new landscape and its wildlife. A talented musician as well, she was into her twenties before she declared herself for art. 'If you can leave art alone – sort of take it or leave it,' she said, 'it isn't the real thing.'

The art of the gum tree in Australia had come a long way since the days of John Lewin and John Glover. True, eucalypts' portraits sometimes bore little resemblance to anything that was native to Australia – fine lush green leaves rather than their pendulous leathery gum-leaf shape. But more and more, artists were finding ways to capture the place and its trees.

In the time of Ferdinand Mueller, a Swiss painter called Louis Buvelot began working in Melbourne. He called the gums 'so poetic' and was celebrated as 'the first to point out how admirably the despised gum, box, peppermint, and stringy-bark trees will lend themselves to pictorial treatment when judiciously handled'. Critics stared into his canvases, forgetting Lewin and Glover, and declared that 'for artistic purposes, indeed, he may be said to have discovered these trees. Previously, people looked upon them as containing so many tons of firewood.' The writer Marcus Clarke gazed at their landscape and saw 'the Grotesque, the Weird – the strange scribblings of Nature learning how to write. Some see no beauty in our trees without shade,' he confessed, but those who lived beneath them saw 'the subtle charm of this fantastic land of monstrosities' and became 'familiar with the beauty of loneliness'. Those who lived beneath them learnt to 'read the hieroglyphs of haggard gum trees'.

As the first volumes of *Eucalyptographia* were published, the artist H. J. Johnstone finished a painting of red gums on the Murray. The first picture purchased by South Australia's art gallery, it was actually a version of one of his other paintings – a 'backwater of the Murrumbidgee near Gundagai, NSW' – renamed as a South Australian subject. From the moment it was hung, it was a hit, and it became Australia's most copied painting as class after class of aspiring painters filed in front of it and were told to paint it from memory. One of the gallery's own directors was sacked for allegedly getting spots of paint on the original while he painted a copy himself.

Then, as May Gibbs' family arrived and settled on their various farms, came the whole troupe of the Heidelberg School, who confessed that it was 'largely through Buvelot' that they 'realised the beauty' of Australian scenes. 'We owe much to him,' they concluded, 'and we should love him accordingly.' As travellers arrived and found themselves astonished that 'the universal eucalyptus, which I expected to find grey and monotonous, was a Proteus in shape and colour,' Frederick McCubbin painted gum leaves rich with colour and intricate delicacy, while reinforcing the alien sense most people had of the bush – and their fear of it – with his iconic series of 'lost children' images: small people in a strange place.

The continent stretched towards becoming one nation; the economy strengthened and the population grew; the republican movement appeared, and there was a demand for paintings of local subjects, done in a 'national style'. Debate raged over which pictures should be painted, which poems written. Suddenly more people were having more conversations about what exactly might make up Australian culture.

The bush-balladers, Henry Lawson and Banjo Paterson, threw their ideas in – in one short story, Lawson had a defiantly anti-Australian Australian overcome with homesickness on coming around a corner in New Zealand to find a blue gum sitting there, a long way from home. Students were urged to find 'in the teeming plant life and the curiously organised animal structures of Australia, examples which they may utilise in every branch of the decorative arts', and bits of gum tree turned up on everything from cornices to vases. They were also directed to consult *Landscape Painting from Nature in Australia*, an instructive work, recommending colours for sky, clouds, distant mountains, smooth waters, and so on, and containing a detailed appraisal of the eucalypt:

> We often hear of the 'everlasting gum tree', but its merits have rarely been acknowledged. Few trees are, in truth, so graceful in form and of such variety … twenty species may be found growing in the space of a few acres. Some shoot up into the air straight and smooth like a ship's mast; others have rough and shaggy bark, and the trunks twist and turn in endless convolutions; many are of a bright red colour, or spotted like a leopard, while others shed their bark, which hangs around them in weird festoons, revealing, so to speak, the creamy-white flesh.

These trees, it was now declared, should be seen as a colourful compendium of possibility which, while not very useful for shade, were certainly ornamental. In this, *Landscape Painting* ventured, a gum resembled 'a fine lady, which the Eucalyptus may be said to personate in the world of trees'.

As Sydney Long, who painted his eucalypts art-nouveau, described it in 1905, the gum tree 'with its changes from silver, brilliant yellows and flesh tones, will yield its story, and the flowers and birds, so quaint and different from those of the old world, will provide graceful and original fancies for the creation of an imaginative school that will be truly Australian.'

May Gibbs had been finding those 'graceful and original fancies' for years before Sydney Long predicted them – she was just having trouble getting them into the world. As Long described a 'truly Australian' imagination, she made her second trip to London and was taking classes at the best school for line-drawing.

She'd lamented the lack of Australian stories for Australian children for some years, taking well-known nursery rhymes and adapting them to a eucalyptic environment, tying human characteristics to the unique shapes of Australian animals. But there was as little call for these in London as there was for the services of a female illustrator of any subject, and May Gibbs sailed back to Western Australia again in 1905. Hating Perth, hating its limitations, she kept her spirits up with long trips back out to the bush she'd ridden through and drawn when she was a little girl, twenty years before. Australians were more wrinkled, she thought when she came home, and they talked in a tall thin way. The trees were tall too – and the flowers, and even the horses and pigs.

She took any commissions she could get and wrote half a manuscript called *Nursery Rhymes from the Bush* before abandoning it. Then she tried a fictional correspondence between a boy in rural Western Australia and his pen-pal in Switzerland, realising how little the other side of the world knew about Australia. She wrote about bushfires and mosquitoes, lizards and possums, and the trees: 'The bush is sad – sad and strange – most of the flowers are queer shapes – nearly all have hard stiff leaves – they are beautiful but strange too.'

'When I stayed with my cousins in the Bush, I amused myself and them by telling stories about the little people I imagined to be there,' she remembered later. 'They always took the form of sturdy, common-sense little persons living the same practical busy lives as ants and other intelligent bush creatures. Never did I find the elegant star-browed fairies that my old-world books showed me. The bush suggested things grotesque, mirthful, cunning and quaint. Even the flowers held an eccentric charm for me, rather than an appeal by their beauty.'

In 1907, she saw an exhibition of Ellis Rowan's lush and detailed wildflower paintings. Rowan had made the journey from Australia to London to take art classes, more than 30 years ahead of May: 'continue to work steadily from nature,' she had been advised, 'rather than [switch] to formal landscape or portraiture.' Briefly celebrated as the country's foremost artist, her pictures of Australian plants had won gold medals all over the world and beaten canvases by Tom Roberts and Frederick McCubbin in Australia's Centennial Exhibition twenty years earlier. But in Perth, in 1907, 'They simply refused to look at my exhibition,' Rowan said. The reason, she suspected, was 'because so many of the ladies over there paint wildflowers themselves.'

May Gibbs had never stopped painting flowers. She didn't turn away from Rowan's images: she peered closely at their intricacy and accuracy, the way their beauty combined with their botany. She decided to try London again.

London's publishers looked politely at the ideas Miss Gibbs presented and shook their heads: they weren't interested in stories about Australia, and they cared even less for its trees and animals. They had no idea what these creatures were supposed to be. 'We need something with an English setting,' they told her, so she took one of her pieces, changed the heroine to a little girl who lived in London, changed the bush setting to inner-city Chimney Pot Land, and changed the creatures to cats and bats instead of snakes and koalas.

She reworked it completely, supporting herself with a commission of drawings for an illustrated book called *Georgian England*. And she found a publisher for this new, English version of her tale. Who knew what surprising thing may happen next, she wrote to an aunt: 'A Publisher may take a fancy to my own style of work before I die – I might even find a good, clean man to love me – I might – have 2 babies of my own ...' But publishers asked her not for anything more from the antipodes, or even another story she had adapted for London. They asked her for more illustrations for another person's history – *The Struggle for the Crown*. Keep cool, she wrote to herself: keep your face to the sun. She completed *The Struggle* and sailed back to Australia not long after, assured by English doctors that she'd become consumptive if she stayed. But she wasn't returning to Perth: she was going to Sydney, which felt like it had more potential.

By the end of the year 1913, she was settled on Australia's east coast, had designed the jacket for a novel and been commissioned to produce 25 magazine covers. She was relishing the ferry ride across Sydney Harbour from Neutral Bay to her studio in the city, and she'd found the rich bush up around Blackheath in the Blue Mountains. It was then that the gumnut creatures began to emerge. As part of Gibbs' cover for the Christmas edition of the *Sydney Mail*, she included a chorus of blank baby-faces among the gumnuts that decorated it. For an illustration to go with a short story, she created another smattering of Australian bush sprites. Something sparked. The gumnut babies arrived at the centre of her imagination, burrowing in and taking hold of her. She was trying, at the time, to come up with an idea for a bookmark – she always had her eye out for new commercial ventures. There was the Australian gum leaf, she thought, 'which was an ideal shape for a bookmark and a pretty thing. If only I could make it interesting on both sides.'

In her rented rooms on the harbour's north shore, May Gibbs went to bed. And in the middle of the night, she woke up and saw, in front of her, that bookmark shape. The clear, distinct green of the leaf, its strong central vein, its fine tip and its chunky stem. Except that peeking around the stem was a round face, two huge inquisitive blue eyes, star-like eyelashes and a button nose – a baby face wearing a green gumnut cap, its pudgy fingers clinging onto the edge of the leaf. It was her first meeting with a proper Gumnut Baby.

In the morning, in her studio, she painted up the front of her leaf – and turning it over she realised it needed the bare backside of her bush sprite's body: its back, chubby legs, chubby bottom, and two little feathered wings poking up over the huge green roundness of that full gumnut helmet. She 'hand-painted them, and the Roycroft Library sold them for me at five shillings each. They became so popular, later we printed them and sold thousands of them for six-pence.' As to who had found whom, she thought it was hard to say: 'I don't know if the bush babies found me or I found the little creatures.' It was a late birth – Gibbs was already 36 years old.

With their wide eyes and their chubby little shapes, the bookmark babies were singled out by one journalist as 'The Spirit of the Bush'. Within a year, that single baby had wiggled off its single-leaf perch and onto a cover Gibbs drew for the literary magazine *Lone Hand*, multiplying into a whole clutch of sprites peering through their gum leaves. It had transmogrified into a brace of other illustrations and postcards, spawned a family tree of floral relatives – the flannel flower babies, the wattle babies, and the Christmas bell babies – and become an instantly recognisable Australian character. Commenting on their speedy capture of the public's imagination in December 1914, the *Sydney Morning Herald* wrote: 'That she uses all Australian flower and leaf forms in her artistic work is one of the chief charms which Miss May Gibbs manages to infuse in all she does.

'This kind of work is so womanly, in the best sense, that it is a fresh proof of the deep feeling for nature, which is nourished by living in such beautiful surroundings as we enjoy in Sydney … As a woman artist "with a way of her own", Miss Gibbs has carefully made her mark.' It was 'the gum tree flowers' that held 'pride of place as public favourite of all her rare original work,' said the press.

Things happened quickly in this new country: the 1000 people who had landed in 1788 had grown to be a population of just under 4 million (80 per cent of whom were born in Australia) as the newly federated country headed into the 20th century – and the speed of the gumnuts' popularity was similarly rapid. It was something to do with their own Australianness, and something to do with their innocence. And it was also perhaps to do with the beginning of a desire to incorporate a love of the landscape and the things that populated it into what was regarded as nationally significant – the things a good Australian should feel proud of. The country was in the last moments of the optimism it had from being quickly settled, quickly successful, and far enough from the rest of the world to ignore its misery. It was still a place of slightly utopian ideals, a place that believed its typical values were to be found in the bush and in bushlife.

As World War I began, and as ship after ship took Australian men to its fronts, a reference to gum trees was like a shorthand for patriotism, nationalism and identifiable Australianness. Like the girls who had assured Charles Darwin that they were Australian – not English – 80 years earlier, more and more people were claiming the country as their heritage rather than identifying themselves as British. To make the distinction absolutely clear, people born in Australia differentiated themselves as 'gumsuckers' – and one of them was even moved to write a poem about it.

Our Gum Trees comprised six stanzas in which Nathan

Spielvogel captured a hundred-odd years of white interactions with the eucalypts, and turned them all into one call to war. The first settlers, 'from the war-stained North', who arrived in the 'bush king's realm', set about their clearances, and all the while 'thought of oak and of ash and elm; / They looked at the gum and sneered.'

Then came the gumsuckers, those new white sons of Australia who could claim to be 'kin of the gnarled Gum' because they played under the trees as children, and would be buried under them at the other end of their lives. Dismissing the oak and elm, as 'fair-day friends / that smile when the sky is clear,' Spielvogel knew the gum – or rather '*our* gum stands firm thro' the winter cold – There's never a change in him.' He was a tree who 'gives his best, like a comrade bold.'

> We stand alone, like our own great tree,
> Afar from the nation's hum.
> Come brothers! Keep our homeland free
> As limbs of our austral gum.

In the war's first bustle of khaki uniforms, of young men pressed into straight lines and weapons training, there was a cluster of unusual recruits among the Armed Forces' intake. Down at the end, scuffling awkwardly with their rifles, were Gibbs' babies, the Gumnut Corp. They even had their own chant:

> *We are the Gumnut Corp*
> *We're going to the War*
> *(We'll make things hum by gum!).*

Mothers and wives and sisters and sweethearts would often send a real gum leaf in their letters to the front – to be touched, smelled, maybe even burnt as a tiny reminder of home. The armed forces commissioned its own series of gumnut postcards from Gibbs to send with hand-knitted socks and woolly balaclavas. They must have been a strange sight arriving in the middle of the mud and blood or heat and sand of the war's various battlegrounds, these beamingly cherubic things with their flimsy clothes and their chubby arms and legs, all pretty fleshtones and delicate watercolours. But the 'Gumnut Corps' was credited with keeping a lot of chins up and spirits high thousands of miles away from Australia.

By Christmas 1916, May Gibbs had released two slim volumes explaining who the gumnuts were and what they did. *Gum-Nut Babies* and *Gum-Blossom Babies* sold out as soon as they reached the shops. Gibbs, primarily an illustrator, had a simple plan for getting the gumnuts into words: she would draw the pictures first, and then weave the stories to fit them. Pictures first, she said, because the pictures will sell the book.

The gumnuts, on the basis of these 22 pages of illustration and story, were lauded across the continent. *The Bulletin* held them up as 'a genuine and original contribution to our Australian folklore' and said they were 'as distinctive as the Kewpie'. The *Evening News* praised the 'quaint individuality' Gibbs gave each of the babies she drew, and hoped that the world was not getting too materialistic for inventions like these. As the sales of the two booklets passed 65,000 in less than five years, it seemed unlikely.

In the yardstick city of London, an Australian voice in

the *Sunday Times* endorsed her as 'an institution of which we are unreservedly proud, and we want the other side of the world to know about her'. Australia's idealism might have been fracturing beneath the war, but it clung harder to its friendly gumnut babies.

As the war rolled into 1918, Gibbs, having added short booklets on wattle babies, flannel flower babies and boronia babies to the two gumnut tales, turned her mind to something more substantial. She had been thinking for some time of writing the story of a young gumnut called Snugglepot, but she was stuck for a name for his little friend. As had happened when the first gumnut baby arrived, she solved the problem in bed. There was Snugglepot; there was the shape of him – and suddenly one night, next to him, there was Cuddlepie. She could write her book. 'Here are the adventures of Snugglepot and Cuddlepie,' she began. 'They were foster-brothers, and this is how it came about …'

Her drawings showed rows of gumnut and gum-blossom babies enthralled by the kookaburra's tale of humans, who carried fire around inside themselves and breathed it out through their mouths, who had layers and layers of skin that they could shed right down so they looked like pale frogs. Snugglepot sat entranced, Cuddlepie cautious.

'"I want to see a Human," said Snugglepot.

'"In the distance," said Cuddlepie.'

It was extraordinary just how many uses the gum

babies had for pieces of eucalypt: the scribbly barks, of course, were newspapers (gumnut editors, Gibbs revealed, 'generally write backwards, because they say it takes longer to read that way, and the people think they are getting more news'). The leaves were clothing, boats, hammocks, baths – they could be curved as luges to slide down the smooth trunk of a tree or sewn together into splendid dancefloors. The nuts were cameras, kettles, cups, cauldrons, glasses, chimneys, wheels, pipe bowls, necklaces and prams.

The book also proffered a vocabulary of the bush: scores of characters whose favourite word, as an exclamation, an adverb or an adjective, was always some variation on 'gum'. 'Isn't it gummy!' in exclamation. 'Gum it all! Gum it all!' in exasperation, and later, as Dr Stork delivered a human baby, he had to confess to Mrs Kookaburra that he 'hardly like[s] delivering the goods … them Humans is so gum careless of 'em.'

'My little book is out,' May Gibbs wrote back to Perth one Wednesday in November 1918. 'I was excited about it, once – ages ago in the early days of November 1918. It is now as if I had never slaved for it, worried over it, shed tears because of it. Nothing matters – the War is Over.'

But war or no war, Snugglepot and Cuddlepie (or 'Snug and Cud', as she abbreviated them) did matter – almost immediately – to quite a lot of people. As much as the gumnuts – or Snugglepot – wanted to see Humans, the Humans wanted to see them, Australian ones at least. *Tales of Snugglepot and Cuddlepie* sold through three editions almost immediately; within twelve months of publication, almost 14,500 copies had been bought in Australia.

The *Age* said Gibbs caught 'the breath of the bush, the stirring of gum leaves and the twittering of feathered inhabitants' so that readers lost 'the reality of trains, desk and the countinghouse.' Adelaide's *Advertiser* wrote: 'May Gibbs – naturalist, psychologist and artist-explorer ... has mapped out a world of her own – and conquered it completely.'

Naturalist. Psychologist. Artist-explorer. Here was the breadth of voices Gumnut Town had found for itself. Reviewers attempted parallels between the creatures May Gibbs wrote about and the leprechauns of Ireland, but her stories were totally Australian. And it wasn't just the koalas, the kangaroos, the kookaburras and the other big animals that took their roles in Snugglepot and Cuddlepie's adventures: it was in the botany of her gumnut babies themselves.

You could trace their eucalyptic origins. Majestic marris (*Eucalyptus calophylla*) from Gibbs' childhood, with their large woody nuts, with long, glossy dark green leaves sliced by a red stalk and spine, grew into the shapes of Snugglepot and Cuddlepie. The nuts and flowers of red bloodwoods (*E. gummifera*) and spotted gums (*E. maculata*) – the trees she lived among in Sydney – fed them. She made careful notes on the history of the eucalypts, their collection by Cook's surgeon on his third voyage, their dominance of Australia's forests. 'Nowhere else found,' she noted: 'grow everywhere under every condition; a race apart and in their variety, usefulness and adaptability no equals.'

She wanted accuracy all the way down to the particulars of a gumnut's growth, and she drew Snugglepot, Cuddlepie and all their gummy friends to show clearly the three stages in the life of a eucalyptus flower. 'Apart from her charming humour and style,' commented the *Medical Journal of Australia*, 'Miss Gibbs is a naturalist of class. She knows every leaf and twig of the Australian bush.'

She wasn't the only person publishing new sorts of eucalyptographies: one prominent member of the Victorian Forest League, Russell Grimwade, was very keen to promote the protection of 'living things we have scorned to cherish'. By which he meant the eucalypts in particular. His interest took two different directions. Professionally, he was a director of the eucalyptus oil company established by Joseph Bosisto and Mueller; privately, he was working on his own book about gums. His book made no claim for totality – 'the vast areas they occupy,' he wrote, 'and the difficulty in collecting specimens from trees that tower three hundred feet into space from rugged mountainsides are only two of the many causes that delay the winning of a full knowledge of the genus.' Instead, he chose 79 species, photographing their leaves, flowers and fruits. He made himself a cupboard out of eucalypt timber to keep his specimens in – and, rumour had it, if he couldn't find a suitable specimen for his project, well, he would plant a seedling in his garden and wait until it grew big enough to be photographed.

Published in 1920, his book, *An Anthography of the Eucalypts*, was a critical and public success, breaking the curse both Robert Brown and Mueller had suffered with their poorly selling botany books. Grimwade modestly hoped it would 'awaken public interest, stimulate research, and promote the cultivation of the Eucalypts.' There was nothing, he felt, that a gum tree couldn't do – and he never left Australia without a pocketful of seeds to press into some obliging foreign soil.

With her altogether different enthusiasm for the eucalypts, May Gibbs' name as an illustrator and storyteller was made: the National Art Gallery of NSW (as the Art Gallery of New South Wales was then called) requested an original watercolour from the *Gum-Blossom Babies*' cover for its collection and she agreed, while commenting that she didn't 'like being represented by that little bit and will they please buy at a large fat price very soon – a large, fine masterpiece in Gumnuts I have in mind.'

But there was never so much interest in her pictures if they did not have a Cuddlepie peering out of the corner, a blossom baby trying on a new hat, or a story attached. Invited to exhibit at the Society of Women Painters Exhibition in 1921, she submitted a number of watercolours, headed with a portrait study of her new husband, James Ossoli Kelly, whom she had married just after her 42nd birthday in 1919. The reviews were less than ecstatic.

In the next year's exhibition, her watercolours were singled out as 'exceedingly creditable … considering the difficulty of painting portraits in this medium', while the *Sydney Morning Herald* said simply that her entries were 'enhanced by the presence of one of her excellent "gum nut" illustrations'. When her work wasn't even selected for the Society of Artists' exhibition two years later, she gave up submitting altogether.

Australian art between the wars had branched into modernism – taking the gum trees with it – through the work of women like Thea Proctor, Clarice Beckett, and

Grace Cossington Smith. Critics would later contrast the 'moodiness and psychological depth' of Jessie Traill's gum tree etchings with 'the untroubled blueness of Arthur Streeton', while Margaret Preston admired the 'gum leaf's sharp triangle' as a fundamental shape in Australian art and advised white Australian artists to trawl the Aboriginal palette and traditions for inspiration before artists from another country marched in and appropriated them – as Matisse and Picasso had in North Africa. The sense that Australia was unique and that, as one critic put it squarely, that uniqueness came mostly from the gum trees – 'exclusively ours! ... all and solely Australian' – was growing stronger.

In a more traditional vein, Hans Heysen was looking after the eucalypts' interests particularly well. He had arrived back in Adelaide from a European study tour in 1903 and dumped European landscapes from his mind's eye immediately, taking up the 'straggling unconformity of gum creeks and stringy-bark ridges'. One of his first canvases – *Red Gold*, a portrait of two gnarled, twisted red gums – had won the New South Wales art gallery's Wynne Prize for Landscape in 1904. He had made the trees domestic (his eucalypts looked positively paternalistic, with cows wandering among them), and monumental. A tree 'full of vigour', one critic described a Heysen eucalypt, its 'head erect, surveying the whole countryside'.

Through the first decades of the 20th century, Heysen had contented himself with painting gum trees around his property at Hahndorf, just out of Adelaide. If the local council muttered about chopping one down, he'd been known to slip £100 to a councillor to ensure that it was left alone. There was, to him, 'something immensely exhilarating when tall white gums tower into the blue heavens – the subtle quality where the edges meet the sky – how mysterious'. Their main appeal, he said, was the 'combination of mightiness and delicacy – mighty in its strength of limbs and delicate in the quality of its covering. [As well], I know of no other tree which is more decorative, both as regards the flow of its limbs and the patterns the bark makes on its main trunk. In all its stages the gum tree is extremely beautiful.'

A quarter of the way around the continent, on the south coast of New South Wales, the recently arrived D. H. Lawrence struggled with the 'indescribable, the age-old silence of the Australian bush' and 'the sombreness of gum trees, that seem the same, hoary for ever, and that are said to begin to wither as soon as they mature', as he worked on his novel *Kangaroo.* While science would explain how the leaves followed the sun's path through the day, Lawrence saw the leaves as 'sun-refusing … like dark hardened flakes of rubber'. His main character, an Englishman named Somers, was terrified of the bush, which 'scared him … so phantom-like, so ghostly, with its tall pale trees and many dead trees.' (Australian farmers had for some time been in thrall to the idea of ringbarking as the most effective way of clearing land – hence Dorothea Mackellar's reference to ringbarked forests in her famous poem.) In the moonlight, Somers sensed the 'spirit of the place … biding its time with a terrible ageless watchfulness, waiting for a far-off end, watching the myriad intruding white men'.

Later, in the face of the 'magical range of Blue Mountains [and] all the hoary space of bush between,' he commented on 'the strange, as it were, *invisible* beauty of Australia, which is undeniably there, but which seems to lurk just beyond the range of our white vision.

'You feel you can't *see*,' he said, 'as if your eyes hadn't the vision in time to correspond with the outside landscape,' while Somers' wife observed that this was a country, a landscape, that 'feels as if no one has ever loved it.'

Here were those old, alienated first impressions Australians seemed to be shrugging off as people like Heysen – loving the land, loving the trees – painted eucalypts that were described in terms such as majestic, dignified, lordly, regal and heroic. They would even be seen as 'Rubenesque'. No one, Heysen was assured, had taken on these trees as their one, absorbing and ongoing subject. He was, to his followers, the 'leader, the pathfinder' whose 'faith and vision' had to be praised. He was, to his detractors, the rather charmless successor to Roberts, Streeton and the Heidelberg School's version of Australian landscape, 'irrelevantly extolling heroic rural labour and eucalyptus ad nauseum'.

Approaching 50, Heysen stood at the apogee of Australian painting. And he wanted new landscapes, new eucalypts to paint. In 1926 he made his first trip to the Flinders Ranges. Whatever Australia's landscape made D. H. Lawrence's characters feel, that 'spirit of the place' made Heysen 'curiously conscious of a very old land where the primitive forces of Nature were constantly evident,' and he had days of 'crystalline purity when the eye could travel, as it were, to the end of the world.' He went back again and again – there would be ten trips between 1926 and 1933, including a 'most disconcerting' excursion in 1928 when he arrived and found the place bathed in green grass after rain – and the region's eucalypts jostled into his canvases.

One, *Red Gums of the Far North*, Heysen painted to a design he'd used a lot on trees around Adelaide: by chopping them off at the canopy rather than getting their whole shape onto the canvas he emphasised their solid trunk and made them seem to stretch forever, beyond the frame, even beyond the sky. These trees, his 'red gums', were *Eucalyptus camaldulensis*, the most widely distributed tree in Australia – the trees Major Mitchell had learnt were the water-marking 'yarra'.

His popularity, his acclaim and his currency soared. *Red Gums of the Far North* won him the Wynne Prize for the eighth time (out of his record total of nine); he made £11,000 pounds from just four exhibitions, and he had so many imitators that his own art threatened to disappear behind theirs. One canvas alone would endure 11,219 copies by 1975, and an admirer feared his work would be lost behind a 'tangled scrub of little gum tree painters'.

In the area of material success – and imitation – Gibbs was also proving herself. While the first story of Snug and Cud went through reprint after reprint, she wrote another two volumes of their adventures (*Little Ragged Blossom and More About Snugglepot and Cuddlepie* and *Little Obelia and Further Adventures of Ragged Blossom, Snugglepot and Cuddlepie*) in the first years of the 1920s, and licensed their characters into every form of merchandise and ephemera she could think of – and sued for breaches of copyright. The gumnut people became handkerchiefs, postcards, calendars, colouring-in books, cartoon books, omnibus editions, babies' booties, badges, dolls, printed fabrics and pottery. She toyed with the idea of tea cosies and hot water bottles and even earmuffs.

Readings for radio were made, and there were several unsuccessful attempts to turn Snug and Cud, at least, into movie stars. The nuts – and Gibbs – were prospering in their Australian market.

One young father wrote to say that, he hoped she wouldn't mind, he and his wife had used strips of her newspaper illustrations to make a frieze for their baby's room because they looked so lovely. Her secretary wrote back that this was certainly a breach of copyright, that there was an official May Gibbs frieze that could be purchased, but that Miss Gibbs was willing to overlook the infringement this time – so long as it was just a one-off incident.

Out of Gumnut Town she lured more gum-baby pairs: Nuttybud and Nittersing, Chucklebud and Winkydoo, Bib and Bub. She even let a Scotty-dog loose in Gumnut Land. In books, in cartoons, in stories and merchandise, the eucalypts had been let loose on the imaginations of year after year of Australian children. Every so often, she crossed the harbour to Sydney's Central Station and took a train out of the city ('Big Bad', the city was called where Snug and Cud lived, with strikes and trams and no one to notice the beautiful pictures Cuddlepie drew on the ground), across the plains that even by Major Mitchell's day had been choked by so many unmanaged eucalypts that a man couldn't ride between them and were now beginning to fill with more and more suburbia, and up into those blue mountains that had been impenetrable for so much of Sydney's beginning. Through the lower villages named for the three white men who had crossed their sandstone first, through Katoomba, and on, her notebook bristling with images and ideas even before she arrived.

Then at Blackheath, just before the pass began to wind

down towards the pasture and wide open space, May Gibbs got off the train and walked into the bush. It was a combination of 'memories of Western Australia and trips to Blackheath,' she said, that fed her bush babies. She trawled the space for leaves and nuts and bits of bark; she jotted sketches in notebooks, lines here and there.

For a while, she thought she'd build a home there: by the early 1920s, she owned two adjacent blocks in Blackheath, and plans were drawn for a cottage. The bricks for the foundations, her architect said, had already arrived. But the plans were never completed, the house was never built, and by the beginning of the next decade – with the Depression biting harder – she was trying to sell the land with Rodriguez and Thew, Auctioneers, Estate Agents and Valuers in Blackheath, who told her she'd be lucky to get £30 for either block.

It wasn't only May Gibbs who championed the Blackheath wildlife and made it part of people's imaginations. Much more practically, people climbed down over the rosy sandstone of its cliffs to the foot of the valley, thick with *Eucalyptus deanei*. This tree is the blue gum in New South Wales – not the same species as Mueller's blue gum, nor the same as the tree called a blue gum in South Australia or Queensland. But it's Sydney's blue gum – and it grew so thickly in a bower several hundred feet below May Gibbs' land that the place was called the 'Blue Gum Forest'. An elegant place of slender trunks with shimmers of light coming down through the leaves.

Walking through the sheen of silver-blue trunks at Easter, 1931, a group of bushwalkers from Sydney's Mountain Trails Club heard an axe hitting a tree, and found Clarrie Hungerford ringbarking a gum. Well, he said, he had every right to, because he'd bought the lease to the area. His long-term plan, Hungerford told the walkers, was to clear the forest altogether and plant a grove of walnut trees – although, Hungerford's descendants suggested later, this may have been something he thought up on the spot to outrage the bushwalkers and provoke them to demand that he on-sell his lease to this 'unimproved land', rather than make any attempt to work it.

In either case, the club's next meeting included a request that everything possible be done to prevent the logging of the forest. Hungerford was contacted, and said he wanted £150 for the lease. By the time he named his price, a special Blue Gum Forest Committee had been formed, including club member and Australian conservation pioneer Myles Dunphy. The price was too high, Dunphy wrote back to Hungerford, but he did say that the new committee was happy to keep negotiating while it also lobbied the Department of Lands to have the forest declared a public reserve.

Letters went back and forth between Hungerford and the city, and in November 1931, another group of bushwalkers went into the forest to meet him. They found that he had felled a blue gum just that morning. A hundred and thirty pounds, said Hungerford, with a £25 deposit upfront. Fine, said the bushwalkers. They had it paid out within twelve months – and they convinced the Department of Lands to change the land's title to public reserve. One of conservation's first victories.

May Gibbs had been passionate about conservation for years. 'Humans,' she said in her first gumnut book, 'please be kind to all bush gumnuts and don't pull flowers up by the roots.'

'Did you think they were alive?' May Gibbs would ask people of her nut babies and all her other bush characters. 'Because to me, they always were.' She cherished them like family, pouring her attention into the quality of their printing, their colours, their paper, their design. 'Do not let the Babies be suffering from measles as in the cover design of old,' she wrote to her publisher, 'as this is very distressing to their mother. Let all the inks be strong and dark in the inside pages; discard any colour that inclines to paleness.'

As *Snugglepot and Cuddlepie* went through edition after edition, the number of drawings was reduced in some print runs and stripped out of others altogether. But the book remained in print. And Gibbs had more than enough gumnuts to be going on with. By the 1930s, she had three weekly commissions to meet: a cartoon strip about the gumnuts Bib and Bub, a cartoon strip about a pig called Tiggy Touchwood (this was the least eucalyptic, and most short-lived, of her children's characters), and *Gumnut Gossip: Extracts from the 'Daily Bark'*, a weekly column for newspaper readers all over Australia.

This was Gibbs' regular report from Gumnut Town – the *Daily Bark* was, after all, that record written backwards on the scribbly gum: Gibbs was merely transcribing the news from its trunk. Delivered in a newspaper's style of short reports, a couple of stories, with one supporting illustration, it meant more reading – and writing – than the series of frames that made up the strips.

But, after more than a decade as the most prominent contribution to Australian children's literature, there was some new competition for the gumnuts – and a looming depression. A merger of newspapers brought the two Gibbs cartoons into the one Sunday edition, and the editor suggested that all the creatures be transferred into one strip. No, said May Gibbs. Then there was the question of position: her gumnuts had always had the front-page of the children's supplement, but the merger meant that Bib and Bub would appear in the same paper as some red-headed thing called Ginger Meggs, and the editor was adamant that Meggs, not cherubic bits of gum tree, would take the prize position.

Suddenly publications were withdrawing from the syndicate that published her work, and the magazines that still carried the drawings were offering her reduced fees. Outraged by the refusal of editors to consider her requests, she resigned altogether from the Sydney press. (One editor commented that the sight of her delivering her demands, furious, from the well-wrapped depths of a fur coat, put him in mind of one of her own bush creatures.)

The cartoons continued in New Zealand, South Australia and Queensland, as did *Gumnut Gossip* – although she was paid less in all publications. Her income was dramatically cut.

There was nothing for it, she thought. Capturing the imagination of various generations of Australian children was all very well, but now the gumnuts had to find new fans. As 1932 opened, Snug and Cud found themselves packed up and sent off to England to be chaperoned by one of Gibbs' husband's relatives, while another friend took them off to America. Looking for their big break.

May Gibbs sat by Sydney Harbour and waited.

At first the US seemed to have the edge. Snug, Cud, and their representative arrived in one piece, and, even in the middle of a deepening depression, their representative found himself a job as an engineer. Prospects seemed good, and as he wheeled the gumnuts through a succession of publishing houses, he was pleased to be able to write back to Gibbs that 'everyone admired her penmanship and ideas'. But, he had to confess, 'nothing practical has come up'. He submitted the books to six companies and, six months later, had nothing to send her but six rejections.

Everyone liked the books, she was assured, but times were so bad (as she knew, with her income falling in Australia), 'they do not want to publish any new books in 1932'. Then there was the cost publishers would have to foot to take the gumnuts on: the vast majority of childrens' best-sellers in America were, she learnt, 'cheap juvenile work, that have a large circulation and sell for US$1'. The gumnuts, on the other hand, could be produced and sold for nothing less than US$4, 'twice the price' they went for in Sydney. Beyond which, 'parents just have not the money to spend on good books for their children'. Publishers looked at the numbers of books the gumnuts sold at home and were 'astounded'.

In the end, it was the problem she'd had trying to sell Australian versions of nursery rhymes in the first years of the 20th century: 'Publishers will not accept foreign talent.' 'Although individuals like it,' the final summing up was definite: 'It could never be placed here.'

Across the Atlantic, the babies weren't doing much better. British readers' reports dismissed them as 'quite good of their kind – for Australian children', and said that English parents wanted books about English trees and animals over books about antipodean ones. Publishers seemed worried about the fact that the babies were naked. Mothers who were consulted complained that they wanted 'very pretty babies' and that Gibbs' did not measure up. The British Incorporated Society of Authors stated that 'The only possible difficulty … is that the creatures with which the books deal are limited entirely to those to be found in Australia.' Which wasn't really a surmountable criticism.

In the end, May Gibbs turned her attention to getting Bib and Bub back into the Sydney papers, while her husband sank into such a depression that he could see nothing for it but to join the right-wing extremists of the New Guard. Plans for an animated version of Bib and Bub fell through; her publishers allowed the stocks of her books to run out for the first time, and her cartoons brought her £5 or £6 against the £40 or £50 paid for Ginger Meggs. In 1935, she lost her position as Gumnut Town's correspondent when the *Gumnut Gossip* column was discontinued. Wistful, she wrote of being 'the artist who died of drawing gumnuts while she wanted to be drawing clouds.'

But other artists were also looking after the eucalypts' place in Australia's imagination.

Hans Heysen's *Red Gums of the Far North*, on winning the Wynne Prize, had been bought by Sydney's National Art Gallery for 120 guineas. And in 1935 they staged an exhibition of his work, where the photographer Harold Cazneaux saw the *Red Gums* hanging, and singled them out for praise. A photographer with a wide range of interests – his portraits were well-renowned, as were his images of industry and life around Sydney Harbour – Cazneaux was fascinated by the Flinders Ranges, having seen the edge of them earlier that year, driving out around Whyalla on a job for BHP. Their huge shapes, blue and curved, rose up from the flat earth and caught at him. He began to plan a trip. And he sought advice from the master of those shapes: Hans Heysen. He thought it possible, Cazneaux ventured in his introductory letter, that Heysen might know him by name, and hoped that the painter would 'help me a little with a few personal hints as to a fair way of getting about with my car and the best time of year to visit the place.'

In replying, Heysen was as informative as a regional tourist bureau: of course, taking a trailer was so much more preferable to relying on hotels, and it was better to go via the Pitchi-Ritchi Pass, and the best time for the light was either between eight and ten in the morning or '*very late* towards evening', and the Automobile Association of Adelaide maps were perfectly reliable. Loving the Flinders, talking it up.

While Heysen sat in Hahndorf writing this letter, Cazneaux prowled Sydney's gallery, inhaling the Heysen exhibition. 'I jot these numbers down after going round several times as my favourites,' Cazneaux said in his next letter. More than a dozen needed special mention, and there was one canvas that he liked so much he listed twice. 'No. 20,' he enthused, '*Gums of the Far North*, a fine composition in line and rich in Australian colour. The modelling of the gums in these studies is superb.' There was, he said, 'no doubt, Mr Heysen, no one handles foliage like yourself of our gums as seen against the sky or against the light. You do this with such great simplicity. I feel that I already know your far north country from your pictures, and armed with your personal advice to me I intend to go there at my first opportunity in the near future.'

He headed off before the year had ended, but between creeks in flood and squalls of red dust, he couldn't get into the Flinders Ranges. 'I shall see it yet,' he assured Heysen.

Finally, then, in 1937, with his wife and son, Harold Cazneaux saw those mountains and their hills and trees. The way up towards the edge of Wilpena Pound, halfway along the Flinders themselves, was a jolting trip, and Cazneaux was frequently stopped by this image, that view, that light. Just near the Pound, at the top of a hill, he stopped the car again. He got out. He felt the immensity of the sky arching over him and saw pushing up into the light below him, one massive, gnarled tree, its red heart hollowed out. Slightly apart from the other trees' trunks and branches, it looked as if it was growing in its own spotlit space. He took out his camera, framed the shot, clicked, and drove down the hill towards the tree.

It was an old river red, *E. camaldulensis*, and the bank of the creek it was growing into crumbled down one side, exposing its roots in a dusty mess. The leaves stretching out from its branches were so light against the hard-edged definition of the trunk that they seemed to belong to another tree altogether.

'This giant gum tree,' Cazneaux described it, 'stands in solitary grandeur on a lonely plateau in the arid Flinders range, near Central Australia, where it has grown up from a sapling through the years and long before the shade cast from its giant limbs ever gave shelter from heat to a white man. The passing of the years has left it scarred and marked by the elements – storm, fire, water,' he listed. Yet 'although aged, its widespread limbs speak of a vitality that will carry on for many more years … when the sun shone hot and strong,' he remembered, 'I stood before this giant in silent wonder and admiration. The hot wind stirred its leafy boughs and some of the living element of this tree passed to me in understanding and friendliness, expressing the Spirit of Australia.' The distinct nose-shaped ridges of the edge of Wilpena Pound ran down to the left-hand corner of the lens, the tree leaned slightly. His camera out again, Cazneaux framed his gum like a Heysen with its canopy chopped off, accentuating its size. His shutter clicked.

In the early 1900s another photographer, Nicholas Caire, had travelled through the big, old forests of Victoria, snapping the mighty *Eucalyptus regnans* – overestimated (by about 100 feet) at more than 400 feet by Mueller and his collectors – before they were felled. 'Without doubt in future years scientific men in all parts of the world, when studying varied aspects of plant life, will come across references to the giant trees which once existed in Victoria and will send to our grandchildren, or maybe our great-grandchildren, for authentic records of the same,' he wrote. 'Finding that they can get no satisfactory information, they will naturally conclude that the so-called giant trees existed only in our imagination, and originated in the early days, from stories told us by the aboriginals.' His photographs stood as evidence against that.

Cazneaux's picture was a sort of evidence too. Here was a definitive, quantifiable gum, and of all the Cazneaux images that he saw, Heysen particularly admired this one: 'I like your groupings and feeling for light in some of the Wilpena ones,' he said. 'It's a fine thing with the old gum standing alone with roots washed bare and Point Bonney in the background.'

It had an immediacy too. Heysen painted trees that represented stability, resilience and fortitude: all the things people loved in his pictures, but they still had to be *painted* by him. Cazneaux's image was more direct again. Here was the tree. It stood for these things – and this was what it looked like.

And the immediacy of Cazneaux's photographs could attract the highest artistic praise: Sir Arthur Streeton, Cazneaux had heard, told someone 'he was astounded that the chap Cazneaux could turn out such outstanding pictures by photography – he considered them real works of art.' Yes, said Heysen, 'You cannot help being an artist – despite the mechanical process, you manage to get your personal expression into the results.'

The outbreak of World War II created a new fondness for purely Australian things, just as World War I had, and May Gibbs found a new picture book in Gumnut Town. New editions of the old adventures were printed.

Cazneaux, too, worked with his one big river red, exhibiting it again and again in Australia and abroad. Praise flooded in from critics, and it was immediately popular with the public too. He called it *A Giant of the Arid North*. He called it *A Mighty Gum*. Then, in 1941, he submitted it to a magazine as *The Spirit of Endurance*. It was, he felt at the time, 'my most Australian picture'. Photographer Max Dupain hailed it as 'heroic in stature and endeavour' and the new name stuck. But to Cazneaux, it was still a work in progress: in 1950, he flipped the negative in the enlarger. The left-to-right composition became right-to-left.

'By reversing the composition of *The Spirit of Endurance*,' Heysen assured him, 'you have given it another kick up. This was always a fine thing, and now it's better still.'

'I feel sad,' Cazneaux wrote to Heysen in 1952, 'very sad, that I may never see and feel the great Flinders again.' It was the war, he said simply: 'I missed so many years through the recent war which upset our plans.' The son who was with him that day at Wilpena when he took his famous photograph had died at Tobruk during those years. But he hadn't gone into battle carrying postcards of May Gibbs' gumnuts. Cazneaux's son had carried with him a copy of his father's *Spirit of Endurance*.

Cazneaux told Heysen he had written to the man who ran the station up at Wilpena to ask him if 'that grand tree still stood there … He wrote back and said the tree still stood and it was now known as the Cazneaux tree and that it would be looked after. Well, if ever I had a lift up this news gave it to me.'

In the ever-growing suburbs of Australia, May Gibbs' gumnuts went through the war's rationing and petrol shortages and air raids and wardens and everything else with the rest of Australia. One of Gibbs' koalas took up knitting socks (when asked by the shop assistant if she'd like 'green or yellow or red' wool, Mrs Bear replied patriotically that she wanted 'red, white and blue'), while other characters politely invited each other into their newly dug bomb shelters.

These were the suburbs George Johnston would remember and recreate for his character David Meredith in *My Brother Jack*. They were the places where a six-bob sugar gum could prove a fine tool for territorial and conjugal upheaval. Wasn't it 'rather ordinary' and 'so drab', Meredith's wife complained as the gum tree went into the middle of her front yard. Why couldn't he have planted 'something decorative' like 'one of those Japanese dwarf maples', she wondered, relishing it when the next-door neighbour complained that the gum dropped leaves into his yard and thrust its expansive roots under the smooth cement of his driveway, and the offensive tree had to be taken out.

But domestic disapproval didn't tarnish Gibbs' gumnuts, and the three Snug and Cud books were combined into one omnibus edition – printed on such dreadful wartime paper that the Nuts themselves apologised to their readers:

Dear Everybody,

Our pictures were not printed in a fog or a sandstorm. It's the war. Nobody could get us the right paper. But our story is just the same.

Signed.
Snugglepot and Cuddlepie

It didn't matter about the paper or the printing. The creatures Gibbs drew from her gumnuts, leaves and trees were embedded in Australian folklore. She was famous, but never wealthy: when she finally gave up her work in the sixties, the Australian government had to be approached about a literary pension for her to live in some kind of comfort.

In the 1950s, as the resurgent gumnut babies headed into their fifth decade and May Gibbs (in her seventies) still kept up a steady stream of books, cartoons, illustrations and stories, renegotiated contracts, and demanded that her high standards of presentation and production be met, the novelist Kylie Tennant had drawn comparisons between the hard life eucalypts and women both put up with. For both, she said, it was 'a matter of holding on grimly, and good judgment,' as Gibbs knew well.

From her home on the edge of Sydney Harbour, she charted Gumnut Town for generation after generation of Australians, but she could never quite nudge them offshore. In the end, she hardly left her home herself, and occasionally pretended she wasn't there when people came to call. But she still went, sometimes, to places where she could collect her gum leaves and bark. Twelve long khaki leaves sit, wrapped in layers of acid-free paper and bubble-wrap, in an old photographic paper box which is kept in a library's temperature-controlled storeroom under 24-hour security – scooped up from her desk with velvet-soft shavings of scribbly bark after she died in 1969.

With all her stories and characters, she had promoted the eucalypts in a whole new way in their own country. And by the time she died, someone else had come up with a wildly successful scheme to export them to the rest of the world.

trees of man

But there are the trees, quite a number of them that have survived the axe, smooth ones, a sculpture of trees. On still mornings after frost these stand streaming with light and moisture, the white and the ashen, and some the colour of flesh. There is nothing else in the bush ...

—Patrick White, *The Tree of Man*, 1956

The world was a different place after the war. It was a world that was thinking globally, a world craving expansion, progress and technology. It was a world with an eye more keenly locked on the future, on development. The war had left a greater pessimism in it, but there was also a greater sense of potential, of what might be achieved. The League of Nations was becoming the United

Nations, and there were high hopes for what it might be able to do.

Australia was a part of all this. More than that, the generation which reached adulthood during the war, one commentator suggested later, would become 'the first in Australia to believe in its own modernity, to assume its right to comprehend new ideas in literature, art, politics'. In stark contrast to 1918, soldiers coming home from World War II were given living allowances to go to university, instead of parcels of inappropriate land to farm.

When Robert Menzies was elected in 1949 for his second term as prime minister, he arrived with a new wave of rural projects and established the grandly titled portfolio of National Development for things like irrigation schemes, the construction of large dams, and so on. Forestry was a key part of his vision. Australia's restricted immigration policy was changing, and a diverse and ready-made population was beginning to arrive. As the people came in, the trees would go out.

Both the profession of forestry and what it thought its eucalypts were capable of had been changed by the war: when the shipments of softwood Australia had been importing for most of its 150 years (thinking it needed such all-purpose wood in the face of its less useful and almost uniformly hardwood eucalypts) couldn't get through, foresters had looked again at the gums, and they began to see more and more uses they might be put to. If Australia wanted to be a player on the world stage, the eucalypts were something unique it could offer.

The Australian Forestry School was in Canberra, a leafy place with its own forests and arboreta, and a principal called Max Jacobs. Jacobs, a shy man and an enthusiastic forester, had originally wanted to study soil but, being colour blind, 'couldn't tell colour from feel', and ended up with trees instead. He was heading for the top of his profession: he had taken himself to the Northern Territory when he finished his degree to study the least-known eucalypts in the country, and he'd come home with more than a dozen new species. It was great up in the Territory, he enthused: you could collect as many as twenty different species in just half a day up in its far north.

In the thirties, he had taken courses at Oxford and received doctorates from both German and American universities. His holidays were spent travelling in Europe on a tiny allowance, eating one meal a day and taking third-class trains, learning its forests, its trees.

A fellow forester commented on meeting him back in Australia halfway through the war that Major Jacobs, Engineering Staff Officer, didn't look much like an achiever. His uniform was a bit dishevelled (the epaulette on one shoulder was upside down, his gaiters back-to-front), and 'he looked shy and diffident, self-effacing and slightly awkward until he spoke about professional things.' Then, they said, he was all assurance: even people 'who nodded to very few' praised Max Jacobs.

While the war took his full attention – and would influence his arguments on how Australia's forests should be stocked for decades beyond its end – he was enough of a eucalyptographer to notice, while studying aerial photographs of Timor, that the 10,000 foot mountain he was looking at 'could have had eucalypts on it'.

As peace was declared, Jacobs was settling into the mock-tudor principal's residence at the Forestry School in Canberra, ready to lead its first post-war intake of students through the process of becoming Australian foresters. Students followed two years of general science subjects, taken at any university, with two years of specialised courses in Canberra. No one could begin the course without three months' fieldwork under their belt, and the School's three academic terms were interspersed with more field-work, rather than holidays. The program represented an immersion in forestry: Jacobs noted to himself that 'eucalypts should be studied first and given more emphasis' (with less time, he thought, given to talking about trees that were only of interest in America), that more botany should be studied out in the bush, and that 'insufficient emphasis' was given to the question of fire control. 'Equipment such as pumps, tanks, hoses, nozzles, radios,' he jotted down, 'should be described in detail ...'

When asked for his definition of forestry, he sometimes quoted the first comprehensive English textbook on the subject, *Schlich's Manual of Forestry*, circa 1894. 'Forestry,' it decreed, was 'the human action directed to the production and utilisation of forest produce.' Foresters, therefore, were the requisite humans.

As Australia's first white foresters had learnt 50 years before, drawing on information and practices from American and European landscapes, the forest confronting Jacobs' students was unlike any other. Technically speaking, it constituted very little of Australia's continent – less than 4 per cent – only half of which was, as Jacobs put it, 'economically exploitable'. This, on the face of it, made Australia seem unlikely to contribute much to world forestry. But what this under-forested country did have to offer in the way of silviculture was that most of the trees that were scattered across the rest of its countryside were eucalypts.

In the area of reafforestation too – the replanting of land only recently cleared – there was no doubt that Australia had achieved a questionable reputation. 'In no other country has the natural equilibrium … been so violently upset as in Australia,' Russell Grimwade had commented on the plunder committed in Australia's forests. In no other country, he went on, 'does the responsibility of preserving a knowledge of the past rest quite so heavily upon its people.' The American Museum of Natural History had been so concerned about the ferocious removal of Australian trees that it had made collecting from the country one of its highest priorities in the early 1920s. 'In no continent has the devastation been more rapid than that of Australia,' it said of Australia's animal and plantlife, 'owing to three causes: deforestation, an enormous fur trade, and an increasing leather trade.' Forestry, and the person of Max Jacobs, stood ready to right these past wrongs in the management of Australia's trees – and to promote those trees to the world.

Questions about how forests were used and planned (or not) were bubbling up in more countries than Australia as the world began to realise it would face imminent shortages of wood for fuel and building, and ever-diminishing forests overall. It needed answers, and the search for these fell largely to the Food and Agricultural Organisation, a sub-branch of the newly invoked United Nations. It was the FAO's job to help to 'rehabilitate' these 'backwards communities', as Jacobs called them (he couldn't call them 'developing countries', he felt, since the fact that they'd cleared out most of their indigenous forest across generations seemed to him to indicate that they were, if anything, *over*-developed). Country after country was running out of timber as fast as their populations were growing. There was a huge demand for fuel, and there were huge areas – both where native forest had been chopped into firewood, and in climates that were naturally arid – that needed planting.

Enter the gums. They germinated easily, and most of their seedlings survived. They grew well and quickly, which meant they could be cut down quite promptly, and numerous slender new trunks would sprout from their roots. As had become clear during the war, they could be turned to a pretty good range of uses. And they had a country increasingly devoted to researching them: Jacobs himself was expanding his interest from particular questions about timber sway and species identification to work on eucalypts' growth habits. These were just the sort of trees the FAO had in mind and it adopted them with a passion. Not since Mueller had the genus been regarded in terms of so much potential.

In 1951 federated Australia celebrated its 50th birthday. There was a Festival of Trees, and the 'gum tree' entry in the *Official Commemorative Book of the Jubilee of the Commonwealth of Australia* cited them as not only ubiquitous in the landscape, but as having 'by far the greatest range of usefulness' – they had come a long way from the days of those First Fleeters who had accused them of being good for nothing except boiling a pot. Western Australia, for instance, was reported to have three and a half million acres of forest in its south-west corner – mainly the mighty jarrah and karri eucalypts – and it was confidently predicted that a harvest of 600,000 loads could be cut each year for 25 or

30 years from these forests alone. Forests, after all, were for felling.

From the Forestry School in the Jubilee year, Jacobs contributed an article to the *Current Affairs Bulletin* about the future of Australia's forests. With the war still so recent, one of the main points he wanted to stress was the importance of trees for defence. 'Every hundred tons of wood obtained locally means that another hundred tons of ammunition, food or other stores can be moved on a transport system that is certain to be hard pressed,' he argued. 'Defence forests are needed in areas where military activity is likely, irrespective of their soundness as a normal business proposition.' Australia, he said, may have managed so far to provide its firewood from whatever trees were to hand rather than actively growing 'crops' of them. But he could see the day when this would become necessary – particularly across southern Australia where, he said dramatically, 'the remaining shade trees will be cut for fuel to the point of extinction.' He wondered too if 'wood will become an important food,' citing experiments that had transformed it into 'an edible carbohydrate on an experimental scale.'

At an FAO conference in Rome in 1951, thousands of miles from the gums' native habitat, the world considered its shrinking forests, considered its options, considered the eucalypts, and asked the FAO to organise a Eucalyptus Study Tour to Australia. Early the next year, a special treaty was drafted between the United Nations and the Australian government ('for the Provision of Technical Assistance to the Governments of Tropical and Semi-tropical Regions'), to ferry a party of international foresters through Australia's increasingly desirable eucalypt woodlands.

Thirty-four of them came – 'a much larger party than was anticipated', the official report commented – from countries as diverse as Burma and Jordan, the Netherlands and Malaya, New Zealand and Nigeria. Twenty-five countries altogether. Even Libya, 'the newest independent country of the Middle East', sent 26-year-old Sed Sherif, who said his homeland 'had long recognised the value of the eucalypt' while admitting that most of its gums had come from Turkey. Israel sent its conservator of forests to explain how it had taken up a 'vigorous policy of afforestation' to transform 'the appearance of the previously denuded countryside'. In four years, he said, his government had put down more than 600 miles of new roadways – most of which were lined with eucalypts.

Brazil – which had been enthusiastically cultivating the trees for 50 years, thanks to the single-minded passion of Navarro de Andrade, the man employed to ensure that the Paulista Railroad Company had a reliable source of wood to fuel its steam engines and erect posts and fencing along its tracks in the first years of the 20th century – sent page after page of information on what was being done for the 38 million eucalypts it already had growing and the steps it was taking to become 'the top country in the world in eucalypt production'.

The Californians came too, with an even longer-standing interest in the gums: their first eucalypt seeds had arrived in a ship captain's pocket in the 1850s, sparking the enthusiasm of one Ellwood Cooper, who had marvelled (watching his gums grow more than 42 feet in three years) that, thanks to 'the Australian "gum-tree", we can in our generation create forests'. Nowhere other than America could expect such good results, he had said, and beyond their spectacular growth he had captivated people with reports that 'in the wilds' of Australia, 'the gum leaf has often to answer the purpose of the entire medicine chest.' It could provide 'immediate and permanent relief' from rheumatism, neuralgia, gout, sciatica, 'any affliction of the nervous system', fever, ague, and 'all diseases of the liver'. A century on, California – like the FAO – was not asking for these sorts of miracles from its gums. The great list of uses California's first eucalyptographers had suggested for their pet timber had dwindled, and its eucalypt plantations were shrinking 'as a consequence of the removal of many groves from irrigable lands more valuable for agriculture'. Fossil fuels were now so popular that most Californians – even those working in logging camps – no longer used eucalypts as fuel. Yet the trees had been around for so long that some Californians felt as much claim on them as Australians might. 'Say,' an American serviceman had reportedly drawled in Sydney during World War II, 'you got some of our eucalypts here.' What they were great for, the Californian representative assured Australia in 1952, was making windbreaks – fantastic protection for all that delicate Californian citrus.

Meanwhile, representatives from Nigeria (six species had been planted just a few years earlier, although two had failed) and Laos (which wouldn't plant its first gum for another 40 years or so), were at the beginning of their eucalyptic experiments.

The visitors underwent a week of enthusiastic instruction in Canberra. Max Jacobs, having performed the official welcome alongside the Minister for External Affairs and distributed the inordinate amount of literature prepared, gave them an hour's talk on how eucalypts grew, while other experts discussed geography, climate and the eucalypts' tricky classifications. Then the 34 foresters set out, ready to 'familiarise [themselves] with the great wealth of eucalypt species and their adaptability'.

In just under two months they were whisked across 5000 miles of Australia by air, and a similar amount by road. They went from Canberra to Western Australia, back to Adelaide, and then to Victoria. They flew to Tasmania, before returning to the mainland and travelling up the east coast, following the route on land that the *Endeavour* had traced, several miles offshore, 180-odd years before, through New South Wales, into Queensland, and back to Sydney. The route was, as the official report from the Department of the Interior pointed out, 'more of an "off-the-beaten-track" tour of Australia than is usually mapped out for overseas delegations "down under"'.

They must have seen every conceivable eucalypt-based enterprise: pulp and paper mills, hardboard factories, wood distillation and tannin extract plants, sawmills and mills for cutting railway sleepers, a masonite outfit so exemplary it was called 'a romance of industry'. They visited a handle factory and Russell Grimwade's large eucalyptus oil distillery. And they saw almost all the different sorts of forest Australia had to offer, everything from stunted *Eucalyptus obliqua* growing next to the road just out of Dimboola to the red gum forests along the Murray River. They had half an hour among 'virgin *E. regnans* and *E. obliqua* with rainforest understorey' in Tasmania, fifteen minutes to appreciate an 'abrupt change of forest type' near Coolongolook, on

New South Wales' north coast, and saw land cleared for cattle – and bananas – that had failed and was being replanted with gums.

Beyond reports on their own countries' use of gums, the delegates didn't leave much of themselves behind. They commented that the difference in temperatures across the country (from freezing in Canberra at the Tour's beginning, to 90 in the shade by the end of it) was 'rather striking', and said they appreciated seeing 'native bears, kangaroos, emus, platypus and other fauna … without interference with the schedule'. They were all very impressed by the eucalypts.

There was one line, in all the literature they were given, that summed up the reason for this. Celebrating the opening of a pulp and paper mill in Burnie, on Tasmania's north coast, the 'magnificent eucalyptus forests' growing in the vicinity were described as 'the ore reserves of the mill at Burnie, but unlike the ore reserves of a mine,' it was pointed out excitedly, 'they are constantly renewing themselves.' Who could ask for anything more of a resource?

The visitors composed their final report, asking the FAO to publish one large, authoritative tome on the trees, and perhaps set up a certified seed provision service. And then they went home, dreaming of vast plantations and possibilities. This Australian tree family, gushed the Department of the Interior, was 'an ambassador of goodwill abroad for its native land'.

Dr Jacobs received his official letter of thanks from the FAO's project manager for the Tour, singling out his 'wholehearted co-operation in assisting to make the tour a success'. Were the FAO to think of a single man to represent the eucalypts, it was fast becoming Jacobs.

Jacobs was wholehearted about everything to do with trees and forestry and the promotion of both, whether he was receiving more students at the School – where he could be relied on to sing and joke with them – or getting out of bed in the middle of the night to apprehend a man stealing a tree from the street. He stood, in his pyjamas, in front of the man's bike and 'nearly fell with the impact' as the bike steered into him, while the culprit, 'physically hurt and moaning', rode off into the darkness – without the tree. His daughter remembers him dashing home to eat with them at night, and then going back to his work until at least two in the morning. He was committed to the trees at home and to seeing them established outside Australia. It had taken them 150 or so years to get to 56 countries around the world: they would reach half as many again in the next quarter of a century, largely thanks to Jacobs and the FAO.

As Jacobs worked on his book *The Growth Habits of the Eucalypts*, an accumulation of scientific knowledge about the trees that would become a standard text, the French eucalyptographer André Métro began compiling the large reference work requested by the 1952 Study Tour, delivering its 403 pages three years later. The thing about the eucalypts, wrote Métro, was that they turned out 'efficient production of wood in quantity, even if the crops grown do not measure up to the exacting standards of silviculturalists of the old school or truly represent "the forest beautiful".' These trees weren't traditional, and they weren't (at least in Métro's eyes) pretty, but you could grow a lot of them in a short time. Métro included detailed information on 67 select species: diagrams, temperatures, yield tables, the latest information on the technology of the wood itself, and reports from eucalyptus growers in different countries.

India was already pushing the gums hard. With eucalypts dating back to 1790 and plantations more than a century old, it led its own study tours and held its own symposia. It had even hybridised a *Eucalyptus tereticornis*, called 'the Mysore gum' (or, less interestingly, *E. hybrid*), as the most suited to its climate and soil.

Spain, too, weighed in with the 'immense plantations' it had established from the 1860s. Initially planted for the gums' miraculous fever-clearing properties, the trees had to be protected against people trying to rip bunches of leaves off the branches. Prove you were sick, and you could take a switch home. By the 1950s Spain was also looking for more pedestrian functions for its gums – sawn wood, fuel, charcoal – rather than medical miracles.

The story of Ethiopia's first gum trees was imbued with a different sort of miracle: the Ethiopian Emperor Menelik, who had to move his country's capital every time it ran out of firewood, named its first permanent site Addis Ababa – 'new flower' – after the eucalypts that had been planted as a permanent source of fuel. Now Ethiopia was researching how far apart seedlings should be planted, and measurements of how much wood would grow when.

Several countries already had such well-established eucalypt plantations that they thought it would be a nice thing to introduce koalas as well. The FAO wondered whether koalas would be able to cope with 'the carnivorous animals of Asiatic, African and American continents', and the idea was dropped. But as the suggestion of transplanting koalas made clear, there was no change, no introduction, that science couldn't at least consider, and the framework of the FAO gave it enough working groups and committees and reports and briefings to feel it could achieve anything. The obvious bureaucratic descendant of the 1952 Study Tour was the First World Eucalyptus Conference in 1956.

Ninety foresters came from 26 countries, including 29 delegates from Italy alone. Despite the criticisms of some visitors that its gums were 'an eyesore', their 'peeling bark suggestive of unmentionable skin diseases', Italy had long been involved in the eucalypts' story, and had been creative with its use of them. It was in Italy that Australia's most widely distributed eucalypt, the river red gum, had been named *Eucalyptus camaldulensis*, from a specimen flourishing in a Neapolitan garden in 1832. And when blue gum seeds sent by Mueller in the 1860s dried out the marshes at the monastery at Tre Fontane – achieving something that had been attempted without success since the time of Caesar, as Mueller had liked to boast – the monks celebrated by creating a eucalypt liqueur, Eucalitino. 'Personally,' said Max Jacobs, 'I would not recommend it as a regular drink but at least it might make recovery from influenza a little more interesting.'

There was a large Australian delegation in Rome too. Jacobs, whose *Growth Habits* had been published the previous year, addressed the broad topic of 'Eucalypt woodland in Australia'. As recently as 'two decades ago,' he said, 'a eucalypt tree had little money value in Australia ... This is not the case today. The present and likely future value of eucalypt logs makes it essential that full stocking should be obtained in the better forests.' This was the job of Australian forestry: to protect, cultivate, and ultimately harvest gum trees from forests which were as 'merchantable' as possible.

But Jacobs was no advocate of planting just anything anywhere. He urged overseas foresters to study all the available gums (the number was up to about 600 different species by now) before they chose one to plant on a large scale. And he hypothesised that it was Australia's savanna eucalypts – less 'merchantable' in their own country – which would prove best for overseas sites, while the highly valued gums from Australia's southern forests wouldn't be much use anywhere else. He exhorted both Australian and overseas foresters to remember that 'different market conditions may lead to strongly contrasted methods of treatment, each of which is right in its locality.'

Max Jacobs was always a big-picture man. He had the knack of enthusing people to think about new ideas – ideas they might never have considered before – before they realised the scale of what he was suggesting. The timeframe he could think about stretched from where he stood in the 1950s to the end of the 20th century and beyond. He was just as good at identifying what needed to be thought about as he was at communicating what had just been discovered. He stood at the peak of a profession which was itself at its peak.

After the first eucalyptus conference, the trees took

him to more and more places: in 1958, it was Brazil. And what does a eucalyptographer do on holidays? He stands gazing at the tree Brazilians call *Eucalyptus alba* and wonders how and when it might have made its first crossing of the Pacific; he thinks of the trees he saw in those aerial photographs of Timor during the war, of the Portuguese ships that used to sail the Pacific, and he wonders if he would find these trees if he went to Timor.

There was a museum he wanted to see as well. In the region where Navarro de Andrade, that enthusiastic eucalypt-planting employee of the Paulista Railroad Company, had set up his first plantations, local farmers had accused him of creating forests where no native creature could live. The museum was de Andrade's response: cases stuffed full of animals and birds shot within eucalypt plantations to counter their accusations. It was, Jacobs thought, a very fine museum.

His work was expanding at home too. He left the Forestry School to become the head of the Commonwealth's Forestry and Timber Bureau – more of an administrator and bureaucrat, in the disappointed opinion of some people who thought the skills he had 'in great measure for research and teaching would be wasted'. But as this was the organisation that administered the School and advised the Australian government on silvicultural matters, on questions of the import and export of timber, *and* ran most of the country's forest research, he wasn't leaving teaching at all. He was just expanding the number of people he could instruct.

And then it was back to Brazil, chairing the Second World Eucalyptus Conference in 1961 where the trees were described by the FAO's director general as 'one of the most promising means for quickly stepping up supplies of wood and wood products.' From one end of the world to the other, gum trees now grew on more than a million hectares of land. The 1950s push to understand how eucalypts grew in warm, moist countries had led to the FAO's distribution of data on planting man-made forests and using their wood: the pace of the trees' expansion was about to increase again. But there was a note of caution in the director general's introduction. Everyone thought eucalypts were so fabulous, so adaptable, that it was assumed that, if you looked hard enough, you would be able to find a suitable species for every purpose. Not so, he cautioned: 'Experience has shown that there are limits to their usefulness.'

What was still regarded as 'almost unlimited', as Jacobs' own paper to the conference discussed, was the number of different species of gum on offer for other countries to try out. He himself led the session on 'Basic Problems', in which it was felt that 'few points of importance' about how or where to grow gum trees had emerged since 1956. Delegates enthused about how much machinery they now used on their plantations, requested that Métro's *Eucalypts for Planting* be updated, and assured each other that, although there were 'differences between the properties of eucalyptus wood from young, rapid growth plantations ... and the properties of mature trees of the same species in their natural habitat,' these were 'only differences in degree and do not give rise to really new problems.'

In Australia, there was no hesitation, no question about the rise and rise of the gum trees' commercial status, and the status of the men who drove that. Jacobs' foresters were 'riding high as a profession in political, research and education areas', credit for which was laid at his feet. He was also celebrated for creating the first body that would think about forestry and plantations federally, rather than leaving these questions up to individual states with their individually enacted forestry legislation to decide.

Where early foresters had had to fight for the most basic levels of funding, more and more money – from both federal and state bodies – was now pushing into the forests. Talk about job creation and export earnings soared, promoted 'by Jacobs' personal charisma and propped up by a vision which was promoted internationally by the foresters about what their profession could do for modern, industrial societies'.

The gums' conquest of the world shimmered: they were the unquestioned – and unlimited – Australian and global resource. But beyond the scale of that conquest there was still room in Jacobs' eucalyptography for the minutiae. Visiting Timor in 1963, he walked through the back door of the Australian consulate and found himself face to face with an *E. alba*, like the one he had seen five years earlier in Brazil. 'The good Timor eucalypt' he called it, and he hypothesised about how early – the 1500s, the 1600s, years ahead of Banks and the British – Portuguese ships might have taken its seeds around the Cape of Good Hope to Brazil, ready for Navarro de Andrade's planting spree in the early 1900s. Some ship, perhaps, had been an early forerunner of the massive dissemination of trees he was overseeing now.

This discovery was small if set against the scale he usually thought in and the extent of what he dreamed for his country's forestry. There was Australia, paying £70 million a year 'for the privilege of importing forest products,' he said that same year at the fifth all-Australian timber congress, when 'there are very few items of imported forest produce for which alternatives could not be grown in Australia.' What he proposed was simple: self-sufficiency. He was old enough, he reminded his audience, to remember when war had cut off Australia's access to all its imported timber. It would be prudent to begin to plant alternatives in greater numbers now so that, 'within the normal working lifetime of a professional man or a business executive,' future resources could be established on Australian soil. He wasn't talking a two-year plan, or even a ten-year one. How far did you want him to look ahead? He was considering the time when Australia's population might be as high as 50 million people: think of all the trees those people would need.

Beyond planting programs and estimates of yield, the eucalypts were working their way out in other directions. Albert Namatjira was becoming the first indigenous artist renowned for work in a white artistic tradition, the trees he painted stylistically descended from Heysen's gums. His artworks – famous for their emblematic, white-trunked ghost gums, *Eucalyptus papuana* – earned £50,000 between 1945 and 1949, and he became the first Aboriginal Australian to be given citizenship. (He had to pay tax, but still wasn't allowed to purchase land.) After he died in 1959, his work fell from general acclaim.

Later, people like Lloyd Rees would praise 'his eyes [which could] look so far away and seem to know what's there', but most professional artists at the time thought that it was 'tribal' or 'primitive' art that deserved their attention, rather than this work of a tribal artist in a European tradition. Since the 1940s, museums had been keen to collect indigenous gum paintings, but what they wanted was ochre on sheets of eucalyptus bark, not representational gums on watercolour paper.

Around the same time, an Australian artist called Fred Williams came home from America understanding that the patterns being used by abstract painters in New York fitted precisely over the landscape – the trees of the bush – that he wanted to paint at home. Critics looked at his canvases and credited him with 'taking up the problems of Australian landscape painting where Tom Roberts left off in the 1920s, an old man in his seventies painting saplings in [Victoria's] Sherbrooke Forest'. Williams' trees 'spread across scoriated surfaces like notes on a musical score', evoking the Australian bush rather than representing it. He might sometimes have felt the bush was 'flat and featureless', but his work reconciled the two senses it inspired: the feeling of hugely 'broad vistas', and the need – like the delicacy Frederick McCubbin had captured in individual gum leaves – for 'intimate bush detail'.

'He gets closer to the essence of the Australian landscape than most,' approved Patrick White, while John Olsen – experimenting with the look of gum trees across the land, saying they needed calligraphy to catch them – likened Fred Williams' attitude to Buvelot's and lamented that most other Australian artists were 'being driven to be terrified of gum trees.' The very word, he said, had 'been made a term of derision because some people paint them so unimaginatively. The barbarian intellectuals,' he railed, 'have got artists running scared of what is most distinctive, what is most worth investigating about the place.' There was nothing corny about anything Australian, he said, if it was 'handled properly … rephrased in a personal way.' Rephrasing, renewing: 'Freddy Williams loves the gum tree,' Olsen concluded, 'and look how he's renewed the way we see it.'

'Australia,' one playwright commented at the time, 'is not so much what a gum tree looks like as what a gum tree means.'

In all the stories of eucalyptography – of people whose eye, once caught by the eucalypts, never managed to walk clear of their influence again – archetypal stories could be found beyond the botanists or explorers, the artists or poets. Like that of Stan Kelly, an engine driver from Ararat in western Victoria who, in his thirties, found himself launched on a mission to paint a specimen of every single species.

He began accidentally, taken by a huge *Eucalyptus leucoxylon* growing in a friend's garden in 1945. He picked himself a spray, set it up on his kitchen table, painted it and, he thought, it 'came out all right … From that moment,' he said, 'I developed an interest in the eucalypts.' With his first book – 49 colour plates – in 1949, he hoped to 'arouse in [readers] an appreciation for a tree that is characteristically Australian.' The book's editor lamented that, while everyone was busy filling their gardens up with exotics, 'the eucalypts are dismissed as "just old gums".' 'Quite apart from their amazing utilitarian role,' said the botanist who provided descriptions for each picture, 'the gum trees have a strong aesthetic appeal.' No other country 'of like area,' he noted, 'owes so much to a single genus of plants.' Sometime after that Kelly decided to keep going, to paint them all, and through the fifties and sixties he sought them out, one by one. On his holidays, he left his wife and children at home and combed the country on buses, on trains, in four-wheel drives. (The *Women's Weekly* called his wife a 'tree widow', but Kelly said that was 'poetic licence' – his family 'didn't mind. They just took it that I wanted to see these places.')

He travelled to Western Australia, to Queensland, through the Northern Territory (where Max Jacobs had relished being able to gather up twenty specimens in a morning) and the Kimberley. He sat with his back leaning against Burke and Wills' 'Dig tree' and felt, he said, 'an aura about the place. I was looking at the same things that they were looking at,' he thought, 'but from a different aspect altogether.' He went to the Centre, too. He'd 'seen Albert Namatjira's paintings,' he said, and suspected they were 'highly exaggerated, but when I got up there, I found that wasn't the case at all. The colours were absolutely fantastic.'

It was 1965 and he travelled to Alice Springs, on his way to Darwin, on a Vespa. Thirty miles an hour, top speed – the scooter purred along, he said – 'and so I missed nothing. I smelt, saw, felt and heard everything along the way. It was a perfect way to travel.' His was pure enthusiasm and affection for the trees, nothing to do with economics or bureaucracy or science. On that trip it was *Eucalyptus foelscheana* he was after – 'the largest leaves of the genus,' he explained. Out at Howard Springs, 'I found what I was looking for, and on the way home, another magnificent tree I'd always been looking for and admired so much was in full bloom.' He was, he remembered, 'so thrilled at finding it that I climbed right up the tree and sat in among the branches, surrounded by these beautiful orange-coloured flowers … such a thrill to find this beautiful tree.'

Meanwhile, Max Jacobs had an interesting way of charting how botanists thought of eucalypts: in 1965, he drew up a table comparing the origin of the names the different species had been given from L'Héritier on. For the first 80 years, with only four exceptions, they were named for their various botanical attributes – this one's oblique leaves, that one's resinous gum. Then there were names commemorating people or places. The final column in Jacobs' table had only four entries from 180 years of naming: trees which had kept their indigenous names in conjunction with their new '*Eucalyptus*' tag.

There were 742 eucalyptus names in all by now, and still a lot of questions that had to be answered about them. Take Ethiopia: Jacobs, gazing over its vast plantations of *Eucalyptus globulus*, saw the blue gum which Mueller had exalted above all others and commented that it was a popular tree overseas while it was 'not an important tree in its homeland'. (Mueller would have been appalled.) Jacobs had made this particular visit to answer what seemed a simple question: it wasn't a matter of designating the best species for a site, or how far apart seedlings should be planted, or what sort of fertiliser should be pushed into soil. Jacobs was there simply to try and work out why these trees flourished in this place – and in Italy, France, California, South America and other parts of Africa as well.

Staring out at the land, he noticed that the young blue

gums were heavy with their first leaves cascading right down to the ground, while other types of tree had had their leaves stripped for several feet off the ground. The blue gums were one of the few crops that the Ethiopians could plant without the added expense of putting up fences. There were sheep nearby, and cattle and goats. Suddenly he saw why this eucalypt of all eucalypts was the crop for Ethiopia: Ethiopian sheep, cattle and goats didn't like their young blue leaves, although they would happily eat the young leaves of everything else. The gums could grow, unmunched, until they were taller, stronger, and their tasty adult leaves were well out of reach of anything peckish that was passing by. The young leaves themselves were a barrier.

He made his way home, and down to Tasmania where *E. globulus* seedlings were sprouting after a bushfire. There was no doubt, he said, that cattle, sheep and goats preferred the seedlings of any other eucalypt to an *E. globulus*, 'to the extent of giving it a marked advantage even over species such as *Eucalyptus obliqua* which would outgrow it in the absence of grazing.' The Indian Conservator of Forests had noted the same thing exactly a hundred years before: the growth of *Eucalyptus globulus* was 'incredible' – 'especially when the trees are young, the leaves are full of oil glands and even goats won't touch them.' A goat-proof tree was always useful, but the 19th-century Indian discovery that blue gums were goat-proof had never been passed on to other countries: research results didn't always travel.

In 1970, Max Jacobs retired as director general of the Forestry and Timber Bureau, though he was by no means done with his work. He undertook more and more missions for the FAO, was sought out by businesses as 'the world's leading expert on the *Eucalyptus* species', and took up visiting professorships around the world. 'The genus *Eucalyptus*,' he told the University of Washington, 'is one of the most useful genera discovered by explorers who fanned out from Europe during the past 500 years.' Its importance in 'the middle and lower latitudes of the world', he said, would only increase.

But the shape of the world – and of eucalypts within it – was changing in ways that forestry hadn't anticipated. For one thing, in many countries, as the Californians had said as early as 1952, wood was less and less the fuel of choice. For another, countries were beginning to look at their exotic gum trees and see negatives, rather than the glowing positives that twenty years of FAO endorsement had promised them. Most importantly, there was one small word – pulp – which had catapulted eucalypts into a whole new phase of promotions, and problems.

It had begun towards the end of the sixties: a speaker at the FAO's 1967 conference on man-made forests (held in Australia instead of a third conference on eucalypts) had talked of a clear change in what the wood was wanted for – 'although it is not yet clear just how pertinent it will finally become'. What he was talking about was the switch – in his lifetime, he said – from a preference for softwood conifers to hardwood plantations for industrial use. And this change came from 'the changing importance that hardwood is assuming for use as a pulp'.

Max Jacobs had thought about it too: by the year 2000,

he hoped, '50 million of [Australia's] 76 million acres of native forest will be accessible,' opening up vast new areas from which that 'yield' could be taken, and converting more and more of Australia's already sparse native forest into a profit. In the end, money had to be made, and if a handful of cents could be made selling otherwise worthless eucalypts for the pulp needed for books, newsprint and other coated paper, then that was better than making no money from those trees at all.

India, too, was looking at its eucalypts in terms of this growing demand for pulp, and, by the early seventies, it was discovering that the economically attractive idea of being able to sell just about any gum for pulp had some unattractive side effects. A report made to the Indian government in 1960 had recommended 'that 607,000 hectares of most productive land be selected for raising plantations of fast-growing species under intensive management' to meet increasing demands for pulp, and the fast-growing species suggested were gums. To provide this 'most productive land', perfectly complete, functional, and ecologically distinct native forests were cleared. The justification was simple: eucalypts would grow faster than the trees they were replacing.

One of the selling points of gum trees had always been how fast they grew; this had made them an ideal option to provide the timber for fuel that India still needed. A hungry pulp industry meant that any eucalypt intended for firewood or timber might suddenly be appropriated by a larger, more solvent pulp company able to pay growers more money than the people who needed timber or fuel could ever afford. In the first twenty years of a 'fuel scheme' in Indian forestry, it would eventually be revealed, 'not a single log had been allocated to meet the fuel needs of households'. It had all become pulp instead.

In Australia, too, the increasing demands for pulp were changing the eucalypts' world, and not just in terms of the glowing returns that Jacobs had anticipated. In the mid-sixties, he had drawn attention to the Bombala-Eden-Twofold Bay district on New South Wales' far south coast as the spot 'any post-graduate geography group' would pick if they had to recommend 'the most favoured region' to promote for new rural and industrial prosperity. When Japan's Harris-Daishowa company expressed an interest in Australian eucalypt fibre for their pulp and paper industry, the government saw a way of converting Eden's 'unproductive' forests into something very lucrative. The first shipment of their chips went to Japan in 1971.

Whatever symbols or metaphors the gums could be turned into, public apathy about forests had a long history in Australia. Experts like Mueller had wanted to talk about the responsibility of conserving trees as resources and had complained that their statements fell on 'deaf ears'. In the early 1970s, that apathy was turning, and for the first time people seemed to question forestry's sense of itself as playing a seminal role in the history of conservation. New words were creeping into the vocabulary people used when they talked about Australia's gum forests, and where the foresters had always referred to their role as 'protecting' trees, they found themselves suddenly referred to as 'the main destroyers of remaining natural forest', using methods which had 'a bad, and at times disastrous, effect on forest values other than wood production'.

Suddenly the trees found themselves accorded a value that had nothing to do with money. Suddenly, the whole notion of forestry, managed forests, supply and demand, was under attack. As people began to pay a different sort of attention to their eucalyptus forests, they found they weren't entirely happy with what they saw. To take a single tree out of a forest was one thing, but the way logs were removed now didn't need anywhere near as delicate a process, and the foresters – who had regarded themselves as conserving the forests, or preserving them for future needs and returns at least – found themselves accused of their wholesale and wanton destruction. More than that, even their future plans were dismissed: what need was there to plant stand after stand of exotic pines in the place of native gums and in some vain quest for self-sufficiency? the new green movement asked. If Australia ever achieved such a thing, conservationists pointed out, it would be the '*only* trading nation in the world which is *self sufficient* in forest products'. At what cost would this be achieved – and did it need to be?

By 1973, Max Jacobs had to be employed to explain to both federal government ministers and the media why 'a managed forest is a happy place', against more and more arguments that forestry's forests were fairly unhappy. The following year he was called in to vouch for the work of the Australian Pulp and Paper Mills company in a pamphlet called 'The Forests We Care For'.

The most organised and annotated attack on forestry and its practices came from a book by Richard and Val Routley called *The Fight for the Forests*, which accused foresters of being paternalistic, secretive, in bed with the wood industry, lacking expertise in and knowledge of ecological matters, and incapable of considering trees in terms of any value other than that of wood production. Most foresters bitterly resented the book as the first major attack on both their public image and their professional status. All they were doing, they argued, was what had always been expected of them, and hadn't they been the people who'd cared for the trees all along, who'd tried to get people to think about how many of them there needed to be? Hadn't the founding members of their profession, in every state of Australia, spent the end of the 19th century and the beginning of the 20th fighting the popular idea that forests were either inexhaustible or an aggravating hindrance to the country's development? Obviously the public, the conservationists, these new environmentalists, didn't understand this.

But people did understand pictures. When old-growth forest was flooded to create lakes Gordon and Pedder in Tasmania, the images of dead tree trunks poking through the water's surface were powerful. Photographs of clear-felled land were even more effective – the earth stripped bare, back to mud, and the charred stumps of trees; the land bulldozed and burnt to nothing. 'This is not a battlefield,' one caption read. 'It's a view of the Eden wood chip project.'

It wasn't just this new generation of conservationists who took issue with these operations: some of the old timber-getters questioned it too. Trees were being ripped out now, they said, that they'd've left as malnourished saplings, and these bulldozers and chainsaws that ripped through everything without a moment's hesitation completely severed not only any tree trunk unlucky enough to get in the way, but the workers' connection to the trees they were harvesting.

The strange thing was – even as the voice of conservation and concern for the environment grew – how little many people noticed. Even someone like Stan Kelly, who certainly paid more attention to trees than most people, could move through the decade without really knowing what was going on. In 1978 he published the second volume of his *Eucalypts* (the first had appeared in 1969) and declared himself at the end of his project. He had painted more than six hundred species. 'I began painting the eucalypts as a hobby,' he wrote in his preface, 'little dreaming that thirty-two years later … I would realise my dream of painting the whole flora.' The eucalypts, he said, were 'Australia's greatest asset and finest ambassador.' His books were published in America and the UK. Copies found their way all over the world, and he had fan letters from as far away as Israel, where eucalypt saplings had been sponsored by Jewish schoolchildren in London. It was well into the eighties, he said, before he became aware of any of the treatment being accorded many of those ambassadors. He lived on a great open plain in western Victoria which had been stripped bare for years. It was only later, he said, that he went up into the bush and saw what was happening – whole areas denuded not only of the trees but all the scrub, all the young trees, all the regrowth. It was, he said, 'a shock. It was unbelievable.'

As Kelly's final contribution to eucalyptography was published, Max Jacobs was in Rome, revising the FAO's 1955 *Eucalypts for Planting*. The number of eucalypts growing outside Australia had increased fivefold in the 25 years between editions. 'The stream of new species does not cease,' he encouraged the world's foresters, lamenting that 'there is not more land in the southern hemisphere with a latitude of 35-40°S, since there are some excellent species available for such conditions.' He finished work on the manuscript in 1979, and went home. But before its long-anticipated publication at the end of that year, he died. He was 74 years old. He'd had 'a feel for the forest', colleagues said in their tributes, 'the earthy and intimate forest understanding of a good silviculturalist'. And they remembered him emerging from a square of plantation with a brush hook or an axe in his hand 'and a goodly cover of sweat and leeches', having tidied up or trimmed some wayward growth. 'There,' he would say, 'that looks much more like it.'

After his death, the problems, occasionally hinted at but usually ignored in the face of all that eucalypts promised, were ready to explode. America had found the gums wanting as timber as early as the 1900s, and accepted that there were things they couldn't do. Some Brazilian farmers had questioned them in the 1950s, but had been assured they were a miracle crop. Now, with the continuing problem of trees intended as firewood being sold for pulp instead, India's farmers were questioning more and more why all their land was given over to these trees which gave them nothing in return. One forester even suggested that, for all the information the FAO went to so much trouble to disseminate, there wasn't really a single eucalypt suited to their humid, tropical conditions. 'Are we justified,' he asked, 'in keeping the people guessing on the suitability of the species based on unsound and uncertain experimental data and casual observations?'

It might be wise, too, another Indian forester suggested, to undertake 'careful impact studies on the welfare of tribal populations' before the trees were slapped in the middle of the places they lived. However fast they grew, whatever economic incentives people liked to dream about, there was 'a strong and valid criticism that the choice of *Eucalyptus* as one of the major species in social forestry is not to the advantage of the common man in need of fuel, fodder' and so on. More and more stories about how they monopolised any water, any nutrients an area had, were offered up against them.

Behind all this, India saw a culprit: the FAO. India's passion for eucalypts had been driven, they said, by 'Western technical advice from agencies like the FAO on forest management in tropical areas which are scientifically ill-understood.' Furthermore, they alleged, Western advisers had 'played an aggressive role by framing development projects for the forests, often with little thought for their long-term effect or for the social impact of these schemes.' The World Bank, another gum promoter, also stood accused: with more than half its forestry budget going to tree cultivation (mostly of eucalypts), its projects for the reconstruction of rural ecology were called 'marginal' at best, and 'destructive' at worst.

Whoever was to blame, the eucalypts stood squarely in the middle of the mess, while Indian researchers said bleakly that their country was lousy with official environmental experts who would 'fabricate … convenient data' to serve the interests of 'the power and profit of the few' and legitimise more ecological destruction.

As forestry split between social foresters and industrial or commercial foresters, the division was even wider between foresters in general and conservationists, who decried the wholesale removal of gums in Australia, and their wholesale introduction everywhere else. While Bob Hawke won victory for Labor with the help of promises to save the forests along Tasmania's Franklin River and *not* build a very large dam, farmers overseas were increasingly looking for leaders who would get rid of as many eucalypts as possible as quickly as possible. In India, a book on its 'eucalyptus craze' was called, tellingly, *The God That Failed*. In Spain and Portugal, where huge terraces had been bulldozed out of native forests for the gums, farmers led protests against the symmetrical grids of seedlings, equating them with the right-wing politics of Franco's era.

Grow this crop, country after country had been told, and make fast money from it – and the social costs of introducing rows and rows of eucalypts had disappeared under the hunger for everything the 'miracle trees' would deliver. By the mid-1908s, a review of the ecological effects of planting gums was saying diplomatically that there could be 'no universal answer, either favourable or unfavourable, to the planting of eucalypts. Nor should there be any universal answer: each case should be examined on its own merits.'

Nine years after Jacobs finished revising *Eucalypts for Planting*, the FAO released another book on its endorsed trees: *The Eucalypt Dilemma*. With large type and big pictures, the pros and cons of gums were reduced to point-form in 26 pages. True, it said, no other tree had been so widely propagated. And true, eucalypts could provide quick benefits. But they might affect the soil. And the water supply. And wildlife. And they might 'upset local values or traditions'. In the end, if you lived somewhere that wasn't Australia, and you were thinking of putting in a stand of gums, the new FAO advice was this: 'each judgment will be specific. In some areas eucalypts will not be appropriate; in some areas eucalypts will be very useful. Such decisions are complex, and no one knows all the right answers ...'

The days of the unquestioned promotion of the gums were at an end.

with the giants

There is, there was, a country, that spoke
in the language of leaves ...

—Judith Wright, 'Falls Country'

The trees found themselves in a fast-changing world. As farmers from India to Spain, Thailand and Portugal argued against their invading gums, more and more arguments were being made for them to be left alone in their own country. White Australia, heading towards 200 years of occupation in 1988, started to wonder why what was left of the eucalypts as they had been before James

Cook and the *Endeavour* arrived, before Arthur Phillip and the First Fleet turned up, couldn't stay untouched, rather than becoming the next contribution to forestry's catalogue of resources.

The value of eucalypts – expressed so clearly in terms of imports and exports, profit and loss – found another currency. It was the idea that trees shouldn't be saved from becoming timber and fuel and pulp and veneer by being turned into another sort of resource, like a big playpen for recreation or anything else. The point was that the trees were beyond value altogether. As the Wilderness Society in Tasmania put it, emphasis needed to be placed on 'the philosophical and the eternal' of the matter. It needed to become a question not of promoting 'the wilderness experience ... but the right of wilderness to exist'. Post-materialism, this was called in the late 1970s, and it linked back to early Tasmanian naturalists' sense of the divine in their landscape. 'Heaven grant that we may be able to retain many solitary places in this beautiful island of ours where nature in all her grandeur will reign supreme,' one had written 70 years before, 'and where sulphur fumes, and axes, and jam tins will be forever unknown.' Conservation's battle to achieve this, in Tasmania and across Australia's continent, was only going to increase in the post-materialist age.

In light of which, the eucalypts needed new ways of attracting people's attention, and the solution was an old one, but a good one. What was one of the attributes that people – particularly Australians – seemed guaranteed to respond to? Size. This was, after all, a country that excelled in the construction in fibreglass and concrete of large-scale sheep, fruit, cows, crustaceans and so on. What did the eucalypts have over every other flowering plant in the world? They were the tallest, and the tallest of the tallest lived in a state which was not only comparatively free from man-made big things (it only boasts the Big Penguin, the Big Coffee Pot, and the Big Tasmanian Devil), but had a relatively large forestry industry among a relatively small population. They lived in Tasmania.

Among the flood of mainland activists who had gone to Tasmania during the Franklin River campaign in the eighties was Geoff Law. A Victorian, he had the kind of upbringing that led him away from the cities most Australians lived in, and into something wider – or wilder. Camping, bush-walking, white-water rafting, cross-country skiing: he was brought up, he says simply, 'with a love of the natural environment.' The sort of kid who'd borrow books on Tasmania from the library to gaze at pictures of Precipitous Bluff.

In 1981, during a holiday in Tasmania, Law had stood on the top of a mountain in the south-west, looking across to the east. 'I saw a hillside that had been scalped,' he says, 'and I felt absolutely shocked. I didn't know that people were allowed to do that.' More and more things were changing in his landscape – bushwalks would end in a clear-fell coupe, in the middle of smouldering logs; walking trails would become forestry roads busy with trucks and machinery. Somewhere, too, he saw a poster with the line 'Don't Flood the Franklin'. 'Looks like a spectacular river,' he thought, 'pity they're going to dam it, pity it's just going to go' – just presuming, he says, 'that nobody could do anything about it.'

Still, he travelled south to join the campaign for the Franklin, and settled, and stayed, taking the first of a series of jobs working to protect Tasmania's forests, and sleeping on future green federal senator Bob Brown's kitchen floor. The campaign was a training program, he says: people learnt to write press releases, stage protests, run PR campaigns, hold meetings – they learnt how to organise. He thought he was a bit spoilt, too, coming in on the end of a successful campaign, expecting that you would always win, always get the top story on the night's news. But there was no doubt he was one of the best people for this job: within a few years, new campaigners referred to themselves as 'small players', and Geoff Law as the man they learnt from: he was becoming one of the state's most effective environmental campaigners. And his passion, his effectiveness as a campaigner, comes, in Brown's opinion, 'from his direct love of and knowledge of and relationship to the forests themselves.'

Something about Tasmania's forests, about the scale of its trees, had always registered with European eyes, right from the first ones to have seen them. Not only had Tasmania provided both the *Eucalyptus obliqua* specimen for L'Héritier to name and the seeds Kew was growing before the end of the 18th century, it was Tasmania's coast that the French had traced by ship, 'filled with wonder at the sight of these ancient forests in which the sound of the axe had never yet been heard'. It was Tasmania where they had marvelled at 'trees of immense height and proportionate diameter'. *Eucalyptus obliqua*, now commonly known as the messmate, grew hundreds of feet. *Eucalyptus regnans* grew even higher – the name translates as 'the reigning eucalypt' – with its head above the other trees. More regal than was implied in Tasmania's common name for it, 'swamp gum', or even the Victorians' tag of 'mountain ash', some of these trees, the French sailors said, looked 'as old as the world'.

In the trees' arsenal of ways to attract people's attention, age had already proved useful, even if early estimates by Mueller and others that a mountain ash might be more than 3000 years old were inaccurate. While Mueller's poetic description of trees standing 'already in youthful elegance while yet the diprotodon was roaming over the forest ridges encircling Port Phillip Bay' was exaggerated, there is still poetry in the great age of these trees, Tasmania's in particular. This one a seedling in 1480, before Shakespeare was a boy; that one already well established when Abel Tasman sailed by in 1642.

Three hundred years later, it was Tasmania's forest – 'dark and gloomy as it looks from a distance, [but] exquisite in its beauty as you pass through it,' according to one early bushwalker – that had been tagged magnificent 'ore reserves' for paper mills in the fifties as the FAO's Eucalyptus Study Tour trooped through. And it was Tasmania's eucalypts – the curvy, sinuous trees John Glover painted which were later dismissed as unrealistically exaggerated and were now being endorsed again as not only important but representative colonial art – that artists were taking up again. Some even took Glover's own gum images as starting points and ringbarked them, or updated their background to an urban setting.

It was to Tasmania's forests, too, that Law and Brown took the federal environment minister, Graham Richardson, in 1986. Flying over clear-felled and old-growth land, walking through the forests while they showed him King Billy Pines and crushed sassafras for him to smell,

Richardson declared himself sympathetic to the calls of the conservation movement and its bid to limit old-growth logging. 'Having been shown the awesome forests,' he wrote, '... I wanted to become a warrior for the cause. By the time we arrived back in Hobart, I was a convert ... Trees have always been popular, so saving trees was bound to be even more popular than the trees themselves.' To Richardson, it was one of those occasions when 'what was right was also popular'. (Three prime ministers since have declined invitations to visit the place and look at the big old gums: 'I saw what happened to Richo,' said Bob Hawke simply.)

It was also in 1986 that Geoff Law took a trip out to the area around Mt Field and Mt Mueller, less than two hours west of Hobart. There were trees he wanted to see in a working forest, vast tracts of gums behind huge padlocked gates growing around the tanin-stained waters of the Styx River and out through its valley, just beyond the town of Maydena. The forest was being harvested by a paper company, Australian Newsprint Mills, which leased the land from the government, and its gums were coming down to satisfy the worldwide demand for pulp that had been booming and booming since the sixties. If you wanted to make paper with the best surface for printing on – like newsprint – then the best fibre to make it from was a shorter hardwood fibre. And the best example of that was eucalyptus fibre.

Law pulled up at the boomgate just outside Maydena, asked to be allowed through, and was given a photocopied map. It was only ANM that had the keys to the padlocks on the gates: not even the Forestry Commission could get in without their permission. He drove past the log yard and into the labyrinth of forestry roads, feeling more like an unwelcome, surreptitious trespasser than a tourist, even though this was technically public land, much of it listed on the Register of the National Estate.

After half an hour on potholed gravel roads, he arrived at a small sign: 'The Big Tree.'

Whatever he expected, whatever he thought was behind those padlocks and gates, he was awestruck, standing amongst the long legs of tree trunks, leaning far back to take in their height and the sheer distance to their canopies and leaves above. He was amazed that people hadn't heard of this place. These massive trees, he thought, which no one knows are here. These massive trees – due to be logged for newsprint. In the article he wrote about his visit for the Australian Conservation Foundation, Law calculated that should the tallest of these trees be logged, the government would receive about $200 for it. It seemed small money for such grand and unique objects. 'One of the richest tracts of forest in the entire country,' Law wrote, 'much of it still in wilderness condition' – and both access to it and management of it was in the hands of one company who leased it, Law calculated, for $4 per hectare per year, to turn it into newspapers.

The river and its valley had been called 'Styx' – and noted for its 'thick forest' – for more than 150 years before Law first saw it. It had survived unsuccessful gold prospectors, people looking for exotic-sounding osmiridium (used to make pen nibs), and talk of slicing it with a railway to link Tasmania's east coast with the west. The area it sat within had endured decades of logging, from the first years of the 20th century when the trees were taken out individually by axe and cross-cut saw to be used for housing frames, walls and floorboards, to the later demands of the pulp and paper mills. One of the most extraordinary trees ever turned into newspapers had come from above the Styx, in the Derwent River Valley. The massive diameter of its felled trunk was measured by the height of a man standing with his arm above his head, plus half an axe handle, plus the full length of another man's arm reaching down from where he lay at the top of the tree's circumference. It had germinated, it was calculated, in 1548, and had been felled almost 400 years later in 1942. The two men took two and a half days to cut it down – it had been left by early millers as too big, a 'venerable veteran'. Workers for miles around 'downed tools for a moment, almost in reverence to the mighty tree that was no more', while the company in charge of logging (it was ANM even then) said it was only the war that had justified such an action, and how sorry they were that the tree had been cut.

The history of wrestling eucalypts to the ground was filled with solid labour. Neat slots cut into a trunk in three or four axe-strokes. Boards wedged in that men used to climb the height of the tree – to top it or to fell it. And these were big, old trees they were dealing with. In the country around the Myall Lakes, up north of Sydney, between 1890 and 1916, men cut eucalypts – 'best hardwood in the world,' says the poet Les Murray – into sleepers for the Russian czar's great Trans Siberian Railway. (Some came from Tasmania's forests as well.) And it wasn't a matter of dropping a tree and feeding it through a mill to spit out regular rectangles at the other end: each sleeper was cut by a man with a broadaxe. 'There's probably still some under that railway,' muses Murray: 'it's so cold up there.' By the time of World War II, the northern New South Wales timber cutters reckoned they were taking the second-rate stuff – logs their fathers would have walked away from. The logs judged as ready to harvest 40, 50 years later? 'Bloody telephone poles,' the old axemen sniffed. 'We wouldn't have looked at anything that small.'

By 1986, as Law stood among the Styx's trees for the first time, the woodchippers had arrived – no axes, no cross-cut saws: just bulldozers, chainsaws, enormous trucks and helicopters. Tasmania's foresters knew these trees were tremendous. They had described towering mountain ashes in the Styx Valley as early as 1960 and, two years later, three surveyors from ANM measured a bunch of 'extremely tall trees' in the same area. The tallest came in at 98.26 metres: definitively Australia's tallest tree. Fourteen trees were given their own 15-hectare reserve in which to sit, protected. It was a tiny patch of space in the middle of an old-growth forest thousands of times its size, mostly untouched and, in Law's immediate opinion, just as important to preserve. 'Why continue to clear-fell our remaining virgin forests when the benefits to the community from doing so are diminishing,' he asked in his 1986 article, 'and when public demand for wilderness and natural forests is on the increase?' Behind those locked gates, he wrote, 'are some of the world's most beautiful wilderness forests.' It was time 'to protect the forest giants of Tasmania's south-west by adding them to the World Heritage Area', the boundaries of which were then under hot debate.

In the late eighties, the listing of Tasmania's wilderness as a World Heritage site occupied much of the Tasmanian conservation movement's attention. The campaign, on which Law worked, began in earnest in 1987, when a Wilderness Society member came back from a bushwalk with stories of an amazing forest out near Wylds Craig, on the island's west coast. At its heart sat a huge messmate, whose shaggy trunk sprang into three prongs ten metres or so up from the ground. It was scheduled to be logged. The Wilderness Society called it the Trident Tree, and when images of it began to appear, support for its salvation came from all directions.

'The feeling expressed in the newspaper editorials was that these trees were living cathedrals and to destroy them would be an act of vandalism,' Law remembered later. He quoted Yehudi Menuhin's proclamation on the matter, that destroying the tall forests of Tasmania to make paper was akin to gassing the Jewish people and boiling them down for soap: 'there aren't too many people who can get away with a statement like that.'

It took a year for the logging to be stopped – and it had come within half a kilometre of the Trident by then. As far as Law was concerned, much of the credit for the campaign's success lay with this individual gum: seeing it, he said, gave people 'a taste of something that exists beyond the rat race of everyday life, something which we need.'

But the area listed as World Heritage reserve in 1988, white Australia's bicentenary, was a compromise – two of the three commissioners appointed to investigate which parts of Tasmania's tree-rich wilderness should be saved nominated only 10 per cent of the area under consideration. The third said everything that had been nominated should be preserved, as well as some other areas that hadn't been suggested. In the deal that was finally done (it took more than 14 hours of cabinet meetings) 70 per cent of the proposed area was nominated, but this represented only 30 per cent of the forests suggested. Law could think of magnificent stands of eucalypts in more than four locations around the island that had not been saved. And those tall trees in the Styx were among them.

There was no doubt they were the tallest known examples of *E. regnans*: a survey of the state's wet eucalypt forests established that in the same year. Calling for immediate further reservations to be made for their conservation, the survey observed that 'fortunately, reservation of wet forest as a whole … is possible within the area directly adjacent to the present World Heritage Area'. It could simply be enlarged.

Law knew that the future of the tall forests was a good issue for a campaign. He had seen the most committed people lose interest when campaigns came down to the thick language of bureacracy. But this 'was something that people could focus on,' he felt, 'something a bit more spectacular and inspiring than just talking about forests generally.' As Bob Brown says, 'these forests, the tallest forests, gave us something to home in on, a symbol for everything we were fighting for.'

At least the Trident Tree stood safe, becoming itself a symbol of success and a source of inspiration for both conservationists and the public.

In July 1989, prime minister Bob Hawke stood at the junction of three states – New South Wales, Victoria and South

Australia – on the banks of the Murray River, and declared his vast new environmental plan: the One Billion Trees program, a scheme to plant a billion trees across Australia between 1990 and 2000. It called for 400 million trees to be planted as seedlings, with 600 million more sown as seeds or regenerated naturally behind the protection of fences. City newspapers did the maths and scoffed that the program would need to plant 11,415 trees every hour for a decade. It sounded scary – until you realised that a single nursery could produce 10 million seedlings a year, that planters could handle 150,000 tea-trees in a single day. And it was only an American billion that he wanted planted, after all – not the million-million of a British one.

Hawke planted some nice *Eucalyptus camaldulensis* saplings to kick-start the whole scheme, and unveiled a plaque commemorating the moment. It sounded so grand, so mathematically precise. And certainly, experts agreed, there was 'plenty of scope for one billion trees to be profitably and usefully planted in Australia': between 12 and 15 billion trees had been lost from the Murray-Darling basin alone. Yet from the outset there were questions about the small amount of funding the plan had received, the tree-planting methods that were going to be used, and even whether anyone knew which trees should be planted where.

And where the idea of a billion trees could be taken up on this kind of bureaucratic level, it was still much easier to think about single gums. If someone could identify a eucalypt as somehow theirs, if they could name it and claim it – personalise it, anthropomorphise it – then they would feel a lot more attachment to it. Once the Trident Tree was given a name and stopped being an anonymously shaggy messmate somewhere along an unknown track, people had something to focus on and care about as they took in the conservation arguments from one side, forestry's from the other.

These things had been on Peter Solness' mind for some time: through the 1980s, into the early nineties, he toyed with the idea that trees were, for Australia, very real – albeit possibly dormant – 'cultural icons'. There were connections between people and trees, he suspected, that sparked deeply held stories. Intimate stories. Confessional stories. Subconscious stories. As a photographer, he thought there might be some good pictures in that. He thought about the way people reacted to their own personal trees – trees they had planted, trees that were a memorial to something they cared about, or belonged somewhere they felt they belonged. He thought about the way people could stand, indifferent, to trees they perceived as nothing to do with them, like the vast tracts of Australian bush carelessly dismissed. He thought about the way trees' stories had distilled into the voices of development against the voices of conservation and vice versa, and wondered if there was something beyond the politics, the economics of those two opposing positions.

If he could photograph whatever these things might be, he thought, he might be able to shift the ways people thought and talked about trees. He might be able to give them a new value. As part of his Tree Stories project, he photographed Geoff Law under the heritage-listed Trident Tree in 1997. 'For years people around Australia had been buying newsprint without knowing that pristine old-growth forests and some of the tallest trees on the face of the earth were literally being turned into rubbish,' Law explained to him.

There was another tree Solness wanted for his collection. He wanted to photograph the tallest tree in Australia, in the Styx Valley. You'll need the key from the paper company, Law told him, and they should have a map to tell you how to find it.

It was late in the afternoon. Solness borrowed a bunch of keys to those padlocks Geoff Law had opened eleven years earlier, and set off. And there it stood, set back from the road, the old sign still at its base, and Peter Solness beside it. Coming on for dark, on his last day in Tasmania.

It was impossible to get back away from it and see it properly. All he could see was a trunk, carrying up to the sky – 'like a rocket, it just goes straight up.' He could get no sense of its character from the ground. On a wet day, 90-odd metres is enough height to make rain drops look impossibly slow as they fall next to the solidity of a trunk. Large, perfect drops from so high up.

The tree itself is too tall to fit it in a single photograph. The light needs so much adjustment between its base and its crown that Solness had to split it into four single images that would join up into one long, thin picture, heightening the effect of its monumental reach while catching the lush detail of the ferns, the moss, the tiny plants that grew in its deepest shadow. Up close, the *E. regnans* bark is tiny threads and shreds of every shade of the warmest brown. Further up the trunk, the roughness pares back into smooth, creamy shapes of grey-green, looking, as William Anderson had described this species on Cook's third voyage, as though it had been peeled.

In his quest for tree stories there were trees that had meant more to Peter Solness (aesthetically speaking, he thought this one looked a bit too much like an overgrown telegraph pole), but this was the photograph that mattered most, the scale and place he wanted to best recreate for people to see.

The competition about which Australian state owned the tallest eucalypt had raged for years. It had begun when Mueller had made grand claims for Victorian trees in excess of 'half a thousand feet', conceding that he hadn't actually measured them himself. Nicholas Caire, photographing Gippsland's disappearing forests – also *E. regnans*, or mountain ash as the Victorians called it – guessed at tree heights of more than 300 feet. Then New South Wales claimed to have a taller tree – an *E. grandis* (flooded gum) – in its north-east forests, while Western Australia drew everyone's attention to its south-western forests of karri trees (*E. diversicolor*), one of which was measured at 88 metres.

There was no doubt that scale would always help the trees make a case for their own fame and importance, and whichever was going to turn out to be biggest in Australia – in the end it was Tasmania's – the country was united in wanting its eucalypts to be the tallest trees in the world. When those aggravating redwoods from California, the sequoias, pipped them at the post, consolation was found in the fact that the sequoias were softwood trees, and that the mighty eucalypts could still stand as the tallest hardwoods anywhere, the tallest flowering plants on the face of the earth.

In 1998, the year after he sent Peter Solness in search of the Big Tree, Geoff Law went back to the Styx himself, driving in with Bob Brown. The heavy gates were still there, and as they went in, Law was again astonished by the size of the trees, by the fact that most people still didn't know they were there, by the scars of the new roads built to let the foresters in further and further, by whole hillsides that had still never seen an axe, let alone a bulldozer or a chainsaw. These cathedral forests, he thought, with enormous eucalypts – maybe, somewhere among them, there were those mythical, elusive eucalypts that would clear the height of any sequoia – all still unexplored.

Law had years of Tasmanian forest campaigns behind him, and he knew you could get ground down by all the pushing and lobbying and arguing. On the one long break he'd taken, he had gone to Ladakh in the Himalayas: 'no trees,' a fellow campaigner pointed out. Now, in the thick tallness of the Styx, all his passion for what he had been trying to do, trying to show people, trying to save, was suddenly reignited.

'We all have this bond with nature,' says Brown, 'it's a very acute thing. It's why we put pictures of flowers on our walls, not pictures of chainsaws … and it's our bond with nature that keeps us in there, campaigning, and that helps us to keep the morale of other people up as well.

'The big party politicians, they're frightened of forests – they go in and put their hard hats on, worry about the mud on their shoes, can't wait to get back to the pub or the cafe. We go in, and we always want to stay longer –

wish we'd brought a tent. It's freedom; it's inspiration; it's adventure.'

Geoff Law rang ANM: he wanted to talk to them about those padlocks. Here was the Wilderness Society, launching a huge campaign to encourage people to visit the forests, he said, producing maps, galvanising public interest in these places – this was, after all, public land – yet more gates with padlocks were going up. Couldn't some of them be removed, or at least moved to open up the road to the Big Tree reserve?

The company baulked: those gates cost $2000, it said, and it had no obligation to provide access to anyone.

He wasn't saying they were legally obligated, Law countered: he was just making a request – in the interests of people's access to magnificent forests, in the interests of the company's own PR. And he left it at that.

He took a phone call a couple of weeks later. The main gate had been opened. Another gate had been installed, barring access to new logging operations, but leaving the path to the Styx's increasingly famous trees open. Not long after, in the wake of the 1997 Regional Forestry Agreement, ANM stopped logging the Styx. But the government itself, Forestry Tasmania, began logging – 'on behalf of the public,' as Law describes it.

The Wilderness Society, with Law as its campaign manager, launched its battle for the Styx in 1999, the same year international criticism of the 'vandalism' meted out to Tasmania's forests was voiced at a Royal Geographical Society meeting in London.

For eight months Wilderness Society members explored the valley, rafting the river. (Law, says Bob Brown, is 'the most travelled wilderness explorer and activist: he's made extraordinary treks into wild and remote areas.') They discovered a eucalypt they christened the Chapel Tree, and a lovely spot for picnics they called Shingle Bend. They traced the logging roads, took the local council in to show them what they lived alongside, and built short tracks through to Shingle Bend and the Chapel Tree so that people could visit them more easily. They began to make a photographic record of the valley's features, recording its trees, its birds, its land, its complexity. They planned to bring people in on guided tours and to distribute thousands of maps so that people would take themselves there. The Styx was set to become a household name.

As the Wilderness Society called a meeting to tell residents near the Styx about the logging and the trees it involved, one of their members came up with the perfect way to catch people's attention. In the top of a big old *Eucalyptus regnans*, they would string up a beacon: lengths of wire spotted with lights, a star that measured four metres across, lit by cutting-edge solar-power technology. A team of climbers spent eight days in wind, rain and sleet, scaling the 77 metres to the top of the tree, weaving dots of light (they were actually 3000 'fairylights' the size of beachballs) around its branches and its trunk, and fixing the star at its apogee which would shine above the forest each evening. The tallest Christmas tree in the world, the Wilderness Society said proudly – although the *Guinness Book of Records*, taking a very Euro-centric view, said it couldn't be a Christmas tree unless it was a spruce, and refused to argue the point.

One of the world's most renowned botanists and environmentalists, David Bellamy, thought it counted. It would be even better, he said, if the Tasmanian government made 'a lasting present to all the children of the world by stopping the logging of these magnificent forests, and setting Tasmania and the whole southern hemisphere on a new course of sustainability into the new millennium.'

'It was a beautiful metaphor,' says Law. 'We thought it was a symbol of hope for the forests.'

Through the first months of 2000, hundreds of people took the Wilderness Society's guided tours through the forests, and hundreds more followed its self-drive maps. The trees became familiar. There were tours and trips and fundraising benefits. With every rally held to try to save these trees, the number of people who turned out increased, and another brace of celebrities would go to see the trees. Like Graham Richardson in the forest that had become the Tasmanian Wilderness World Heritage Area, they came back converted.

In response to the campaign, Forestry Tasmania was making its own study of the tall trees in southern Tasmania which would conclude that, yes, the world's tallest hardwoods were growing in the Styx. In the meantime, it had agreed to delay the logging of the Christmas Tree – first in response to a request from the Derwent Council, then because Geoff Law found a wedge-tailed eagle's nest nearby, which (as one of four rare or threatened species known to exist within the valley) couldn't be disturbed. In April 2000, it was announced that logging of the Christmas Tree would be delayed 'by three years or more'.

Somewhere in this sat the theory that people could quite easily *not* think about trees they had no specific connection with, no name for, but that once something was identified, given something that distinguished it, it was remembered and cherished. So while logging did go on in the Styx, and was even increased in some areas, Law noticed that it was only 'trees we hadn't explored yet, trees in unnamed forests' that were being taken now. Trees that had been personalised – the Chapel Tree, the Christmas Tree – were being left alone.

And where were they going, these unnamed lengths of eucalypt? They were going to be woodchipped and sent to Japan. Tasmanian mills don't take native old-growth chips any more – their timber is either '100 per cent plantation', Law explains, or they import it. (Despite those imports, it would have pleased Max Jacobs to hear Bob Brown argue that, with two million hectares of plantation timber available, Australia has achieved that self-sufficiency in timber that he always desired. It's harder to guess what he would have thought of the fact that 30 million members of Consumers Japan, that country's largest consumer organisation, had written to each woodchip company and government in Australia asking that no old-growth forest be destroyed to supply Japanese papermakers.)

The whole shape and size of the industry had changed from the great days when the Eucalyptus Study Tour was taken to admire the shiny new mill at Burnie and the forests that would feed it. That mill had closed down, and the Burnie wharf now exported woodchips and other forest products from Tasmanian forests overseas while importing pulp for Tasmania's mills to process.

As 2000 ended, Forestry Tasmania announced that it had a new policy for its forests. Any tree taller than 85 metres high would be protected. 'Very tall trees fascinate people,' it said, and 'Forestry Tasmania acknowledges the cultural value of the tallest trees in Tasmania and seeks to enhance protection and encourage appreciation of the tallest trees on State forest by the following actions.' It would measure them, it would conserve them, it would maintain registers of 'the ten tallest extant trees on all its lands and the ten tallest trees ever recorded in Tasmania', and it would involve itself in the design and implementation of a 'statewide tourism strategy for tall tree appreciation'.

Next to forest, plantation is a strange-looking thing. A line of trees growing up the side of a hill with each eucalypt exactly the same height, exactly the same age, exactly the same shape: this is the symmetry of plantation. The futures for these trees – as veneer, as pulp – sit at odds with the grand height they themselves achieve, looming above their tiny information signs.

Just around the corner from the tallest trees' 15 hectares of sanctuary, things are different again. The place looks not symmetrical but like a warzone – like a photograph from World War I of mud and charred fragments of things that used to be alive. The soil is munched up into paste by the huge machinery moving through. It's that 'denuded desert' that astonished Stan Kelly, and it looks like an alien monochrome, blanched of living colour. 'A vast and tedious panorama of splintered nothingness,' the writer Bob Ellis called it. This is the clear-felled landscape of modern forestry.

There is no broadaxe or timber-getter: in a clear-fell, the chainsaws and bulldozers arrive first. They take down every tree – if the coupe is on a steep slope, cable-loggers are brought in to winch out the severed trunks. The best logs are trucked out for sawn timber, others go for chips, pulp, veneer, and the rest of the razed mess is left to dry.

After that comes a helicopter, raining thousands of balls of fast, flammable chemicals like napalm that explode on impact. Every animal is killed, and every piece of plant is burnt. Then the helicopter returns, this time to drop eucalypt seed that's been genetically selected to grow quickly. Neat little piles of carrots are left around the edges of the seeded area. Doused in 1080 – a poison which turns the carrots blue and is banned in most countries – these will kill any animal or bird that eats them. In twenty years or so, according to the economics of it, you can do it all over again rather than having to wait the 1500-2000 years it is estimated that it would take for a clear-felled forest to recover all the 'structural and habitat features of the original'.

You can see the logic in forestry's rush to claim land in this way: once an area has been cleared and replanted, it can't be taken back and protected. Once the timber has been taken out, the land becomes forestry's to work, which fed environmentalists' suspicions in the last year of the 20th century that every single eucalypt that could be cut down and chipped and sold – no matter for how little – was being rounded up.

The economics of conservation and forestry argued with each other. There was one suggestion that if a hundred dollars was collected from every Green voter in the Commonwealth, the lease of the whole Styx Valley might be bought, just as bushwalkers had bought the Blue Gum forest in Sydney's Blue Mountains back in the thirties.

If you wanted to talk bottom-line dollars, said conservation, the Styx could inject eight million tourism dollars into an area that badly needed the money. And there would be jobs too – up to 150, they argued, claiming that the forestry industry was overseeing the largest export of woodchip by the smallest number of workers for the smallest returns. Conserving jobs was always given as a reason for keeping the logging going, but to environmentalists like writer Richard Flanagan 'the one thing that's really clear is that the forestry industry doesn't deliver jobs or prosperity for anybody.' Go out to the forestry towns, he said, they weren't like the mining towns in WA where 'you might see a certain amount of wealth trickling back to the workers. There are no BMWs in Maydena.' There are 3000 jobs directly related to wilderness and forest tourism now, says Brown: 'that's more than the total number of jobs in old-growth logging these days.'

Forestry argued that two-thirds of the old-growth forest on public land around the Styx had already been reserved, saying too that these thousands of hectares of new national parks and reserves would make 'more intensive management of wood production forest ... necessary to compensate for the increase in reservation.'

Geoff Law replied that it wasn't enough to reserve forest that forestry itself had no interest in, and that the promised new national parks had, in reality, meant a

1000-hectare extension of an existing park taking in trees at the edge of the Styx which were nowhere near as impressive as the ones at its heart – the ones named 'The Valley of the Giants'. In February 2001, the Wilderness Society launched a campaign for a 'Valley of the Giants' national park.

Law stood in the middle of the valley and described what he saw for an ABC radio crew: 'the tall eucalypts emerging from the rainforest down in those deep gullies. Somewhere out across there, there might be Australia's tallest tree, maybe even the world's tallest tree; certainly trees taller than 90 metres. It's just that no one's ever been out there to seriously measure the trees and have a look.'

For the uninitiated, he says, 'for the casual observer, it's easy to look round and say, "there are already so many trees in Tasmania: why argue to keep these ones?"' But why, he asks, with such a tiny fraction of old-growth tall eucalypt forest left anywhere, and with so much effective plantation and regenerated eucalypt timber now available for forestry – why do these last pockets have to be taken as well? He knows that people have a sense that old-growth eucalypt forest is important, 'that if it's untouched now, it should be left that way.' The Wilderness Society commissioned an opinion poll in the second half of 2001 that showed that 70 per cent of Tasmanians supported the protection of old-growth forest. Seventy per cent is a lot of voters; promises to end almost all old-growth woodchipping in Western Australia had changed that state's government earlier in that year.

But there are other ways to look at the economics of trees. While research slowly established which eucalypts would earn farmers 'premium financial returns' as a forestry crop, much like a crop of wheat (spotted gums topped the list, with sugar gums not far behind), there were more and more reminders that the most valuable use for eucalypts in most parts of Australia was to leave them growing undisturbed in their native habitats. They were as essential to the survival of other flora and fauna, to the preservation of soil and the provision of clean water as they were to the preservation of the scenic value of wilderness or as a unique genetic repository. Thanks to their other uses, the timber was going to construction, railway sleepers, electricity poles and fence posts. Some timbers, like the jarrah, come with a lush deep red-brown colour which makes them attractive for top-quality furniture. Others – red gums, boxes, ironbark and even Baron Mueller's blue gum – are used more and more for flooring, although it's tallow wood (*E. microcorys*) that's best for this purpose. It comes naturally waxed, greasy, and ready (particularly) to dance on.

In Tasmania, a group of artists undertook a striking project to demonstrate how much a single gum might be worth beyond pulp and chips. The 'One Tree Project' took a single 86-year-old messmate (felled in southern Tasmania during the construction of a road to allow clear-felling to take place), and distributed pieces of it to more than 50 artists. Forestry valued the tree at a couple of hundred dollars: the One Tree Project produced $14,500 worth of items, calculated by the reserve price set for each piece by its creator. There were baskets, bowls, a guitar, golf clubs, textiles, puppets, furniture, paper, and that medicinal eucalyptus oil. (The eucalyptus oil industry had gone off-shore by now – Australia provides only 5 per cent of world requirements, overtaken by producers in Asia. And while claims that it could deal with cancer, gonorrhoea and malaria have fallen away, the oil holds good for all sorts of simple tasks like washing dogs, deflecting colds, and removing chewing gum.)

Look at the quantity of land Australia had already cleared and found not much good for what it was being made to do, other people point out. That land could be 'farmed' with gums (if someone came up with an incentive scheme to tide farmers over the three or four decades they would have to wait for returns). And the old-growth timber could be left alone.

So much felling in so short a time – estimates reckon that only 10 per cent of Australia's pre-settlement old growth remains – left Australia with one of the highest rates of land clearance in the first world. Conservation drew parallels between the continued logging of the Valley of the Giants and the destruction of the Bamiyan Buddhas in Afghanistan. 'The Taliban blew up the Bamiyan Buddhas because they didn't understand them, because they saw them as evil,' says Brown. 'Is there any difference between that and chainsawing the tallest living creatures in the southern hemisphere?'

It seemed to writer David Foster, pinning his own imaginings to the dark green of a European oak tree, that 'we European settlers don't as yet have eucalypt dreaming,' while another writer, Drusilla Modjeska, charges the country with having both art and literature redolent with gums, but a population who 'day by day hardly notice them.' Is it, she asks, that they are such an intrinsic part of the landscape – of the people – that it takes something more dramatic, less commonplace, to jog people's attention? Is it that most Australians feel too guilty to be able to simply stand and reflect among eucalypts? 'The optimistic view,' she says, is that 'after 200 years in the country we are finally understanding the value of the environment we have crashed into; there are signs of ecological consciousness all around us.

'The gloomy view would be to say that the ecological consciousness doesn't extend far enough if there's a conflict over profit or our comfort.'

It was easy to be gloomy back at that spot on the Murray River where Bob Hawke had planted the first river red gums of his billion trees. Certainly, a billion trees had been planted. But on the whole, the program had been judged as more of an apprenticeship, a useful exercise to learn how to revegetate areas better next time. The wrong trees went in, many of them planted incorrectly. At the same time nothing was done about the rate at which land was bulldozed for agriculture, or about the enormous problems of salinity or the watertable – often caused by the removal of trees in the first place. (A single sugar gum could pump 1100 litres of water through the ground in a day.) Mr Hawke's trees at the Murray site had died, were replaced – three or four times – and died again: by the new century, ten gums grew cautiously nearby, behind a fence.

While the Billion Trees project grew partly from a government trying to attract people's attention to their trees, in Tasmania a huge plan has been formed by people trying to attract their government's attention to what they would like – for their environment, among a whole host of issues. After consultations with every community around the state, 'Tasmania Together' identified a number of goals, one section of which dealt specifically with ensuring 'natural resources are managed in a sustainable way now and for future generations.' The wording is simple. A standard was established 'to sustainably manage old-growth forests and to phase out clear felling in those forests'. It aims to end 'clear felling in areas of high conservation value old-growth forest by January 1, 2003' with the 'complete phase out of clear felling in old-growth forests by 2010'.

'The benchmarks were released, a progress board was set up to implement the whole thing, and we're in a kind of limbo,' says Geoff Law. 'Waiting to see what happens.'

Among the arguments about how best to take care of gum trees, ideas come and go about how they might be commemorated or preserved. Where one of Australia's giants once stood, an *E. regnans* in Gippsland, there is now just a tall metal pole with the depressing statement in letters at the top: 'the world's tallest tree.' Yet sometimes it seemed possible that nothing need ever be lost again – that old river red gum on the banks of the Murray, carved by the first white men to walk the overland route from Sydney to Melbourne in 1824, had fresh shoots harvested from its very top in 1998. The following year, clones were produced. Where seed collected from this tree in the 1930s had produced hybrids, it now has offspring that carry its exact genetic material.

'Our greatest need at the moment as human beings,' says David Foster, 'is for a reawakened religious sense. And I do think it'll come out of a reawakened respect for trees. The only thing that's going to stop the earth being totally deforested is a worship of trees.'

That respect was there in the way the artist Rosalie Gascoigne talked about her work – great plains of images that took not the extremities of Australia's extreme landscape, but the hinterlands, the fringes of domestication. Calling the gums' landscape 'elegant and spare', and dismissing any idea that they all look the same ('they're doing a ballet, all gesturing'), she was interested in recreating not the look of the place and the trees but, more on Foster's level, the feel. 'The weathered grey look of the country gives me a great emotional upsurge,' she said. 'I am not making pictures, I make feelings.'

The artists push on. The research pushes on. While one group in Tasmania looks for the genetics that control things like growth, wood quality, resistance to pests and diseases in the mighty *Eucalyptus regnans*, with a view to controlling those genes through artificial selection and breeding (transgenic eucalypts have been proposed to increase pulp production since early 1999), a study for the Melbourne Museum found that a single river red gum, out on the Murray River near New South Wales' Moira State Forest, was home to more than 4000 insects and other invertebrates alone. One tree: more than 320 different species of living things, dependent on it. Four thousand creatures in one tree? One scientist had already suggested that there could be 'hundreds of such invertebrates completely unknown to science in each coupe of Tasmania's forests'. They could come and go, unstudied, unnamed, unknown.

'There is considerable information available on a few of these insect species,' the zoologist Alan Yen and his co-authors wrote of the eucalypts in general in their work on that one tree in the Moira State Forest, 'but there have been relatively few studies on the total fauna.' For such a common tree as the river red gum – the most widely distributed of all Australia's gums – 'there are no published studies on the composition of the arboreal invertebrate fauna associated with this species.'

As Geoff Law sees it, forestry is a bit like whaling: it was 'a hugely important part of Australia's development, with great people involved, fantastic old salts, and a whole rich history and literature. Yet now, in Australia at least, no one would suggest that we should start killing those giant mammals again.

'It's been accepted over the years that these giant trees have to make way, for things like paper, for things like building. Now we have plantations, we have huge forestry areas that have been logged and regrown. We have alternative resources, sustainable resources. There's not a lot of forest left in pristine condition – why does forestry need these last bits?'

He can't see what it will take to change forestry's mind. But he does believe that, one day, something will happen and its arguments and defences will 'collapse like a house of cards … Forestry's interested in dollars and cents. They know that the public relates to old-growth eucalypt forest as something beyond money, and they have to try to relate to that in their public statements while they also argue that the primary functions of a forest are about material aspiration and industrial requirements. Most of those industrial requirements have long since passed [in Australia] – now we're talking about meeting the needs of distant papermills in Japan. But they can't come out and say the only thing these trees are good for is woodchip, because the public would reject that.'

And so he waits. Another huge tree is found in a logging coupe – a swamp gum with an 18.7 metre girth, it could be Australia's stoutest – and is given a 'temporary protection order' by Forestry Tasmania. Another election is called, and while the government is returned, the Greens increase their vote by 80 per cent and their representation from one seat to four. There will be no softening of policy on forests as a result of the election, the premier says on his victory.

Visitors come to the Valley of the Giants. Bus tours come: the Wilderness Society's tours won a highly commended prize in John Howard's inaugural environmental awards. The celebrities come – Roger Woodward, Rachel Griffiths, Olivia Newton-John, John Williamson, Jack Thompson. Tibetan monks have given the place their blessing; Japanese Ainu have visited as well. And among all these people, Law has never known a single one to arrive in the Styx's forest and say, go ahead, chop it down. Not one. 'But the onus is always on us to come up with something new to get people's attention. And that can get very wearying.'

Still, he believes that a change will come, and others believe that he has changed a lot already. There are 'thousands of hectares that wouldn't have been saved if you took Geoff out of the equation,' says Brown. 'He's given his life to fighting for wilderness and forests.'

Along the Franklin in 1982, Brown recalls, 'both major political parties were in favour of the dam. So were the unions, big business, the newspapers. The churches were silent. It was almost the same configuration as we have now with the Styx – and then suddenly, 18 months later, the Franklin was protected and free. So the question is not if logging stops, but when – and our aim is to bring that forward as much as possible. This is not something that we can leave for future generations to fix: it's up to us to do something about it now.'

In the Valley of the Giants, the fairylights have been taken down, but the single star still shines out from the Christmas Tree. Five minutes every night – a living light on one tall gum tree.

the ancient kingdom of fire

It's the gum-trees' country. They had it before we came,
They'll have it again when we're gone.
Ages they've had it. ... crooking their green fingers
At life again when the fires have burned them black ...
They're growing now, while you and I shout in their shadow

—Douglas Stewart, *Ned Kelly*

On the mainland, just over a million hectares of gum trees (that's the size of some whole countries, like Belgium, and Brunei) achieved the World Heritage Commission's nod to become the Greater Blue Mountains Heritage Area in December 2000. Identifying it as 'a natural laboratory for studying the evolution of the eucalypts', the submissions claimed 'the largest area of high diversity of eucalypts on the continent is located in south-east Australia'. The Greater Blue Mountains Area, they said, 'includes much of this eucalypt diversity'.

As Christmas 2001 came on, the countryside and its eucalypts were, as David Foster put it, 'in heat', waiting for 'the kind intercession of Jupiter's thunderbolts; dry storms over dry forests'. On December 3, a huge storm formed. It dropped buckets of rain and hail over the coast north of Sydney, but in the mountains, it was just electrical. Across the parched Blue Mountains, it threw down seventeen lightning strikes and pretty soon trees were alight.

By three in the afternoon, fires were burning across five areas, and the Rural Fire Service had declared great tracts of blazing land 'rural fire districts'. For three weeks, fires burnt across the mountains and around Sydney. Some were contained; some were fought; some, under fairly calm weather conditions, were left to burn. No houses or people sat in their paths – there were only trees and their wildlife.

Lightning, which starts fires mostly in summer, can do several things to a tree. It can burn off a strip of bark, down the length of the trunk, injuring the tree's internal tissue and its roots. It can kill an upper trunk and branches outright, while the rest of the tree stands unaffected. Sometimes there's no apparent damage, but the tree will die months later – again from internal injuries. 'Cold' lightning, which strikes at 20,000 miles per second, can make a tree explode. 'Hot bolts' – that's 25,000° Farenheit – will make an entire tree burst into flame. Some trees, it seems, are more prone to lightning strikes than others – some people suggest it's the level of oil they carry; others the way the bark reacts to heat.

Australia is carved into patches of fire season – different lengths of time at different times of the year, the long, dry weeks when the multicoloured semicircles of fire danger signs flick their needles into the red of Extreme and sit, locked there, for days. Any story about this continent, its ecology, its history and its gum trees, must talk about the unavoidable interconnectedness of Australia and fire.

There's a dangerously cosy relationship between eucalypts and fire. Most have bark that will protect them; fire can produce the perfect situation for the eucalypts to germinate and all but twelve or fifteen of their species carry lignotubers, new shoots that can push their way out through superficially burnt grass or the trunk; plus they drop between a third and a half of their leaves annually with their 'peak drop' in late spring, early summer – perfect fire-season time, in most places. The trees' litter dries out and covers the ground as ready fuel (three centimetres of leaf litter can cause the kind of conflagration you get from a centimetre of refined gasoline) – and most of them have the kind of open crowns that can whip up an enormous updraught in no time.

Some gums have shreds of hanging bark – stringybark or candlebark 'filigree strips' – that dangle like firebrands and can be carried ten, twenty, up to thirty kilometres ahead of a firefront by the wind to spark new flames. Others carry high levels of flammable oil in their foliage and their twigs.

In some species, the bark that's supposed to protect the tree carries fire straight up into the canopy of the forest, creating the most volatile of fires, a crown fire. Other species can cause fires to behave like huge whirlwinds, spinning furiously and sucking (at about 100 kilometres an hour) large logs – even whole trees – metres up into the air, where they disintegrate in a great gassy explosion that you can hear miles away. They have been known to suck every speck of soil off a sizable piece of ground.

Eucalypts are designed to survive deteriorating soils and unreliable water, which makes them (as it has been bluntly put) 'fireweeds'. They can pull nutrients out of the ground and direct them straight to new, post-burn growth. Opportunists, they'll burn readily, greedily and gratefully. Perfectly suited to survive fire, they require it and they thrive in it. But when people start talking about these trees, and their fires, they're not usually so complimentary about these clever adaptations.

Opportunistic? The eucalypts, says David Foster, 'are cunning – they've got the situation sussed. In winter, they won't burn; two weeks later, you'll find yourself in high fire danger and you can't burn. The fuel builds up and builds up – and they seem to work the climate well so they don't burn when it's convenient to you.' He knows the eucalypts: he fights them for his local rural fire brigade – the brigade in Wingello where one firefighter was killed and five others horrifically burnt in 1998 in an explosion of grey ironbark, white gum and white stringybark. Which made him 'hate stringybark with a passion'.

By Christmas Eve 2001, the Blue Mountains were heading for the middle of their annual fire season. Not only were those first fires still burning, some were burning more ferociously, and more were alight, some deliberately lit. Burning closer and closer to Sydney, closer and closer to houses and towns.

The Rural Fire Service was already weeks into fighting these fires, but for the newspapers, the radio and television stations, the story was just beginning. People had only just begun to talk about the flames, the weather, the danger. This is how it works, says Lyndsay Holme, the National Parks and Wildlife Service's 'fire technical officer' up in Katoomba, where fires had been fought for three weeks already. Fires that burn anywhere where there aren't people, anywhere remote, rarely make the news. Holme had woken up at two that morning and heard another storm overhead. Rain, he thought: just let it rain. Before dawn, with the air already tasting of smoke and winds coming in from the north-west, a lightning strike hit the summit of Mt Hall, about 20 kilometres south of the Three Sisters and their famous eucalyptus-blue space.

The trees growing on this one lush peak are a perfect example of how the definition of what should belong to the genus *Eucalyptus* – what should count as a eucalypt – had changed since L'Héritier had first made up the word. There are yellow stringybarks, *Eucalyptus oblonga*. There are turpentines, which a lot of people think are eucalypts, but which belong to the genus *Syncarpia*. There are red bloodwoods like Solander and Banks sampled at Botany Bay – but in the latest suggestion for making the genus *Eucalyptus* a manageable size, a separate genus has been suggested for the bloodwoods and their name, in this system, is no longer *Eucalyptus gummifera*, but *Corymbia gummifera*. And there are some misleadingly tagged Sydney red gums: these are *Angophora costata*, once gathered up as eucalypts themselves in some long-abandoned botanical scheme but now also their own genus.

One of these trees sparked and caught, and a major fire was under way: you could see its glow from the houses in the mountains that night. Another fire sparked across on Brereton Ridge, and National Parks sent a helicopter to fight it. Within a day and a half, at least 75 fires were burning around the state. Helicopters were pulled out of the wilderness and sent to save houses: in any case there was so much smoke that the chopper near Mt Hall had trouble just staying up in the air.

The Mt Hall fire burnt on, running east and blasting a path as it jumped from ridge to ridge: the fire services watched it from spotter planes, when the smoke was clear enough for them to fly, and from 822 kilometres up in the air when SPOT satellites passed overhead. They marked its movement with texta lines on maps. At its height, it blazed through land around Warragamba Dam – yet it left lines of casuarinas untouched. This is the strange thing about a fire's fury: it doesn't leave uniform destruction, a place razed. The effect it drags across a landscape is inconsistent, which makes it hard to recreate or imitate it in the prescribed burning programs with which different agencies try to maintain Australia's landscape.

The next day, in the mountains, and across New South Wales, firefighters left their Christmas lunches. Homeowners packed their Christmas presents. A Christmas angel sat abandoned and unburnt in the middle of a charred backyard. Across gullies, in view of the mountains, people stood up from their Christmas tables and watched the flames shearing through the landscape. It was all glowing, they said, and 'it was kind of beautiful'. It's always inspiring, says

Holme. 'People stand with their mouths open. In any fire there's a sense of danger – and sadness – but it's also amazing, watching this other part of nature.'

In the course of that Christmas Day the fires sparked and spread wildly, down on the south coast, out around Sydney's southern dams, up in the Hunter Valley. Across the state the total firefront doubled in a day from 630 kilometres to more than 1300. Two fires met – one from the Blue Mountains, another from further south – to form a single 60 kilometre front. Another blaze, further south, covered 60 kilometres to the coast in less than six hours. The Mt Hall fire – already 25 kilometres wide – turned to press north through its national park, flaring out of control in its isolation. Sooner or later it would meet up with a fire that had been deliberately lit at Bluepool.

Across the rest of the mountains, gum after gum sparked and caught and burnt in the face of other firefronts. Bulldozers and chainsaws and firefighters moved in from Boxing Day, starting to carve 140 kilometres of firebreak around the back of houses that abutted the bush – houses built on the strips of land technically called the 'urban interface', that complicated place where backyards and gardens butted into the bush of eucalypts. There was an urgent concentration about it: shifts dripped twelve hours of sweat, hacking their way across the surface of the land in search of another shift working through the understorey a few kilometres away, hacking at anything that might burn. Residents watched the firefighters and machines plough through, trees falling to make a path as wide as a two-lane highway in some places. They loved their bush, they said, but they found all this very reassuring. They expected their houses to be the first hit by the Mt Hall fire when it left the Blue Mountains National Park.

The New South Wales' Rural Fire Service chief, Phil Koperberg, listened to weather predictions for days with humidity as low as 5 per cent, temperatures close to 40 for 48 hours, and winds of up to 50 kilometres an hour. He was heading for the worst firestorm conditions in 33 years. 'In terms of a weather pattern that sustains fires of this magnitude,' he said, 'I have never seen anything like it … who would have thought things could deteriorate to such an extent?'

In the Blue Mountains, other fires flared and turned and houses were burnt. One couple heard a knock on the door and thought it was emergency services, not flames. 'When we tried to open it,' they said, 'the fire had created a vacuum, and we couldn't.' They smashed their way out as the fire hit their loungeroom. Down the road, on the same day, a 'highspeed destructive fireball' was razing homes in its path. 'It's a weird country,' said Koperberg reflectively to one man whose house had gone: 'You wonder what the hell we're doing here.'

Koperberg issued statements for residents about the terrible days they would face. It would be 'really frightening,' he said. 'There will be a lot of noise, a lot of smoke, a lot of terror, a lot of sparks.' And it would be hot, 'really hot, uncomfortable, and you're going to be standing in burning embers [with] things dropping on you … you will wonder what on earth is going on.' He knew it was a big thing to ask, he said, but if people stayed they could stand and save their houses. 'If you can't cope with this,' he advised, 'then pack those things which are most important to you, lock your house, and go to the beach.'

And then, nothing came of it. The 48 hours passed;

one threatening fire sat in the trees in the bottom of the valley, stifled by the stillness of a day when the expected winds didn't turn up.

The days dragged on into a week, heading for New Year's Eve and 2002. More fires flared and people told stories of watching flames come down mountains like lava. Stories of walls of flame a hundred metres high, black smoke so thick it obscured the flames altogether and left them in a dark world with just 'the roar and crackling of the leaves'. Stories of setting their bums on fire with hankies flapping out of their back pockets while they fought for their homes, of facing 'this big bloody truckload of flame'. They said it looked like something out of *Star Wars* or *Mad Max*.

The Mt Hall fire inched towards the edge of the Blue Mountains National Park; length after length of firebreak was carved out of the bush. It was the key to protecting the mountains' towns, Koperberg believed – this 'southern strategic line', as it was called. Geoff Luscombe from National Parks wondered if it might create the longest backburn in history. Certainly, he said, it was the most resource-hungry: 'long, monumental and a colossal effort of sweat and hard work.'

From the Katoomba Fire Control office, Lyndsay Holme watched the Mt Hall fire move. From his window, it looked like the whole world was on fire – smoke and flames filled his vision 'from two degrees right round to 180', and way over in the distance he could see new fires, little fires, 'pumping away'. Going out into the night to go home, the 'big steaming dragon' breathing its fire at the end of the road, he shivered more often than not. Wintry winds were whipping up after scorching hot days. 'It was the weirdest thing': freezing winds at the same time as this fire from Mt Hall – which everyone had known had to happen one day. Some of the area hadn't burnt since 1944.

New Year's Day, says Holme, appeared to be the day the Mt Hall fire would push through, and the place he lived in looked set to 'cop the brunt of it. It was barrelling through firetrails, heading for the place we'd designated as a weak point. If you can't hold the weak point, you can't hold the fire anywhere.'

He would come home after every shift, the latest fire map in his hand, predictions drawn onto its topography, and sit in neighbours' kitchens along his road, discussing what they should do next. The anxiety is always there, he says, no matter how many times you've been through a fire.

On New Year's Day, the fire was taking off: 'We thought we'd have ash dropping any minute. There were billowing flames and huge cumulo-nimbus clouds of smoke above that. Then, at one o'clock, it died off.' The point held, and a break that had been burnt no more recently than six years before held for more than a day as well.

Two days later it pushed forward towards a swamp, and was stopped by water dropped from a helitanker. A fire crew caught near the front was doused too. The fire stalled, then circled and pushed on – it 'slunk into Bedford Road' and was licking at the back of Lyndsay Holme's place in Woodford by evening.

'The crews from South Australia started arriving,' he says, 'and the town brigades, and the helicopters. And we all stood, and watched and waited.'

'We saw the ferocity of it and last night the red rim of it,' one resident said. 'I just can't see us getting away with nothing lost.'

There was its noise, of course: 'People use all those descriptions,' says Holme, 'like stream trains, or thunder. And that's what it's like. You hear the crackle of the trees, and the different crackle of the undergrowth. You see the deep red licks of the flame.' But every fire is different, and Holme had never before stood 'watching bush burst into flame *downhill* from the fire. It was very dry and the wind was behind it, but still, a fire will usually run up a hill and die, or run up and make a leap. It doesn't usually run downhill.'

He stood with his neighbours watching the flame move. There were two creeks below them. They watched the flames head for the water and thought, that'll check it. But the fire just kept coming: 'it was moving through a fairly moist rainforest gully, and that was having absolutely no effect on it.'

The noise built up again, huge flames billowed towards them and the fire made its rush. And 'all of a sudden it was all over. There was no fuel left in the area. You're standing there so anxious one minute,' says Holme, 'and the fire's gone the next.' The flames came no further.

He walked down the road an hour or so later. It was dark – no electricity – and it was calm. He registered the embers, the smoke, the patches where the fire had spotted across the road, the path it had taken in its run against his home. The bush's understorey, nicely recovering from the last fire six years before, was all gone.

The front had slowed. There was more water-bombing, and the winds eased, and the last sections of the southern strategic line were connecting. It was completed on January 6 – the work of a thousand firefighters working twelve-hour shifts for ten days. At 7.52 pm on that same day, Geoff Luscombe stepped back from the maps and the ash and the firefighters and the smoke and declared the Mt Hall fire contained. At its centre it was still burning fiercely, but every edge of the fire had a control line marked sharply along its perimeter. Luscombe looked at those edges and made the call, just before the end of his shift.

No property had been lost, but it had burnt through roughly a quarter of the World Heritage Area's million or so hectares. 'The Sad Destruction of Our World Heritage Site', said the newspapers. Which was a long way from the truth.

It had taken six years from the completion of the first full assessment of the Blue Mountains and their surrounding plateaus for the World Heritage site to be declared at the end of 2000. But the idea of conserving such a vast chunk of the area was much older than that: those first bushwalkers who had raised the money for the Blue Gum Forest in the early 1930s had also made the first calls for a Greater Blue Mountains National Park.

Listing had been argued on the basis that the area had 'universal aesthetic qualities' (a list of seminal Australian landscape paintings of the region, including John Lewin's *Evans Peak*, was included), that it provided 'a living record of the development of a largely endemic sclerophyll flora, including the spread to dominance of the eucalypts', that it represented 'present-day Australian (and global) biodiversity of temperate, eucalypt-dominated sclerophyll ecosystems', and that it contained 'outstanding diversity of the genera *Eucalyptus*'. The final area (1.03 million hectares) contains 91 different kinds of eucalypt – more than 10 per cent of the total number of eucalypt species. The importance of this was simple: no existing World Heritage area had been listed 'primarily for their eucalypt forests and woodlands'. Almost two dozen eucalypts on the list of rare or threatened plants are found within its boundaries, and there are as many as 65 different sorts of gum in each half-degree-square portion of the Blue Mountains and its surrounding plateaus.

What all this meant was that the World Heritage listing had conserved one of the most potentially conflagrant environments in Australia.

In the Blue Mountains, says Geoff Luscombe, 'it tends to rain a lot, which builds up fuel. It has thin sandstone soil, which dries out very quickly and, over a long period of time, very completely, and both these things make it predisposed to burn. You can measure fuel loads three years after a burn and they'll be back to 80 per cent of the pre-existing amount.'

Eucalypts turn up in Australia's fossil record around 80 million years ago, along with charcoal fragments. The smell of burning eucalyptus leaves had been in Australia's air for more than 35 million years. Then, between roughly five and two million years ago, when Australia's vegetation was already 'essentially similar to what it is today', the climate changed again. Drier conditions set in: the rainforest retreated towards the continent's coast and the eucalypts, fearsome and increasingly fire-prone in the new dry environment, expanded in its wake.

In the next geological era – still running as recently as 10,000 years ago – everything that the eucalypts needed to explode into the vast number of species and locations they would occupy was in place. The landscape was passing through periods of great aridity; the climate was melding into predictable seasons; and the fires were well and truly burning. There were humans too – humans who began to influence both the landscape and its plants through the way they used fire. What would become known as 'firestick farming' had begun.

As the environment changed and changed again, a new, precise and fragile interdependence was established between eucalypts and fire. Most gum trees need to burn at some stage during their seed-bearing life. Some need heat to release their seeds (a risky business, timing the release of a capsule which is smaller than a centimetre and has to protect the seed 'sufficiently long in the holocaust of raging crown fires'). Some – it's only recently been found – need smoke to activate them. Most need the ash to provide a clear, soft bed for their seedlings, free from any competing plants. They require, and promote, fire. And they accommodate it. Even in the worst bushfire, a eucalypt forest only risks a tiny fraction of itself as fuel – 95 per cent of its biomass stays locked away in its trunks, which might char but will not, even during the most intense fire, be consumed. They accommodate the very severity that they encourage.

For all that early British Australia had pined for the annual rebirth of deciduous trees, the rebirth from lignotubers and from carpets of sun-hungry young seedlings is even more miraculous. No bushfire story can be told without shoots sparking from black stumps, the fluffy bright green of their first new leaves, against grey soil and the memory of trees that looked dead in the black-and-red of the fire. As the artist Rosalie Gascoigne described it: 'After the flames had died down it was amazing to see what was standing and what was burnt to a cinder. All of the gums looked shattered, but you get those blue-green shoots after, it's very gentle.'

Every ship that skirted the edge of Australia, from Abel Tasman's, through Captain Cook's and Banks', and on to those carrying the people who landed and settled, had noted the prevalence of fire – from campfires up. Cook, after his first sighting, had written in his diary, 'in the afternoon we saw smoke in several places by which we knew the country to be inhabited.' His New Wales, he had said, was 'The Continent of Smoke.' The First Fleet's Governor Phillip arrived and announced that you couldn't go as far as a mile into this new place without seeing a tree blackened up its trunk. Yet it wasn't until two years later, in 1790, that the First Fleet endured a summer with the temperature surging through the forties and a wind pouring from the north-west as if from an oven. Even then, when it was so hot that birds and flying foxes died mid-flight and the white men collapsed into their beds in the swelter, Sydney did not burn: a grass fire which bore down hard on the settlement could be easily routed.

Two years later, though, with indigenous burning regimes more interrupted, the bushfire season saw the space around Sydney 'everywhere on fire'. And in 1797 there was such a blaze that chain gangs of convicts were promised a pardon if they would stand and battle the blaze. They fought through the night, shackled together, beating at the flames with boughs of eucalypt branches. By morning, the fires were contained, and the men were freed.

In the northern part of the world, where all those men came from, fires bore as much mythology as forests. In England the fires, like the land, had been domesticated. Fires were about hearths and warmth and controlled flames; large fires were indicative of the Apocalypse itself. To a Eurocentric mind, fire meant one thing: big, bad, destructive danger. To be avoided at all costs. As one of the governor's officers put it, attempting to survey the newly crossed Blue Mountains in 1814, 'the mountains have been fired; had we been on them we could not have escaped; the Flames raged with violence through thick underwood …' The burnt trees, he complained, 'tear our clothes to pieces, and make us appear as Natives from the black dust off them.'

To suggest that fire might be a positive thing for the land and its vegetation, a constructive thing, a necessary thing, was as impossible then as the idea that trees might have grey-green leaves that hung on all year and still be beautiful. To suggest that the 'Natives' may have had sophisticated patterns for using fire to control their vegetation, to keep the fires themselves in check, was similarly impossible. Yet some people had suspected there might be a link between the two. Drawing together the high rate of fire, and that sparsely-treed park-like appearance the country running out to the mountains had first presented to its white arrivals, Major Mitchell commented that 'fire, grass, kangaroos and human inhabitants seem dependent on each other for existence in Australia, for any one of these being wanting, the others could no longer continue.' During his own time in the country, he had seen that 'the omission of the annual periodical burning by natives, of the grass and young saplings, has already produced in the open forest lands nearest to Sydney, thick forests of young trees where, formerly, a man might gallop without impediment.'

It was just three years after Mitchell's observation, on February 6, 1851, that bushfires swept through Victoria and showed their potential magnitude for the first time. 'Black Thursday', they were called, and one artist who painted them commented that 'in the town of Kilmore the inhabitants thought the end of the world had come, and clinging to one another bade each other, as they supposed, a last farewell.' So fierce were the fires that people all the way across Bass Strait in Tasmania watched the sky darken, while leaves charred to ash, their veins still visible, floated across the ocean from the mainland and fell from the sky. Black Thursday was followed by Red Tuesday (February 1, 1898), Black Sunday (February 14, 1926), Black Friday (January 13, 1939: a popular fire – enterprising aeroplane owners offered sightseeing flights over the flames, for 30 shillings, from Essendon airport), Black Tuesday (February 7, 1967), Ash Wednesday (February 16, 1983), and Black Wednesday (October 16, 1991). Not to mention the enormous fires in 1919, 1951, 1968 and 1977 that didn't get names, or the blazes that blackened 15 per cent of the entire continent in 1974–75.

The kind of names they were given remained constant, but white Australia's approach to fire rollercoastered from foresters convinced that fire could and should be eliminated from the Australian environment, to foresters convinced that they themselves should set patches of the country alight every so often. On the whole, though, fire was 'the enemy'. Farmers and pastoralists tried to restrict it by getting rid of their trees. Anti-fire foresters argued that there was 'not a shadow of a doubt that [forests of gum and wattle] can be as completely protected from fire as the average house in the city.' It was 'solely a matter of organisation'. A character in H. A. Lindsay's novel *The Red Bull* suggested that the best thing for controlling fire would be to clear out the pyrophitic natives and plant incombustible 'green belts' of oak and ash and hickory in their place.

As recently as 1937, Max Jacobs had assured foresters that 'complete fire protection is not impossible or impracticable, but an inevitable development,' while his predecessor as principal of the Forestry School said flatly that the belief that 'a fire through the bush is a good thing [has] no solid basis in fact.' It was 1947 before a climatologist uncovered 'immutable geographic circumstances that make large fires so routine a phenomenon in Australia,' and 1981 before evidence for the role of fire in the development and maintenance of Australia's plant population was systematically examined for the first time.

In 1994, fires burnt around Sydney and beyond, under the worst conditions white Australia had seen, it was said, for ten days. The *Sydney Morning Herald* plugged for calling them the 'Black Friday' fires on their fourth day, but as they inconveniently kept burning until the following Monday, the name became redundant. The Rural Fire Service was reformed in its wake; new action plans were devised; data were analysed to add to what people knew about how fires might behave, and the New South Wales government even rewrote its Bushfires Act, which hadn't been revised since the days when fires were fought with wet sacks.

In the first days of 2002, as 175 firefighting units, three mighty and popular helitankers, and more than four thousand salaried and volunteer firefighters arrived from other states – even other countries – few went into the World Heritage Area. The reason was very simple: the fire was good for it, said one Rural Fire Service officer. Some of it hadn't had a good burn for decades. 'The Sad Destruction of Our World Heritage Site?' It was just doing what it needed to do.

'We tend to forget,' says Lyndsay Holme, 'that even with a sketchy understanding of 200 years of fires – and most of that is anecdotal – and 50 years of more scientifically based information, we still understand only the tip of the iceberg. We are dealing with ecosystems that have been evolving across millions of years.'

The reaction of the different eucalypts to fires, says Phil Cheney, the CSIRO's leading bushfire researcher, are quite well understood: 'We've known about eucalypts' responses to fires ever since the work of Max Jacobs in the 1950s.' What needs to be understood are the fires themselves: the way they move through the eucalypts, the way they grow and accelerate, all the variables that can affect what they will do and when.

'We've been underestimating the potential of high-intensity fires burning under extreme weather,' Cheney says, approaching the end of Project Vesta, an enormous six-year study designed to understand how fires behave, particularly when they're ravaging bushland in the middle of summer. 'There had been observations of fires that defied our predictions, and people had shrugged and said, "well, fire's an erratic thing." That just adds to the myth that fires are unpredictable. Certainly they're variable – but you can find explanations for them.'

Project Vesta's premise is simple: the more accurately you can predict what a wildfire will do, the more effective your control measures can be. The 1994 fires in the Blue Mountains had spread much faster than the official 'Forest Fire Danger Meter' (designed in the sixties) predicted. Project Vesta wanted to know why – and it became increasingly obvious that a lot more than that was unknown.

Assumptions about wind, fuel load, even the way fire spreads went quickly out the window. 'We didn't appreciate that a line of fire doesn't accelerate constantly from zero up to its full potential – yet we should have known better,' says Cheney, 'because a fire has no mass. The idea that fires, starting at one point, go through a growth period – and that the rate of spread grows over hours – is firmly ingrained in all of us. Yet when the wind changes and turns a long flank of fire into a headfire, that fire spreads at its potential speed straight away, and the only change is in the size of the flames.

'This is a very important factor in explaining a number of fatalities, like Wingello ... which boiled down to the fact that the firefighters didn't appreciate how close the fires were. Fires in the forest always look further away than they are, up to double the actual distance – and people expect a time delay during which the fire will build. Often they don't react until they see flames.'

As the results came in and the data were analysed, Project Vesta could already boast that 'our suspicions about high-intensity fire in a forest were correct, their potential rate of spread being three to five times more than previous predictions.' It had also discovered that a fire which started from a line more than 100 metres long would burn at its potential rate immediately. And all these things edged towards being able to answer more questons about how fires would behave when you were in the middle of one.

In the all-important language of economics, the project was declared to have 'a benefit to cost ratio of 80 to 1', with eighteen months or so to go before its final 'National Fire Behaviour Prediction System' for dry eucalypt forests was released. This announcement was made the day after Geoff Luscombe declared the Mt Hall fire contained.

Fire, says Phil Cheney, is all about practice – 'even I have to go through what I call a practice-recalibration phase: I need to get a few fires under my belt – I need to reawaken myself to the relativities of fire that are difficult to explain with mathematical guidelines but become obvious when you've burnt a few.'

The problem with practice is that so few people are getting any. The most fire-prone continent in the world now sports the most urbanised population – the majority of Australians spend their lives in the cities and then look 'for a lovely isolated block to retire to, without any idea of the landscape it's in, the behaviour of the place,' says Cheney. People experience so little fire because fire organisations are so much better at extinguishing small blazes before anyone sees them – whereas 'thirty years ago, fires were much more commonplace and most country people had to burn off to protect themselves.'

Now, no one even wants to see a controlled burn, a hazard reduction burn, a prescribed burn: 'People simply don't like black trees, they don't like smoke in the air, or they go into denial once they've survived one fire, or they rely on interstate forces to be shipped in,' says Cheney, 'all these things are typical recipes for disaster.'

No matter how much is learnt about fire and eucalypts, he says, it is only humanly possible to control 'fires that are at two to three per cent of their maximum intensity.' And no matter what research had been done over the last ten, twenty, or 50 years, 'there is still no good theory that explains how a bushfire spreads.' To have a force – the wind – that runs horizontal at increasing speed, heats up to 1000°C, turns through a sharp angle and then shoots to the top of the trees in a turbulent environment: well, says Cheney dryly, 'it's not mathematically easy to explain what's happening there, or to be precise.'

As the smoke cleared from January 2002 and New South Wales' 24 days of fire emergency, it seemed people knew as little as ever about the trees they built their houses among. Concerns about the 'damage done' to the World Heritage Area and their trees were countered with polite explanations, repeated by at least two spokespeople, that no one had to worry: eucalypts actually regenerated with fire. It was usually good for them.

'Fire adaptation was one of the things that was special about the place,' Geoff Luscombe points out. 'Fires aren't damaging to the World Heritage listed scenery. The way they could have an impact is if they were too frequent, or too infrequent – which would lead to longer term changes.'

Demands and accusations flew about prescribed burning programs, with residents retrospectively sure that not enough had been done and the fire agencies pointing out that, not being clairvoyant, they could hardly know precisely where to burn in anticipation of the next summer, and they could hardly burn everything, because residents would dislike that even more.

Then buy more helitankers, people said, and Phil Koperberg pointed out bluntly that all the care and responsibility for keeping people safe from bushfires could not be passed on to the firefighters themselves. 'Heavens above,' he exploded as the newspapers asked 'Black Christmas: Was It Preventable?': 'You have to look at where you build your house.'

Even the praise for that 140 kilometres of firebreak, essential to protect life and property, turned into questions about the slapdash way it had been put through – some thought it might devalue their houses – and questions about why it hadn't been planned and implemented before the Mt Hall fire. As Geoff Luscombe led a taskforce into the area to assess which sections of the break needed to be kept, Phil Koperberg made the point that it had only been possible to get a firebreak put through on such a scale because the threat was so immediate that it could silence any critics.

'Of course the fires have thrown our plans into chaos,' says Lyndsay Holme lightly. 'Here we were, trying to emulate a natural fire regime, and it's gone and done it so much better than we ever could have. We've got a perfect mosaic – areas that are badly burnt, areas lightly burnt, areas hardly touched: there's so much more there than the best prescribed burns could ever achieve. For one thing, we get the seasons all wrong: if we're trying to emulate nature, we should do our burning in summer – but it's very hard to get a fire back into its box when you've let it out, so we burn in spring, or in autumn.

'All this talk about firestick farming,' he says, 'about

trying to do what used to be done. We're all really just guessing.' The calls for increased funding and increased burning settled back into suburban silence. Our attitude to all of this, says Holme, is like an ostrich's. Head well and truly in the sand.

More than two centuries after the *Endeavour* had arrived with its scientific classifications for plants and the British Empire's dreams of outposts, it was suggested that the land – old, dry, infertile – and these hard trees had never been suited to settlement in the first place. If people kept up a nomadic life, David Foster suggests, they could simply move when the eucalypts nearby were about to burst into flame.

'Australian flora, Australian fauna – they've adapted to the fire regime,' says Holme. 'It's we colonials who haven't.'

From above, after the fires, the country sat clearly in hard stripes of colour: unburnt green, the brown-black of the fire's path, blue water. Its contours looked tired, its soil and vegetation more thinly spread, more lightly held, than usual. The way the monochrome of the burnt area ran hard up against pocket-handkerchief-sized backyards, shiny silver corrugated iron and dusty red-tiled roofs, marked clearly the division between the people and the ecosystem they lived next to.

There were the eucalypts. And eucalypts will burn.

'The thing that frustrates me most,' Phil Koperberg said in one interview when it was all over, 'is the failure of the broader community, although not universally so, to recognise that fire is not only part of our ecology – and has been for millions of years – but has in fact shaped our ecology.

'We expect everything to change simply because we're here.'

the land through the leaves

Identity oversimplifies humans.
It denies the hybrid, as trees can't.
Trees, which wrap height in pages
self-knitted from ground water and light
are stood in scrolls best read unopened …

—Les Murray, 'Cool History'

At Botany Bay, where Banks first set foot on that land 'cliffy and barren without wood', where Phillip thought settlement was impossible, the trees have crowded down to the edge of the shore. New bloodwoods. New red gums. New scribblies. The seven D'harawal peace-keepers, multiplying and multiplying again. Up the coast, by the deep blue harbour that took the First Fleet in, an old tree stands in the botanic gardens. Its trunk is silver, and the shapes and shadows staining its bark are rose and purple, like rich blushes or blemishes. It's a forest red gum, one leftover piece of the forest of *Eucalyptus tereticornis* that used to grow around it, and it's thinning on top – grandfatherly. There's so little of its branches and leaves that it's almost all light and air.

It was a sapling in 1788 when the eleven wooden ships of the First Fleet arrived and the view from its crown began to change from the canopies of other eucalypts growing along the land's ridges and streams, from clear distance running out to the blue of the Blue Mountains, to new tall things. Forests of wood and brick, and later glass and concrete and steel, pushed towards the sky with flashes of colour and light.

But it's still alive: the possums have left fresh copper-coloured chinks in its trunk; there's a bee's nest on the side near the water; and, as the afternoon turns, gangs of white cockatoos bulk it up with their white feathers and their noisy voices.

The leaves turn in the breeze, and the light catches their colour and makes them shine.

Up the hill, towards the harbour's mouth, a hundred new forest red gums have been planted on this point that used to be thick with them – sprouted from seeds taken from a tree that stood before Phillip, before *eucalyptus*, before Australia.

Eucalypts feed obsessions, trail questions, and lean against each other in a muddled pyre of ideas and images. Still undecided, they are despised, feared, exalted, grown, pulped, painted, written, and ignored. In all that's been thought of them, done to them, discovered about them, and claimed for them, people were – from the first – trying to find a way of getting hold of the trees, of understanding or capturing something definitive about them. But the stories proved transient, arbitrary: they would change, grow, and evolve, turning towards and away from each other to converge and hybridise as easily as the trees do. They refuse to be contained by a single person's idea, a single person's lifetime.

So Banks' and Solander's botanists' playground became one of the most farflung pieces of the British Empire. A place unique in its flora and fauna became a prison magnificent in its dimensions and position. The space through the leaves that John Lewin painted became the canvases John Glover produced in Tasmania, later dismissed as caricatures – too curly, too exaggerated – while Heidelberg, Hans Heysen, Albert Namatjira, Fred Williams, Rosalie Gascoigne and everyone else took their turn. And as Glover was revived, celebrated, and one of the last of his Australian works to be located was transferred from a private collection to a public one for $1.5 million, the trees around his home on Tasmania's River Nile continued to grow as curved and as curly as they always had.

Characters were reinvented: the first convicts – promised freedom if they stood and fought a fire – became the volunteers and brigades who stand through every fire season. Major Mitchell became wave after wave of settlers, chopping the trees down – and then beginning to plant them again in schemes that tried to rebalance the land.

In the systematics of the trees, the genus was never ruled off as complete. Mueller's *Eucalyptography* was revised by J. H. Maiden; Maiden's by W. F. Blakeley; Blakeley's by L. D. Pryor and L. A. S. Johnson before further works by M. I. H. Brooker and George Chippendale, among others, appeared – and all this took place in Stan Kelly's lifetime. Even his eucalyptography was incomplete in the end: in the decade or so after he declared that he'd painted every different sort of gum (and that was more than 600), at least 150 new eucalypt species had been named. (There wasn't a day he didn't think about going back and adding them in, he said, but he'd moved on to fungi by then.) Then botany took another step, and suggested that several things that had been eucalypts for almost as long as the genus had been invented might really be scooped into another genus altogether. And there went archetypal trees like the spotted gum and the ghost gum and the bloodwood to be *Corymbia.* Even the species' names could change: *Eucalyptus papuana*, so often painted by Albert Namatjira (and arguably now a corymbia anyway), became *E. apparrerinja* – its indigenous name married to its botanical one.

Mueller's passion for the big trees, for their forests, for all the glory that they were and all that they might produce became forestry on the one hand (Max Jacobs and his pupils), and conservation on the other – Geoff Law down in the Styx. The envelopes of seeds he sent to anyone who wanted them became the organised bureaucracy of the FAO. *Snugglepot and Cuddlepie*, the story everyone knew about gums, became Patrick White's *Tree of Man* and then Murray Bail's novel *Eucalyptus* – which itself challenged the success of any eucalyptic export Mueller or Max Jacobs ever made by going into seventeen languages in its first couple of years. The global eucalyptus trade, toned down from the glowing endorsements of the fifties and sixties (by 1992 Australian government publications carried titles like *Eucalypts: Curse or Cure?*) continued, and more than 14 million hectares of the world sported these Australian trees by the turn of the 21st century.

Among all the beginnings, middles and ends, among all these passions, certainties fall away. Even the notion of what defines eucalypt species is quivering under some of the first studies of their DNA, which suggest that the hundreds of different species they have always been supposed to represent might be a much smaller number of trees – genetically identical at their core, but with different nuts, different leaves, different shapes on the outside. And another story begins – always as partial as the glimpses you get through a eucalypt's leaves.

In all the stories, though, you find one set of words: adaptable, diverse, tenacious, interactive, opportunistic, unique. Take them for these people, this place. Take them for the trees.

acknowledgments

Thanks to Paul Bailey and Kathy Bail and the rest of *The Bulletin* people for their patience and generosity.

To Geoff Law (Tasmanian Wilderness Society), Lyndsay Holme and Geoff Luscombe (National Parks and Wildlife Service), Monika Wells and Prof. Rod Home (the Mueller Project, Royal Botanic Gardens, Melbourne), and Senator Bob Brown.

To Les Murray, Fran Bodkin, Phil Cheney and Ian Brooker (CSIRO), Peter Solness, Eric Rolls, David Foster, John Lennis and Ken Hill (Royal Botanic Gardens, Sydney), David Morrison and Noel Sanders (University of Technology, Sydney), Colleen Morris, Dick Turner, Robert Gray, Sally Garrett and Joan Smith, Tim Bonyhady, Humphrey McQueen, Mark Tredinnick, Tony Cannon (The Spastic Centre of NSW), Jennifer Broomhead (State Library of New South Wales), Prof. Peter Pierce, Elizabeth Ellis (Mitchell Library), Dean Nicolle (Currency Creek Arboretum), Rod Seppelt (former Australian Botanical Liaison Officer at Kew), Alan Yen (Melbourne Museum), John Winter (Rural Fire Service of New South Wales), Ben Oquist (Sen. Bob Brown's office), Suzie Pipes (TWS), Michele Field, Barbara Mobbs, Sally

Murray, Meredith Curnow, James Holman, Rob Yezerski, the Adelaide Festival Centre Artspace, Bob Beale, Peter Fray, Helen Suich, Jen Rosenberg, Bec Rohan-Jones, Richard Neylon, Sophie Cole, Ross Warren, Kim Offner, Steve Offner, and to Les and Marilyn Hay.

To the librarians at the University of New South Wales, the Mitchell, the state libraries of New South Wales and Victoria, the Fisher Library at Sydney University, the National Library of Australia, the Archives of the University of Melbourne, and the libraries of the Royal Botanic Gardens in Melbourne and Sydney. To Pamela Lockwood (CSIRO Forestry Library, Yarralumla), and Barbara Glass (the library at the Rural Fire Service of New South Wales). To the art galleries of South Australia, Victoria and New South Wales, the National Gallery of Australia, the Geelong Regional Gallery, and Christopher Heysen.

To Harold Cazneaux's family for permission to quote from his correspondence and for their help and patience unravelling the story of *The Spirit of Endurance*. To Nancy (Anne) Sutherland for permission to quote from her father Max Jacobs' papers. To Gregg Borschmann for permission to quote from *The People's Forest* oral history archives. To the joint owners of the copyright of the works of May Gibbs, The Northcott Society and The Spastic Centre of New South Wales – both organisations have kindly supplied permission to use extracts from the works of May Gibbs. And to Frances Bodkin, for allowing me to use the D'harawal story *Maridyulu'boola Yandel'mawa: The Seven Peacekeepers* in this work.

To the Literature Board of the Australia Council.

To Alex Snellgrove, Penny Evans, Maggie Cooper, Karen Williams and Jo Jarrah. To Michael Duffy and Gail MacCallum.

And to Nigel Beebe.

select bibliography

The reading for this book ranged through a variety of disciplines and eras in the search for its structure and characters. This is a select bibliography, primarily of works directly quoted.

CSIRO Forestry Library, Yarralumla, ACT:
  Papers distributed during the 1952 Eucalyptus Study Tour.
University of Melbourne:
  Grimwade Bequests 1973, Ba SpC/Grim 994 Grim
National Library of Australia:
  Manuscripts
  Papers of Hans Heysen NLA MS5073
  Papers of Harold Cazneaux NLA MS8361
  Papers of M. R. Jacobs NLA MS6336
  Oral History
  Stan Kelly, The People's Forest Collection, NLA TRC2845/63
Mitchell Library, State Library of New South Wales:
  Papers of May Gibbs ML MSS2048
Royal Botanic Gardens, Melbourne:
  The Mueller Correspondence Project
Rural Fire Service NSW Library:
  Clippings relating to the 2001/2002 Christmas/New Year bushfire emergency across New South Wales. Cited by author, publication and date in footnotes

Abbott, Peter S., *The Eucalyptus Oil Industry*, 2000, online @ www.fgb.com.au
ACIAR, *Eucalypts: Curse or Cure?* Canberra: Australian Centre for International Agricultural Research, 1992.
Amadio, Nadine *et al.*, *Albert Namatjira: The Life and Work of an Australian Painter*. Melbourne: Macmillan, 1986.

Andrews, Alan E. J., *Major Mitchell's Map 1834: The Saga of the Survey of the Nineteen Counties*. Hobart: Blubber Head Press, 1992.
Art Foundation of Tasmania, *Glover Appeal*, 2001, online @ www.tmag.tas.gov.au
Australian Conservation Foundation, *Australian Land Clearing, A Global Perspective: Latest Facts and Figures*, 2001, online @ www.acfonline.org.au
Australian Geographic, *Australian Geographic Encyclopedia*. Terrey Hills: Australian Geographic, 1996.
Bachman, Bill, *Local Colour*. Hong Kong: Local Colour, 1999.
Bail, Murray, *Eucalyptus*. Melbourne: Text, 1998.
Baker, D. W. A., *The Civilised Surveyor: Thomas Mitchell and the Australian Aborigines*. Melbourne: Melbourne University Press, 1997.
Banks, Sir Joseph (Paul Brunton, ed.), *The* Endeavour *Journal of Joseph Banks: The Australian Journey*. Sydney: Angus and Robertson in association with the State Library of New South Wales, 1998.
Barrett, Sir James (ed.), *Save Australia: A Plea for the Right Use of our Flora and Fauna*. Melbourne: Macmillan and Co., 1925.
Bassett, Jan (ed.), *Great Southern Landings: An Anthology of Antipodean Travel*. Melbourne: Oxford University Press, 1995.
Beale, Bob, 'Living with Wild Fire', *Bulletin*, 12.02.2002.
Beale, Bob, 'The Secret Life of Trees', *Sydney Morning Herald/Spectrum*, 2.11.1996.
Beale, Bob and Peter Fray, *The Vanishing Continent: Australia's Degraded Environment*. Sydney: Hodder and Stoughton, 1990.
Bentham, George, assisted by Ferdinand Mueller, *Flora Australiensis: A Description of the Plants of the Australian Territory, vol iii: Myrtaceæ to Compositæ*. London: Lovell Reeve and Co., 1866.
Bernhardt, Peter and Robert Holden, *Gumnut Town: Botanic Fact and Bushland Fantasy*. Sydney: Royal Botanic Gardens, Sydney, 1992.
Blainey, Geoffrey, *This Land is All Horizons: Australian Fears and Visions – the 2001 Boyer Lectures*. Sydney: Australian Broadcasting Corporation, 2001.
Blainey, Geoffrey, *A Shorter History of Australia*. Melbourne: William Heinemann, 1994.
Bodkin, Frances, *Maridyulu'boola Yandel'mawa: The Seven Peacekeepers*. Sydney: unpublished, 2001.
Bond, R. W. (ed.), *Australian Forestry*, vol. xvi, no. 2, 1952.
Bonyhady, Tim, 'The Giants' Last Stand', *Sydney Morning Herald/Spectrum*, 23.6.2001.
Bonyhady, Tim, 'A Land of Sweeping Claims', *Sydney Morning Herald/Spectrum*, 27.1.2001.
Bonyhady, Tim, *The Colonial Earth*. Melbourne: The Miegunyah Press/ Melbourne University Press, 2000.
Borschmann, Gregg, *The People's Forest: A Living History of the Australian Bush*. Blackheath: The People's Forest Press, 1999.

Bradstock, Ross A., Jann E. Williams and A. Malcolm Gill (eds), *Flammable Australia: The Fire Regimes and Biodiversity of a Continent*. Melbourne: Cambridge University Press, 2002.

Brissenden, Rosemary and Robert Brissenden (eds), *The Gift of the Forest*. South Yarra: ACF/Currey O'Neill, 1982.

Brooker, M. I.H. and David Kleinig, *Eucalyptus: An Illustrated Guide to Identification*. Sydney: Reed New Holland, 1999.

Brooker, M. I. H. and D. A. Kleinig, *Field Guide to Eucalypts: South-Eastern Australia* (rev. ed.). Hawthorn: Bloomings Books, 1999.

Brown, Bob, *The Valley of the Giants: A Guide to Tasmania's Styx River Forests*. Hobart: Bob Brown, 2001.

Brown, Robert, *Prodromus Florae Novae Hollandiae et Insulae Van Diemen 1810: Supplementum primum, 1830*. New York: Hafner Publishing Co., 1960.

Burgess, Erica and Paula Dredge, 'Supplying Artists' Materials to Australia 1788–1850,' Roy, Ashok and Perry Smith (eds.), *Painting Techniques: History, Materials and Studio Practice*. London: The International Institute for Conservation of Historic and Artistic Works, 1998.

Burke, Edmund (James T. Boulton, ed.), *A Philosophical Enquiry into the Origin of Our Ideas of the Sublime and the Beautiful* (1757). Oxford: Basil Blackwell, 1987.

Burn, Ian, *National Life and Landscapes: Australian Painting 1900–1940*. Sydney and London: Bay Books, 1990.

Burnie Port Corporation, *2001 Annual Report*, 2001, online @ www.burnieport.com.au

Butel, Elizabeth, *Margaret Preston*. Sydney: Imprint, 1995.

Carron, L. T., *A Brief History of the Forestry School*. Canberra: AFS Reunion, 2000.

Carron, L. T., *A History of Forestry in Australia*. Canberra: ANU Press, 1985.

Carter, Paul, *The Road to Botany Bay: An Essay in Spatial History*. London: Faber and Faber, 1987.

Cazneaux, Harold, 'My Most "Australian" Picture', *Australia National Journal*, 1.5.1941.

Chapman, Jean, *Mamie, Also Known as May Gibbs*. Sydney: The May Gibbs Society, 1994.

Cheney, Phil, 'Bushfires – An Integral Part of Australia's Environment', *Year Book Australia*, 1995, online @ www.abs.gov.au

Chippendale, George M. *et al.*, *Eucalyptus, Angophora* (Myrtaceae), *Flora of Australia*, vol. xix. Canberra: AGPS, 1988.

Chisholm, Alec H., *Ferdinand von Mueller*. London: Oxford University Press, 1962.

Clark, C. M. H., *Select Documents in Australian History, 1788–1850*. Sydney: Angus and Robertson, 1950.

Coles, Mary, 'Engine Driver's Unique Work on Eucalypts', *Australian Women's Weekly*, 27.5.1950.

Cook, Captain James (J. G. Beaglehole, ed.), *The Journal of Captain James Cook on His Voyages of Discovery: vol. i, Voyage of The* Endeavour *1768–1771*. Cambridge: The Hakluyt Society at the University Press, 1955.

Cooper, Ellwood, *Forest Culture and the Eucalyptus Tree*. San Francisco: Cubery and Co., 1876.

CSIRO, media releases, online @ www.csiro.au

Cumpston, J. H. L., *Thomas Mitchell: Surveyor General and Explorer*. London: Oxford University Press, 1954.

Daley, Charles, *The History of the* Flora Australiensis *with Additional Letters to Baron von Mueller from Sir Joseph D. Hooker*. Melbourne: reprinted from *The Victorian Naturalist*, vol. xliv, nos. 3–10, 1927.

Dargavel, John, *Fashioning Australia's Forests*. Melbourne: Oxford University Press, 1995.

Dawson, Warren R. (ed.), *The Banks Letters: A Calendar of the Manuscript Correspondence of Sir Joseph Banks Preserved in the British Museum, the British Museum (Natural History) and Other Collections in Great Britain*. London: British Museum, 1958.

Day, M. F. (ed.), *Australia's Forests: Their Role in Our Future*. Canberra: Australian Academy of Science, 1981.

de Foigny, Gabriel (David Fausett, tr. ed.), *The Southern Land, Known*. New York: Syracuse University Press, 1993.

Department of External Affairs, 'Agreement between the Government of the Commonwealth of Australia and the Food and Agriculture Organisation of the United Nations for the Provision of Technical Assistance to the Governments of Tropical and Semi-Tropical Regions in the Form of a Eucalyptus Study Tour', *Australian Treaty Series*, 1952, no. 9, online @ www.austlii.edu.au

Diment, J. A., C. J. Humphries, L. Newington and E. Shaughnessy (eds), *Catalogue of the Natural History Drawings Commissioned by Joseph Banks on the* Endeavour *Voyage 1768–1771 Held in the British Museum (Natural History)*. London/Westport: British Museum/Meckler, 1984.

Doughty, Robin W., *The Eucalyptus: A Natural and Commerical History of the Gum Tree*. Baltimore: Johns Hopkins University Press, 2000.

Douglas, Norman, *Old Calabria*. Harmondsworth: Penguin, 1962.

Ducker, Sophie (ed.), *The Contented Botanist: Letters of W. H. Harvey about Australia and the Pacific*. Melbourne: The Miegunyah Press/Melbourne University Press, 1988.

Duffy, Michael (ed.), *Crossing the Blue Mountains: Journeys through Two Centuries*. Sydney: Duffy & Snellgrove, 1997.

Duggan, Laurie, *Ghost Nation: Imagined Space and Australian Visual Culture, 1901–1939*. St Lucia: University of Queensland Press, 2001.

Dupain, Max, *Cazneaux: Photographs by Harold Cazneaux 1878–1953*. Canberra: National Library of Australia, 1978.

Duyker, Edward, *Nature's Argonaut: Daniel Solander 1733–1782 – Naturalist and Voyager with Cook and Banks*. Melbourne: The Miegunyah Press/Melbourne University Press, 1998.

Earthbeat, *Debate Hotting Up Over Tasmania's Forests*, ABC Radio National, 2001, online @ www.abc.net.au

Eather, H. W., 'An Ambassador from the Bush', *News and Information Bureau – Department of the Interior*, E52/360, 1952.

Edwards, Deborah, *Rosalie Gascoigne: Material as Landscape*. Sydney: Art Gallery of New South Wales, 1997.

Eldridge, Ken, John Davidson, Chris Harwood and Gerrit van Wyk, *Eucalypt Domestication and Breeding*. Oxford: Clarendon Press, 1994.

Elliott, Brian, *The Landscape of Australian Poetry*. Melbourne: F. W. Cheshire, 1967.

Ellis, Bob, 'Slaying of the Giants', *Age/Good Weekend*, 27.1.2001.

Engberg, Juliana, Margaret Plant, Craig Judd, Peter Timms and Terry Smith, *The Real Thing*. Bulleen: Heide Museum of Modern Art, 1997.

FAO, *Unasylva*, various volumes, online @ www.fao.org

FAO, *The Eucalypt Dilemma*. Rome: FAO, 1988.

FAO, *World Symposium on Man-Made Forests and Their Industrial Importance*. Rome: FAO, 1967.

FAO, *Proceedings and Report of the Second World Eucalyptus Conference*. Sao Paolo: FAO, 1961.

FAO, *Report on the Eucalypt Study Tour Held in Australia, September/October 1952*. Canberra: FAO of the United Nations/Commonwealth of Australia, 1952.

Flannery, Tim (ed.), *The Birth of Sydney*. Melbourne: Text, 1999.

Flannery, Tim, *The Future Eaters: An Ecological History of the Australasian Lands and People*. Sydney: Reed New Holland, 1998.

Flinders, Matthew, *A Voyage to Terra Australis … vol. ii, 1814*. Adelaide: Libraries Board of South Australia, 1966.

Forestry and Timber Bureau of Australia, *Progress Report, 1961–1965*. Canberra: Department of National Development, 1967.

Foster, David, *Studs and Nogs: Essays 1987–1998*. Sydney: Vintage, 1999.

Foster, William C., *Sir Thomas Livingston Mitchell and His World 1792–1855: Surveyor General of New South Wales 1828–1855*. Sydney: The Institution of Surveyors, 1985.

Forestry Tasmania, *Tallest Trees Policy*, 2000, online @ www.forestrytas.com.au

Forestry Tasmania, *Regional Forestry Agreement*, 1997, online @ www.forestrytas.com.au

Frawley, Kevin J. and Noel M. Semple (eds), *Australia's Ever-Changing Forests*. Canberra: ADFA, 1988.

Frost, Alan, *Sir Joseph Banks and the Transfer of Plants To and From the South Pacific 1786–1798*. Melbourne: The Colony Press, 1993.

Gee, Helen, *For the Forests: A History of the Tasmanian Forest Campaigns*. Hobart: The Wilderness Society, 2001 [extracts online @ www.wilderness.org.au].

Gibbs, May (with Margaret Walsh and Hazel de Berg), *An Interview with May Gibbs*. Sydney: Bustle Productions, 1986.

Gibbs, May, *The Complete Adventures of Snugglepot and Cuddlepie*. Sydney: Angus and Robertson, n.d.

Gilbert, Lionel, *The Little Giant: The Life and Work of Joseph Henry Maiden, 1859–1925*. Sydney: Kardoorair Press/Royal Botanic Gardens, Sydney, 2001.

Gill, A. M., R. H. Groves and I. R. Noble, *Fire and the Australian Biota*. Canberra: Australian Academy of Science, 1981.

Griffiths, Tom. *Forests of Ash: An Environmental History*. Melbourne: Cambridge University Press, 2001.

Grimwade, Russell, *An Anthography of the Eucalypts*. Sydney: Angus and Robertson, 1920.

Hall, Norman and Ian Brooker, *The Meaning of Eucalypt Names*. Canberra: CSIRO, 1978.

Hall, Norman, *Botanists of the Eucalypts*. Melbourne: CSIRO, 1978.

Hamilton, Jill, Duchess of and Julia Bruce, *The Flower Chain: The Early Discovery of Australian Plants*. East Roseville: Kangaroo Press, 1998.

Hanbury-Tenison, Robin, *The Oxford Book of Exploration*. Oxford: Oxford University Press, 1993.

Hazzard, Margaret. *Australia's Brightest Daughter: Ellis Rowan, Artist, Naturalist, Explorer*. Richmond: Greenhouse Publications, 1984.

Headspace, *A Brush with Landscape*, ABC Radio National, 1998, online @ www.abc.net.au

Heyward, Michael, *The Ern Malley Affair*. St Lucia: University of Queensland Press, 1993.

Hickey, J. E., P. Kostoglou and G. J. Sargison, 'Tasmania's Tallest Trees', *Tasforests*, vol. xii, December 2000, online @ www.forestrytas.com.au

Hill, Ken and L. A. S. Johnson, 'Systematic studies in the eucalypts. 7. A revision of the bloodwoods, genus *Corymbia* (Myrtaceae)', *Telopea*, vol. vi, nos. 2–3, 1995.

Hillis, W. E. and A. G. Brown (eds), *Eucalypts for Wood Production*. Melbourne: CSIRO/Academic Press, 1984.

Historical Records of New South Wales, vol. v, app. A (Barrallier). Sydney: William Applegate Gullick, 1897.

Historical Records of New South Wales, vol. i, pt. 2 (Phillip, 1783–1792). Sydney: Charles Potter, 1892.

Holden, Robert and Andrew Mackenzie, *Snugglepot and Cuddlepie and Other Fairy Folk of the Australian Bush*. Sydney: Museum of Childhood, 1989.

Home, R. W., A. M. Lucas, Sara Maroske, D. M. Sinkora and J. H. Voigt (eds.), *Regardfully Yours: Selected Correspondence of Ferdinand von Mueller*, vol. i:

1840–1859, Bern: Peter Lang AG, 1998; and vol. ii: 1860–1875, Bern: Peter Lang AG, 2002.

Home, R. W. (ed.), *The Scientific Savant in Nineteenth Century Australia.* Canberra: Australian Academy of Science, 1997 (Historical Records of Australian Science, vol. xi, no. 3).

Hughes, Robert, *Beyond the Fatal Shore* – video. London: British Broadcasting Corporation, 2000.

Hughes, Robert, *The Fatal Shore*. London: Collins Harvill, 1987.

Hulme, M. I., *Bibliography on the Utilization of the Eucalypts: Prepared for the FAO World Eucalyptus Conference, Rome, 1956*. Melbourne: CSIRO Forest Products Laboratory, 1956.

Hutton, Drew and Libby Connors, *A History of the Australian Environmental Movement*. Melbourne: Cambridge University Press, 1999.

Hylton, Jane, *Reflections: H. J. Johnstone's Evening Shadows – Australia's Most Copied Painting*. Adelaide: Art Gallery of South Australia, 1999.

IUFRO, *Future of Eucalypts for Wood Products*, 2000, online @ www.ffp.csiro.au

Jacobs, M. R., *Eucalypts for Planting*. Rome: FAO, 1979.

Jacobs, M. R., *The Forests We Care For*. Melbourne: APPM Pty Ltd, 1974.

Jacobs, M. R., *The Genus Eucalyptus in World Forestry*. Seattle: University of Washington, 1970.

Jacobs, M. R., 'The Use and Abuse of Wooded Land in Australia', *The Australian Journal of Science*, vol. xix, no. 4a, 1957.

Jacobs, M. R., *Growth Habits of the Eucalypts*. Canberra: A. J. Arthur, Government Printer, 1955.

Jacobs, M. R., 'Australian Forestry', *Current Affairs Bulletin*, vol. x, no. 1, April 21, 1952.

Jacobs, M. R., *A Survey of the Genus Eucalyptus in the Northern Territory*. Canberra: Government Printer, [193?].

James, Teresa A. (ed.), *An Assessment of the World Heritage Values of the Blue Mountains and Surrounding Plateaus*. Sydney: Royal Botanic Gardens, Sydney/National Parks and Wildlife Service, 1994.

Johnston, George, *My Brother Jack*, London: Fontana, 1971.

Jonsell, Bengt, 'Linneaus and His Two Circumnavigating Apostles', *Proceedings of the Linnaean Society of New South Wales – Journal*, vol. cvi, no. 1, 1981.

Kelly, Stan, *Eucalypts*. Melbourne: Nelson, 1969 and 1978 (vols. i and ii); Melbourne: Nelson, 1983 (new rev. ed.); Ringwood: Viking O'Neill, 1989 (rev. ed.).

Kelly, Stan, *Forty Australian Eucalypts in Colour*. Sydney: Dymocks, 1949.

Keynes, Richard Darwin (ed.), *Charles Darwin's* Beagle *Diary*. Cambridge: Cambridge University Press, 1988.

Kirkpatrick, Jamie, *A Continent Transformed: Human Impact on the Natural Vegetation of Australia*. Melbourne: Oxford University Press, 1994.

Kirkpatrick, J. B., R. J. Peacock, P. J. Cullen and M. G. Neyland, *The Wet Eucalypt Forests of Tasmania*. Hobart: Tasmanian Conservation Trust, 1988.

Koerner, Lisbet, *Linnaeus: Nature and Nation*. Cambridge, Mass., and London: Harvard University Press, 1999.

Kynaston, Edward, *A Man on Edge: A Life of Baron Sir Ferdinand von Mueller*. Ringwood: Penguin, 1981.

Lang, Jean, *Pathway to Magic: The Story of May Gibbs in Western Australia*. Perth: Challenge Bank Ltd, 1991.

Laurence, Janet and Jisuk Han, *Veil of Trees: The Creation of a Passage of Reflection, a Space where Memory is Gathered*. Installation at Mrs Macquarie's Chair, Sydney, 1999.

Law, Geoff, '$222 for Australia's Tallest Tree', *Habitat*, vol. xiv, no. 5, October 1986.

Lee, Sidney (ed.), *Dictionary of National Biography*. London: Smith, Elder and Co., 1898.

Leonard, Gary, *Eucalypts: A Bushwalker's Guide*. Kensington: New South Wales University Press, 1993.

Levitus, Geoff (ed.), *Lying about the Landscape*. Sydney: Craftsman House, 1997.

L'Héritier de Brutelle, Charles-Louis (G. H. M. Lawrence, ed.), *Sertum Anglicum* (1788). Pittsburgh: The Hunt Botanical Library, 1963.

Low, Tim, *Feral Future: The Untold Story of Australia's Exotic Invaders*. Ringwood: Penguin, 2001.

Macdonald, Vici, *Rosalie Gascoigne*. Paddington: Regaro, 1998.

Macinnis, Peter, 'Eucalyptus Oils', *The Science Show*, ABC Radio National, 1997, online @ www.abc.net.au

Macqueen, Andy, *Back from the Brink: Blue Gum Forest and the Grose Wilderness*. Springwood: Andy Macqueen, 1997.

Maiden, J. H., *The Forest Flora of New South Wales*, vol. iv, online @ setis.library.usyd.edu.au

Maiden, J. H., *Sir Joseph Banks: The 'Father of Australia.'* Sydney: William Applegate Gullick, 1909.

Maiden, J. H., *A Critical Revision of the Genus* Eucalyptus. Sydney: William Applegate Gullick, 1909.

Mann, Cecil (ed.), *Henry Lawson's Best Stories*. Penrith: The Discovery Press, 1968.

Maroske, Sara and Helen M. Cohn, '"Such Ingenious Birds": Ferdinand von Mueller and William Swainson in Victoria', *Mulleria*, vol. vii, no. 4, 1992.

McAuley, James, *A Map of Australian Verse*. Melbourne: Oxford University Press, 1975.

McCormick, Tim *et al.*, *First Views of Australia 1788–1825: A History of Early Sydney*. Chippendale: David Ell Press with Longueville Publications, 1987.

McDonald, Roger, *The Tree in Changing Light*. Sydney: Knopf, 2001.

McGregor, Craig, David Beal, David Moore and Harry Williamson, *In the Making*. Melbourne: Thomas Nelson, 1969.

McPhee, John, *John Glover 1767–1849*. Sydney and London: Rex Irwin Art Dealer, and Spink and Sons Ltd and Nevill Keating Pictures, 1986.

McPhee, John, *The Art of John Glover*. South Melbourne: Macmillan, 1980.
Megaw, J.V. S. (ed.), *Employ'd as a Discoverer: Papers Presented at the Captain Cook Bi-Centenary Symposium, Sutherland Shire, 1–3 May, 1970*. Sydney: A. H. and A.W. Reed, 1971.
Métro, André, *Eucalypts for Planting*. Rome: FAO, 1955.
Meyer, Athol, *The Foresters*. Hobart: Institute of Foresters, 1985.
Miller, David Phillip and Peter Hanns Reill (eds), *Visions of Empire: Voyages, Botany and Representations of Nature*. Cambridge: Cambridge University Press, 1996.
Mitchell, Major Thomas Livingston, *Three Expeditions into the Interior of Australia* (1839). Adelaide: Libraries Board of South Australia, 1965.
Modjeska, Drusilla, 'Dots on the Landscape', *The* Australian*'s Review of Books*, April 2000.
Montgomery, Bruce, 'Reprieve for a Forest Giant', *The Australian*, 26.6.2002.
Moyle, Ann, *A Bright and Savage Land: The Science of a New Continent – Australia – Where All Things were 'Queer and Opposite'*. Ringwood: Penguin, 1993.
Mueller, Ferdinand, *Eucalyptographia: A Descriptive Atlas of the Eucalypts of Australia and Adjoining Islands*. Melbourne: John Ferres, 1879–1884.
Mueller, Ferdinand, *The Plants Indigenous to the Colony of Victoria: Lithograms*. Melbourne: John Ferres, 1864–1865.
Mueller, Ferdinand, 'Monograph of the *Eucalypti* of Tropical Australia; with an Arrangement for the Use of Colonists According to the Structure of the Bark', *Journal of the Proceedings of the Linnaean Society. Botany*, vol. iii. London: Longman, Brown, Green, Longmans and Roberts and Williams and Norgate, 1859.
Muir, Richard, *Approaches to Landscape*. London: Macmillan, 1999.
Mulligan, Martin and Stuart Hill, *Ecological Pioneers: A Social History of Australian Ecological Thought and Action*. Melbourne: Cambridge University Press, 2001.
Murray, Les, *A Working Forest*. Sydney: Duffy & Snellgrove, 1997.
National Forest Inventory, *Australia's State of the Forests Report 1998*. Canberra: Bureau of Rural Sciences, 1998.
North, Ian, Alison Carroll and John Tregenza, *Hans Heysen Centenary Retrospective, 1877–1977*. Adelaide: Art Gallery of South Australia, 1977.
O'Brian, Patrick, *Joseph Banks: A Life*. London: Collins Harvill, 1987.
Olsen, John, *Drawn from Life*. Sydney: Duffy & Snellgrove, 1997.
One Tree Project – catalogue and video, 2001, plus information online @ www.onetree.org
Parv, Valerie, *The Changing Face of Australia: The Impact of 200 Years of Change on Our Environment*. Sydney: Bay Books, 1984.
Penfold, A. R., *Eucalyptus: The Essence of Australia*. Sydney: Alfred James Kent, 1930.

Pescott, R. T. M., *The Royal Botanic Gardens, Melbourne: A History from 1845–1970*. Melbourne: Oxford University Press, 1982.

Pescott, R. T. M., *Collections of a Century: The History of the First 100 Years of the National Museum of Victoria*. Melbourne: National Museum of Victoria, 1954.

Powell, J. M., *Mirrors of the New World: Images and Image-Makers in the Settlement Process*. Canberra: ANU Press, 1978.

Powell, J. M. and M. Williams (eds), *Australian Space, Australian Time: Geographical Perspectives*. Melbourne: Oxford University Press, 1975.

Poynter, J. R., *Russell Grimwade*. Melbourne: The Miegunyah Press/Melbourne University Press, 1967.

Pyne, Stephen J., *Burning Bush: A Fire History of Australia*. Sydney: Allen and Unwin, 1992.

Radford, Ron, *John Glover's House and Garden*. Adelaide: Art Gallery of South Australia, 1985.

Read, Peter, *Returning to Nothing: The Meaning of Lost Places*. Melbourne: Cambridge University Press, 1996.

Reed, A. W. (ed.), *Captain Cook in Australia: Extracts from the Journals of Captain James Cook Giving a Full Account in His Own Words of His Adventures and Discoveries in Australia*. Sydney: A. H. and A. W. Reed, 1969.

Roderick, Colin, *Henry Lawson – the Master Story-teller: Commentaries on his Prose Writings*. North Ryde: Angus and Robertson, 1985.

Rodger, G. J., *Annual Report of the Forestry and Timber Bureau for the Year Ended 31.12.1952*. Canberra: L. F. Johnston, 1953.

Rolls, Eric, *Australia: A Biography – The Beginnings*. Brisbane: University of Queensland Press, 2000.

Rolls, Eric, 'The Billion Trees of Man', *The Independent Monthly*, June 1990.

Rolls, Eric, *A Million Wild Acres*. Ringwood: Penguin, 1984.

Routley, R. and V., *The Fight for the Forests: The Takeover of Australian Forests for Pines, Wood Chips, and Intensive Forestry* (2nd ed.). Canberra: Research School of Social Sciences, ANU, 1974.

Rule, Alexander, *Forests of Australia*. Sydney: Angus and Robertson, 1967.

Rural Fire Service of New South Wales, *Statistical Information (Approximate Only) for Section 44s, 20/01/02*, unpublished, 2002.

Ryan, Simon, *The Cartographic Eye: How Explorers Saw Australia*. Melbourne: Cambridge University Press, 1996.

Saxby, Maurice, *Offered to Children: A History of Australian Children's Literature 1841–1941*. Sydney: Scholastic, 1998.

Saxena, N. C., *India's Eucalyptus Craze: The God that Failed*. New Delhi and London: Sage, 1994.

Schama, Simon, *Landscape and Memory*. London: Fontana, 1996.

Seddon, George, *Landprints: Reflections on Place and Landscape*. Melbourne: Cambridge University Press, 1997.

Sharma, J. K., C. I. S. Nair, S. Kedharnath and S. Kondas (eds), *Eucalypts in India – Past, Present and Future: Proceedings of the National Seminar on Eucalypts in Indian Forestry, January 30–31, 1984*. Kerala: Kerala Forest Research Institute, 1986.

Shiel, Des, *Eucalyptus, Essence of Australia: The Story of the Eucalyptus Oil Industry – and of the 'Eucy' Men, and Their Contribution to the Australian Bush Tradition*. Carlton: Queensberry Hill Press, 1985.

Short, P. S. (ed.), *History of Systematic Botany in Australasia*. Melbourne: Australian Systematic Botany Society Inc., 1990.

Sinden, J. A. (ed.), *The Natural Resources of Australia: Prospects and Problems for Development*. Sydney: Angus and Robertson/ANZAAS, 1972.

Smith, Bernard, with Terry Smith and Christopher Heathcote, *Australian Painting: 1788–2000*. Melbourne: Oxford University Press, 2001.

Smith, Bernard (ed.), *Documents on Art and Taste in Australia: The Colonial Period 1770–1914*. Melbourne: Oxford University Press, 1990.

Smith, Bernard, *European Vision and the South Pacific* (2nd ed.). Sydney: Harper and Row, 1985.

Solness, Peter, *Tree Stories*. Neutral Bay: Chapter and Verse, 1999.

Spielvogel, Nathan F., *The Gumsucker at Home*. Sydney: George Robertson and Co., [1914].

Stephen, Ann (ed.), *Visions of a Republic: The Work of Lucien Henry – Paris, Noumea, Sydney*. Sydney: Powerhouse Publishing, 2001.

Tasmania Together, 2002, online @ www.tasmaniatogether.tas.gov.au

Tench, Watkin, *Sydney's First Four Years* (1793). Sydney: Library of Australian History, 1979.

Thomas, Martin (ed.), *Uncertain Ground: Essays Between Art and Nature*. Sydney: Art Gallery of New South Wales, 1999.

Thornhill, John, *Making Australia: Exploring Our National Conversation*. Sydney: Millennium Books, 1992.

Thwaites, R. N. and B. J. Schaumberg (eds), *Australasian Forestry and the Global Environment*. Canberra: Institute of Foresters of Australia, 1993.

Thwaites, Vivonne and John Cruthers (eds), *Karra*. Adelaide: Adelaide Festival Centre, 2000.

Torre, Stephen (ed.), *The Macquarie Dictionary of Australian Quotations*. Macquarie University: Macquarie Library, 1990.

Troy, Jakelin, *Australian Aboriginal Contact with the English Language in NSW: 1788–1845*. Canberra: Pacific Linguists/Australian National University, 1990.

Troy, Jakelin, *The Sydney Language*. Canberra: Panther, 1994.

Turner, R. J., *Identification of Eucalypts* and *Identification of Local Eucalypts: Blue Mountains and Barren Grounds Observatory*, unpublished, 2000/2001.

United Nations University, 'Summaries by Session Chairmen', *The Value of Forests: International Conference on Forests and Sustainable Development*. Tokyo: United Nations University, 2000.

Walsh, Maureen, *May Gibbs: Mother of the Gumnuts*. Pymble: Angus and Robertson, 1994.

Ward, Russell, *The Australian Legend*. Melbourne: Oxford University Press, 1993.

Ward, Russell, *Australia Since the Coming of Man*. Sydney: Lansdowne Press, 1982.

Webb, Joan, *George Caley: 19th Century Naturalist*. Chipping Norton: Surrey Beatty and Sons, 1995.

Webb, Vivienne, *John Glover: Natives on the Ouse River, Van Diemen's Land, 1838*. Sydney: Art Gallery of New South Wales/Australian Collection Focus, 2001.

White, John, *Journal of a Voyage to New South Wales* (1790). Sydney: Angus and Robertson/Royal Australian Historical Society, 1962.

White, Mary E., *After the Greening: The Browning of Australia*. Kenthurst, NSW: Kangaroo Press, 1994.

White, Mary E., *The Greening of Gondwana: The 400 Million Year Story of Australia's Plants* (2nd ed.). Chatswood: Reed, 1994.

White, Patrick, *The Tree of Man*. Ringwood: Penguin, 1978.

Wilderness Society [TWS], media releases online @ www.wilderness.org.au

Wilderness Society [TWS], *The Wilderness Society's Styx Campaign History*, unpublished, 2002.

Wilderness Society [TWS], *Proposal for Valley of the Giants National Park*, 2001, online @ www.wilderness.org.au

Wilderness Society [TWS], *A Fringe of Green: Protecting Australia's Forests and Woodlands*. Hobart: The Wilderness Society, 2000.

Williams, Jann E. and John C. Z. Woinarski (eds), *Eucalypt Ecology: Individuals to Ecosystems*. Melbourne: Cambridge University Press, 1997.

Willis, Margaret, *By Their Fruits: A Life of Ferdinand von Mueller, Botanist and Explorer*. Sydney: Angus and Robertson, 1949.

Wood, Andrew, 'Eucalyptus Study Tour, Australia, 1952', *British Agricultural Bulletin*, vol. vi, no. 25, 1953.

Woodford, James, 'Bob's Gums Have Died, But the Plaque Lives On', *Sydney Morning Herald*, 6.3.2001.

Year Book of Australia, 'Forestry and Fishing: Special Article', *Year Book Australia*, 1926, online @ www.abs.gov.au

Yen, Alan L., Simon Hinkley, Peter Lillywhite, John Wainer and Ken Walker, 'A Preliminary Survey of the Arboreal Invertebrate Fauna of Two River Red Gum Trees (*Eucalyptus camaldulensis*) Near the Murray River', *The Victorian Naturalist*, 2002 (in press).

Zacharin, Robert Fyfe, *Emigrant Eucalypts: Gum Trees as Exotics*. Melbourne: Melbourne University Press, 1978.

Ziegler, Oswald L. (ed.), *Official Commemorative Book: Jubilee of the Commonwealth of Australia*. Sydney: Angus and Robertson, 1951.

notes

The Seven Peacekeepers

page 3

Come up Kelly, in Borschmann, 1999, p. 161.

A French soldier Barrallier, in *HRNSW*, 1897, vol. v, App. A.

page 4

Even before Europeans de Foigny (Fausett, ed.), 1993, p. 43.

page 5

The story of the Seven Peacekeepers, and the story of the names and uses of eucalypts in the D'harawal culture, are the intellectual property of the Bodkin-Andrews family (©2001 Frances Bodkin) and are retold here with the permission of Fran Bodkin.

Becoming Eucalyptus

page 10

Every blockhead Banks, 1998, p. 4.

no people ever Ellis, in Dodge, 1962, p. 18.

page 11

till we fall Cook, in Ward, 1982, p. 32.

many fine smelling Hamilton, 1998, p. 50.

rose in gentle 20.4.1770, in Banks, 1998, p. 18.

the back of 26.4.1770, *ibid.*, p. 20.

page 12

Emmidiatly after Cook, 1955, p. 305.

blacker than any 28.4.1770, in Banks, 1998, p. 24.

page 13

until we compleatly 1.5.1770, *ibid.*, p. 27.

non-descript stuff Hughes, 1987, p. 55.

We sat till Banks, in Diment *et al.* (eds), 1984, p. 8.

page 14

Madeira and Doughty, 2000, p. 25.

The gum distils Dampier, 1688, in Bassett (ed.), 1998, p. 31.

The great quantity Cook, 6.5.1770, in Reed (ed.), 1969, p. 46. This name was probably not decided on until the *Endeavour* had left the Bay and Banks had had time to examine the extent of his collections.

page 15

drawing the plants 12.5.1770, in Banks, 1998, p. 32.

They didn't have Duyker, 1998, p. 189

many of the 23.5.1770, in Banks, 1998, pp. 35–36.

page 16

Most of the 30.5.1770, *ibid.*, p. 40.

He called them Banks, in Maiden, 1909 (*Banks*), p. 22, and footnote.

a narrow-leaved Duyker, 1998, p. 192.

The Woods Cook, in Reed (ed.), 1969, p. 129.

snuggled in among Diment *et al.* (eds), 1984, p. 8.

page 18

immortal Banks Linnaeus, in Dawson (ed.), 1958, pp. 543–544.

a perfect museum Sheffield, in O'Brian, 1987, p. 168.

page 19

renamed 'Banksia' Jonsell, 1981, p. 15.

page 20

Linnaeus wrote Koerner, 1999, p. 156.

whose presence in Cook, in Hamilton, 1998, p. 97.

page 21

The sides of Furneaux, March 1773, in Reed (ed.), 1969, p. 162.

page 22

my surgeon, Cook, *ibid.*, p. 135.

fit for spars Cook, 29.1.1776, *ibid.*, p. 174.

to a great height Anderson, 1776, *ibid.*, p. 177.

page 24

they are the part L'Héritier de Brutelle (1788), 1963, p. xviii.

eu, *meaning* Doughty, 2000, p. 25.

a special work L'Héritier de Brutelle (1788), 1963, p. xxvii.

page 25

enough resources Banks, 1988, p. 89.

Banks advocated Hughes, 1987, p. 57.

page 26

I am inclined Banks, in Hamilton, 1998, p. 97.

sprouting roses Kendall, in Elliot, 1967, pp. 172–173.

each man stepped Collins, in Hughes, 1987, p. 87.

the principal business Worgan, in McCormick *et al.*, 1987, p. 16.

page 27
The timber of Phillip, 1788, in *HRNSW*, vol. i, pt. 2, pp. 127–128.
of universally so bad Tench (1793), 1979, p. 64.
the choicest young *ibid.*, p. 263.
of little use White (1790), 1962, p. 175.
whole face Ross, in Flannery, 1999, p. 82.
page 28
We have *and* Worgan, in Bonyhady, 2000, p. 70.
two companies Zacharin, 1978, p. 51.
page 29
was drawing near Banks to Alströmer, in Hamilton, 1998, p. 90.
one named nine Hall, p. 119.
You are to send Banks, in Frost, 1993, pp. 25–27.
several small phials Macinnis, 1997.
serviceable in medicine White, in Tench (1793), 1979, p. 64.
page 30
Brown reported Webb, 1995, p. 46.
page 31
This is neither Note on a Caley specimen, Harvard Herbarium, USA, in Webb, 1995, p. 120.
Brown envisaged Stearn, in Brown, 1960, pp. xxviii–xxix.
Of Eucalyptus *alone* Brown, in Flinders (1814), 1966, pp. 546–547.
page 32
through forest Blaxland, 1813, in Hanbury-Tenison (ed.), 1993, p. 420.
page 33
shortage of carmine Burgess and Dredge, 1998, p. 199.
along the ridge Elizabeth Ellis, AGNSW, 2001.
page 34
Behold, Hughes, 1987, p. 339.
mammoth collection Barker and Barker, in Short (ed.), 1990, pp. 37, 52.
London kept calling White (1790), 1962, p. 174.
page 35
his examination of Jonsell, 1981, p. 15.
in a pure Cook, in Reed (ed.), 1969, p. 135.

The Explorers' Trees
page 37
The yarra tree Mitchell, in Baker, 1997, p. 153.
page 38
Settlers and sheep Mulligan and Hill, 2001, p. 16; Ryan, 1996, pp. 116–117.
page 39
I could leave Evans, 1815, in Hanbury-Tenison (ed.), 1993, p. 422.

page 40
these flats are Oxley, 1817, *ibid.*, p. 424.
real estate information Seddon, 1997, p. 40.
page 41
our animals Sturt, in Ryan, 1996, p. 83.
the regular report Andrews, 1992, p. 3.
page 42
filling his evenings Foster, 1985, p. 447.
astonished and Janet Mitchell, 4.4.1827, *ibid.*, p. 107.
land of the Mitchell, *ibid.*, p. 119.
page 43
skinning and stuffing Carter, 1987, p. 117.
among all the Gilpin, *ibid.*, p. 115.
a Commission should *HRA*, vol. xi, in Andrews, 1992, p. 4.
denied the possibility *Votes and Proceedings NSWLA*, 1855, in Foster, 1985, p. 199.
page 44
In the Trigonometrical Mitchell, in Andrews, 1992, p. 5.
accidentally on a Mitchell, 1.2.1828, in Cumpston, 1954, p. 58.
page 45
near the place Andrews, 1992, p. 14.
Yesterday evening Mitchell, *ibid.*, p. 17.
page 46
1. To extend *ibid.*
page 47
colonial nomenclature Lang, 1837, *ibid.*, 1995, p. 38.
the natives can Mitchell, in Foster, 1985, p. 202.
by avoiding Mitchell, 1829, *ibid.*, p. 73.
broad and covered Mitchell, 1829, *ibid.*, p. 203.
20 men Mitchell, 14–16.7.1831, in Andrews, 1992, p. 42.
page 48
happy to say Mitchell, Nov. 1831, in Foster, 1985, p. 204.
written my name Mitchell, 1831, *ibid.*
a more romantic Mitchell, 1829, *ibid.*, p. 135.
page 49
a greater treat Mitchell, 1830, in Baker, 1997, p. 39.
to spread the light Cumpston, 1954, p. 74.
impossible to believe Banks, in Foster, 1985, p. 212.
page 50
Consider the east *ibid.*, p. 214.
a surveyor constantly Mitchell, 1855, *ibid.*, p. 217.
page 51
the ardour of 24.11.1831, Mitchell (1839), 1965, vol. i, p. 5.

lost ourselves 28.11.1831, *ibid.*, p. 13.
During the last 9–10.12.1831, *ibid.*, pp. 30–33.
terra incognita 13.12.1831, *ibid.*, p. 34.

page 52

forests of box 16.12.1831, *ibid.*, p. 43.
When almost in 3.1.1832, *ibid.*, p. 65.
I again remarked 6.1.1832, *ibid.*, p. 69.

page 53

whose progress Mitchell, 24.3.1833, in Foster, 1985, p. 164.

page 54

accompanied by Cumpston, 1954, p. 2.
totally unfit Foster, 1985, p. 95.
often interrupted *ibid.*, p. 104.
group of girls Keynes (ed.), 1988, p. 405.

page 55

one horticulturalist Shepherd, in Smith, 1985, p. 292.
rude invasions Tompson, in Powell (ed.), 1978, p. 24.
tallest and most Bowes, in Seddon, 1997, p. 66.
Not so much Thornhill, 1992, p. 145.
in vain seek Watling, in Flannery, 1999, p. 129.
can a painter Field, in Smith, 1990, pp. 35–36.

page 56

It is indeed Wordsworth, in Burke (1757), 1987, p. xxxviii.
Forests of tall Meredith, in Smith, 1985, p. 296.
composed a most Keynes (ed.), 1988, p. 409.
forms that Bonyhady, 2000, p. 73.

page 57

There is a Glover, in McPhee, 1986, p. 5.

page 58

dared to paint *Annals of Fine Arts*, in McPhee, 1980, p. 8.
he finished 300 Bonyhady, 2000, p. 90.
buried in a painting Boyes, in Smith, 1985, p. 260.

page 59

to the artist Bonyhady, 2000, p. 92.
with hideous fidelity *ibid.*, p. 93.
On near examination Strzelecki, *ibid.*, pp. 138–140.

page 60

as a piece Mitchell, 1833, in Foster, 1985, p. 209.
chiefly on Sundays Mitchell, 1855, *ibid.*, p. 205.

page 61

Mitchell launched off Carter, 1987, p. 103.
'in the merry 5.4.1835, Mitchell (1839), 1965, vol. i, p. 163.
new grass 11.4.1835, *ibid.*, p. 171.
almost immediately 5.5.1835, *ibid.*, p. 198.

page 62
the picturesque grouping 1.5.1835, *ibid.*, p. 192.
a green bough 27.6.1835, *ibid.*, p. 245.
contrasting beautifully 3.5.1835, *ibid.*, p. 205.
blades of green 14.8.1835, *ibid.*, p. 313.
soil changing 16.5.1835, *ibid.*, p. 208.
page 63
ascertained only after 25.4.1836, *ibid.*, vol. ii, p. 55.
to a gigantic 25.4.1836, *ibid.*, p. 54.
page 64
We had at length 13.7.1836, *ibid.*, p. 171.
page 65
nothing can surpass Staypleton, in Foster, 1985, p. 286.
instead of rare 4.7.1836, Mitchell (1839), 1965, vol. ii., p. 163.
a new species *ibid.*, p. 175.
the slightest thought 27.10.1836, *ibid.*, p. 314.
page 66
the scenery, 28.10.1836, *ibid.*, p. 315.
another Eden Foster, 1985, p. 323.
He had given Carter, 1987, p. 122.
the Cook of Foster, 1985, p. 315.
page 67
a snug bit Mitchell, 1836, *ibid.*, p. 285.
surpassed any Mitchell, in Carter, 1987, p. 130.
a survey connecting Mitchell, 1853, in Andrews, 1992, p. 346.
page 68
establishing depot camps Cumpston, 1954, pp. 182, 191.
He watched Aboriginal Baker, 1997, p. 188.
page 69
we were not prepared Foster, 1985, p. 421.
many interesting plants 13.4.1835, Mitchell (1839), 1965, vol. i, p. 173.

Baron Blue Gum
All letters to and from Mueller come from transcripts held by the Mueller Correspondence Project, Royal Botanic Gardens, Melbourne, unless otherwise specified.
page 72
loaded up Wilhelmi, in McMullen, in Home (ed.), 1997, p. 326.
page 73
Scientists from Wilkes, 1844, in Bonyhady, 2000, p. 138.
page 74
Sicily and Malta Lee (ed.), 1898, p. 192.
letters of introduction Banks to Swainson, 16.2.1819, in Dawson (ed.), 1958, p. 797.

it is well known Maroske and Cohn, 1992, p. 542.
160 different *ibid.*

page 75

add to our knowledge La Trobe to Gunn, 8.10.1852, in Home *et al.* (eds), 1998, p. 767.
There is an honest Maroske and Cohn, 1992, p. 538.

page 76

It was his heart's Willis, 1949, p. 22.
No doubt, Mueller, 3.2.1853, in Home *et al.* (eds), 1998, p. 141.
It appears to me Swainson, in Maroske and Cohn, 1992, p. 540.

page 77

left without funds *ibid.*, p. 539.
A grumbler La Trobe, 30.6.1853, *ibid.*, p. 541.
Without taking too much Swainson, 1853, in Pescott, 1982, pp. 34–35.

page 78

I have now materials Swainson, 1853, in Maroske and Cohn, 1992, pp. 542–543.
views with regard Mueller to Sir William Hooker, 18.10.1853, in Home *et al.* (eds), 1998, p. 171.
as ignorant as Sir William Hooker, 9.4.1854, *ibid.*, pp. 175–176.

page 79

a matter of Sir William Hooker, 6.3.1854, *ibid.*, p. 171–172, note.
never read before Harvey, in Ducker (ed.), 1988, p. 164.
announced his 'discovery' Maroske and Cohn, 1992, p. 546.
My clever little La Trobe, 30.6.1853, *ibid.*, p. 541.

page 80

not one has Sir William Hooker, 6.3.1854, in Home *et al.* (eds), 1998, pp. 171–172, note.
differentiating 30 Moore, in Home (ed.), 1997, p. 375.

page 81

fully aware *E. globulus*, in Mueller, 1879–1884.
I have a great Mueller to Sir William Hooker, 18.10.1853, in Home *et al.* (eds), 1998, p. 166.

page 82

The last concerted Hall, 1978, p. 129.
the most important Mueller to Sir William Hooker, 6.3.1857, in Home *et al.* (eds), 1998, p. 276.
I do not think Mueller to Sir William Hooker, 15.9.1857, *ibid.*, p. 322.

page 83

For the use Mueller to Sir William Hooker, 6.3.1857, *ibid.*, pp 276–277.

page 84

upwards of a week's J. D. Hooker to Mueller, 22.6.1858, in Daley, 1927, p. 74.
We do look J. D. Hooker to Mueller, 20.12.1858, *ibid.*, p. 91.

page 85

for the amusement Kynaston, 1981, p. 165.

a foundation Mueller to Sir William Hooker, 17.5.1860.
if no unforeseen Mueller to Bentham, 24.1.1862.
page 86
the large folio Mueller to Bentham, 24.7.1862.
temporarily deferred Mueller, 1864–1865.
page 87
cemented together Mueller to Barry, 22.8.1866.
perfectly confused Bentham to Mueller, 18.10.1865.
your investigations Mueller to Bentham, 24.3.1866.
the most acute Bentham to Mueller, 24.7.1862.
page 88
I had been Bentham to Mueller, 23.7.1865.
Circumstances are Mueller to Martius, 22.5.1868.
asphalt would dissolve Mueller to Barlee, 28.10.1867.
mixed with the Mueller to Owen, 25.9.1864.
page 89
gratuitously distribute Doughty, 2000, p. 38.
fresh branchlets Mueller, *ibid.*, pp. 38–39.
page 90
the time would come Zacharin, 1978, p. 57.
One Algerian Cooper, 1876, pp. 18–19.
page 91
a shield with Karl, King of Württenberg, to Mueller 6.7.1871.
Baron Blue Gum *Imperial Review*, June 1880, in Pescott, 1982, p. 47.
many ladies living Mueller to the *West Australian*, July 1883, fn.
most indefatigable *The Gardeners' Chronicle*, 11.5.1872.
could not possibly Maiden, in Gilbert, 2001, p. 170.
well enough known *The Gardeners' Chronicle*, 11.5.1872.
page 92
inexterminable Kynaston, 1981, pp. 277–278.
No city Mueller, 1876, from the Forest Gallery, Melbourne Museum.
page 93
the poor man Willis, 1949, p. 103.
a taste for *Daily Telegraph*, 1.8.1872.
would no one remember Mueller to Thistleton-Dyer, 1.1.1881.
page 94
his messenger Mueller to J. D. Hooker, 7.9.1872.
point de honneur Mueller to Thistleton-Dyer, 1.1.1881.
targeted by Masons Mueller to J. D. Hooker, 7.9.1872.
he was foreign Kynaston, 1981, p. 301.
Baron von Mueller *Imperial Review*, June 1880, in Pescott, 1982, p. 47.
page 95
new specimens of gums Mueller to Ramsay, 26.8.1874.
A professor Oliver, fn to Mueller to J. D. Hooker, 9.7.1879.

a massive Flora Mueller to de Candolle, 24.10.1878.
the long-contemplated Mueller to Berry, 7.8,1877.
more than five Mueller to Bentham, 29.9.1878.

page 96

The issue of Mueller, 1879–1884.
of all generic *ibid.*
In any review Mueller to Gray, 6.9.1879.

page 97

On this genus Mueller to de Candolle, 3.9.1879.
the tallest trees Mueller, 1879–1884.
one of the most *E. amygdalina, ibid.*
can be accomplished *E. globulus, ibid.*

page 98

the ordinary Blue *ibid.*
there will not Mueller to de Candolle, 9.4.1882.

page 99

He was confident 'Brief Remarks at the Conclusion of the Main-Work with its Tenth Decade', 1884, in Mueller, 1879–1884.

page 100

driven out Mueller to Gray, 21.2.1880.
during the many *Argus*, 23.1.1892.
It is but fair *Daily Telegraph*, 26.1.1892.

page 101

Even the Eucalyptus Mueller to Thistleton-Dyer, 7.7.1880.
most plates ready Mueller to Gray, 8.9.1885.

page 102

the subject Mueller, in Maroske and Cohn, 1992, p. 550.
an entire revision Gilbert, 2001, p. 191.
Most of us Maiden, *ibid.*, p. 267

Snug and Cud Inc

page 107

so poetic Buvelot, in Smith *et al.*, 2001, p. 62.
the first to Smith, 1888, in Bonyhady, 2000, p. 159.
the Grotesque Clarke, 1871, in Smith, 1990, pp. 135–136.
The first picture Hylton, 1999.

page 108

largely through Buvelot McCubbin, 1916, in Smith (ed.), 1990, pp. 270–271.
the universal eucalyptus Froude, 1886, in Bachman, 1999, p. 176.
small people Hughes, 2000, episode 2.
national style Roberts, in Thomas (ed.), 1999, p. 133.
Lawson had Lawson, in Roderick, 1985, p. 111.
in the teeming *Sydney Morning Herald*, 18.5.1891, in Stephen (ed.), 2001, p. 86.

page 109
We often hear Daplyn, 1902, in Smith (ed.), 1990, pp. 221–222.
with its changes Long, 1905, in Duggan, 2001, pp. 41–42.
page 111
When I stayed Gibbs, *ibid.*, pp. 44–45.
continue to work Hazzard, 1984, pp. 24–25.
They simply refused Rowan, *ibid.*, p. 106.
page 112
A Publisher may Gibbs, in Walsh, 1994, p. 75.
Keep cool ML MSS2048/10.
page 113
which was an ideal Gibbs, in Walsh, 1994, p. 83.
bush sprite's body Chapman, 1994, p. 4.
page 114
hand-painted them Gibbs, in Walsh, 1994, p. 83.
I don't know Gibbs, in Seddon, 1997, p. 122.
That she uses *Sydney Morning Herald*, December 1914.
pride of place Walsh, 1994, p. 85.
page 115
slightly utopian Ward, 1982, p. 141.
Our Gum Trees Spielvogel, [1914].
page 116
We are the Walsh, 1994, p. 3.
page 117
Pictures first Gibbs (with Walsh and de Berg), 1986.
a genuine and *The Bulletin*, November, 1917.
page 118
an institution Walsh, 1994, p. 85.
Here are the Gibbs, p. 2.
It was extraordinary Bernhardt, in Bernhardt and Holden, 1992, p. 9.
page 119
Gum it all! Gibbs, pp. 34, 74.
My little book Gibbs, 1918, in Walsh, 1994, p. 100.
the breath of *Age* and *Advertiser*, c. 1918.
page 120
Majestic marris Lang, 1991, p. 14.
The nuts and flowers Seddon, 1997, p. 122.
Nowhere else found ML MSS2048/10/3.
Apart from her *MJA*, in Seddon, 1997, p. 123.
page 121
living things Grimwade, in Pescott, 1954, pp. ix–x.
the vast areas Grimwade, 1920, p. 9.
awaken public interest *ibid.*, p. 5.

page 122
like being represented Gibbs, in Walsh, 1994, p. 91.
exceedingly creditable Walsh, 1994, pp. 119, 128.
page 123
moodiness and psychological Radok, in Thwaites and Cruthers (eds), 2001, p. 26.
gum leaf's sharp Preston, in Butel, 1995, p. 54.
exclusively ours MacDonald, in Burn, 1990, p. 100.
full of vigour Plant, in Engberg *et al.*, 1997, p. 55.
something immensely Heysen, in Bachman, 1999, p. 174.
page 124
indescribable, the age-old Lawrence, in Brissenden and Brissenden (eds), 1982, p. 62.
sun-refusing... Lawrence, in Thornhill, 1992, p. 144.
magical range Lawrence, *ibid.*, p. 153.
page 125
majestic, dignified Burn, 1990, p. 48.
irrelevantly extolling North, 1977, p. 10.
curiously conscious Heysen, *ibid.*, p. 13.
page 126
One canvas alone Tillers, in Engberg (ed.), 1997, p. 59.
tangled scrub Smith *et al.*, 2001, p. 113.
page 127
One young father ML MSS2048/64.
page 128
memories of Walsh, 1994, p. 82.
Rodriguez and Thew ML MSS2048/64, ff. 9, 15, 43, 95.
page 129
Easter, 1931 Mulligan and Hill, 2001, pp. 138–141; Macqueen, 1997.
page 130
Humans, please Gibbs, in Bernhardt and Holden, 1992, p. 32.
Did you think Gibbs (with Walsh and de Berg), 1986.
Do not let Gibbs, in Walsh, 1994, p. 138.
page 131
One editor commented Baume, *ibid.*, p. 151.
page 132
everyone admired Waterhouse, *ibid.*, p. 154.
they do not want *ibid.*, p. 155.
page 133
Publishers will not *ibid.*
the artist who Gibbs, *ibid.*, p. 168.
page 134
help me Cazneaux to Heysen, 12.4.1935, ANL MS5073/1/2672–3.

taking a trailer Heysen to Cazneaux, [1935?], ANL MS8361.
page 135
I jot these Cazneaux to Heysen, 28.4.1935, ANL MS5073/1/2683–7.
I shall see Cazneaux to Heysen, 12.11.1935, courtesy of Sally Garrett.
page 136
This giant gum Cazneaux, 1941, p. 25.
Without doubt Caire, in Bonyhady, 2000, p. 249.
page 137
I like your groupings Heysen to Cazneaux, 26.3.1937, ANL MS8361.
Cazneaux's image Roberts, in Thomas (ed.), 1997, p. 134.
he was astounded Cazneaux to Heysen, 1.12.1937, ANL MS5073/3013–15.
You cannot help Heysen to Cazneaux, 11.12.1937, ANL MS8361.
page 138
my most Australian Cazneaux, in Solness, 2000, p. 42.
heroic in stature Dupain, 1978, p. xiv.
By reversing Heysen to Cazneaux, 14.1.1953, courtesy of Sally Garrett.
I feel sad Cazneaux to Heysen, 19.4.1952, ANL MS 5073/1/6321–23.
Cazneaux's son Bonyhady, 27.1.2001, p. 3; Joan Smith, conversation with author, 2002.
that grand tree Cazneaux to Heysen, 19.4.1952, ANL MS 5073/1/6321–23.
page 139
knitting socks ML MSS2048/10.
rather ordinary Johnston, 1971, pp. 261–269.
page 140
Dear Everybody Gibbs, in Walsh, 1994, p. 174.
a matter of Tennant, 1956, in Torre (ed.), 1990, p. 392.

Trees of Man
page 144
the first in Australia Heyward, 1993, p. 43.
changed by the war Jacobs, 16.10.1956, in NLA MS6336/8/3.
page 145
couldn't tell colour Meyer, 1985, p. 62.
you could collect Jacobs, [193?], pp. 1, 3.
he looked shy Carron, 2000, p. 16.
aerial photographs Jacobs, 'The Discovery and Distribution of the Eucalypts', p. 10, in NLA MS6336/8/5.
page 146
Jacobs noted Jacobs, NLA MS6336/3/4.
Schlich's Manual Jacobs, in Rule, 1967, p. vii.
economically exploitable Jacobs, 'Forest Resources', p. 1, NLA MS6336/9/38.
page 147
In no other Grimwade, in Pescott, 1954, pp. ix–x.

In no continent American Museum of Natural History Annual Report, 1921, in Barrett (ed.), 1925, pp. 2–3.
rehabilitate Jacobs, 'The Discovery and Distribution of the Eucalypts', p. 7, in NLA MS6336/8/5.

page 148

developing countries Jacobs, 1956, NLA MS6336/8/3, p. 3.
by far the greatest Ziegler (ed.), 1951, p. 164.

page 149

Every hundred tons Jacobs, draft article for *CAB*, MS6336/1/16.
for the Provision Department of External Affairs, 1952.

page 150

a much larger Eather, 1952.
vigorous policy *ibid.*
the top country CSIRO Forestry Library: Sampaio de Mattos, 1952, pp. 7, 1b.

page 151

the Australian 'gum-tree' Cooper, 1876, p. 16.
in the wilds Cooper, in Zacharin, 1978, p. 111.
as a consequence CSIRO Forestry Library: Duffield, 1952, pp. 2, 6.
you got some Hurley, in Kelly, 1949, p. 13.

page 152

familiarise [themselves] CSIRO Forestry Library: *Report on the Eucalyptus Study Tour Held in Australia Sept/Oct 1952.*
'off-the-beaten-track' Eather, 1952.
a romance of industry CSIRO Forestry Library: *Masonite – A Romance of Industry.*

page 153

rather striking Wood, 1953, p. 65.
the 'magnificent eucalyptus CSIRO Forestry Library: *The Burnie Mill, A Brief Description.*
an ambassador of Eather, 1952.
whole-hearted co-operation CSIRO Forestry Library: Cromer to Jacobs, 8.11.1952.

page 154

nearly fell with Jacobs to Pryor, 24.12.1953, in NLA MS6336/9.
efficient production Métro, 1955, p. 1.

page 155

the Mysore gum Doughty, 2000, pp. 131–132.
immense plantations *ibid.*, p. 45.
first permanent site Hamilton, 1998, p. 154.
the carnivorous animals Low, 2001, p. 157.

page 156

an eyesore Douglas, 1962, pp. 110–111; thanks to Ian Brooker.
Neapolitan garden Hall and Brooker, 1978, p. 15.
the time of Caesar *E. globulus*, in Mueller, 1879–1884.

Personally I would Jacobs, p. 3, in NLA MS6336/8/5.
Eucalypt woodland *Unasylva*, vol. x, no. 3, 1956.
page 157
This was the job Frawley, in Borschmann (ed.), 1999, p. 39.
different market Jacobs, in FAO, *Unasylva*, vol. x, no. 3, 1956.
page 158
There was a museum Jacobs, 'Forestry on Catchments', NLA MS6336/8/5, p. 8.
in great measure Carron, 2000, p. 17.
one of the most Sen, in FAO, 1961, p. 1.
page 159
The 1950s push Doughty, 2000, pp. 175–176.
Experience has shown Sen, in FAO, 1961, p. 1.
Jacobs' own paper Jacobs, *ibid.*, p. 4.
differences between Elliot, in FAO, *Unasylva*, vol. xv, no. 4, 1961.
riding high Carron, 2000, p. 17.
page 160
by Jacobs' personal Byron, in Borschmann, 1999, p. 54.
The good Timor Jacobs, 1970, p. 3.
for the privilege Jacobs, 'To What Extent Should Australian Foresters Plan for National Demand', 1–5.4.1963, in NLA MS6336/9/38.
page 161
stylistically descended Smith *et al.*, 2001, p. 115.
his eyes Amadio, in Amadio (ed.), 1986, p. 6.
page 162
ochre on sheets Thomas, *ibid.*, p. 24.
Fred Williams came home Robert Gray, conversation with author, 2001.
taking up the problems Smith *et al.*, 2001, pp. 413–414, 460.
He gets closer White, in McGregor *et al.*, 1969, p. 218.
calligraphy to catch Michael Duffy, conversation with author, 2000.
likened Fred Williams' Olsen, 1997, p. 163.
being driven *ibid.*, pp. 121–122.
page 163
Australia is not Matthews, 1961, in Thornhill, 1992, p. 157.
came out all right Kelly, The People's Forest Collection, NLA TRC2845/63, 2:2:3.
arouse in [readers] Kelly, Hurley and Willis, in Kelly, 1949, pp. 11, 13, 15.
page 164
poetic licence Kelly, The People's Forest Collection, NLA TRC2845/63, 2:2:3.
an aura *ibid.*, 2:2:2.
and so I missed *ibid.*, 2:1:14.
page 165
The final column Jacobs, 'Notes relating to *Taxonomy and Nomenclature of the Eucalypts*, by Johnson and Marryatt', 1965, MS6336/3.

not an important Jacobs, 1970, p. 10.

page 166

to the extent *ibid.*

'incredible' – 'especially Zacharin, 1978, pp. 76, 79, 80.

page 167

the world's leading Yoho to Jacobs, 20.1.1970, in NLA MS6336/1/20.

The genus Eucalyptus Jacobs, 1970, p. 1.

although it is not Pryor, in FAO, 1967, p. 1002.

page 168

50 million of Jacobs, 'World Trade in Forest Products and Australia's Place Therein', 1968, NLA MS6336/9/38.

that 607,000 Krishnankutty and Chundamannil, in Sharma *et al.* (eds), 1986, p. 445.

most productive Shanmuganathan, *ibid.*, p. 22.

not a single Krishnankutty and Chundamannil, *ibid.*, p. 450.

page 169

any post-graduate Jacobs, in Carron, 1985, p. 43.

fell on 'deaf ears' Mueller, to J. D. Hooker, 16.8.1897.

In the early 1970s Legg, in Frawley and Semple (eds), 1988, p. 223.

the main destroyers Routley and Routley, 1974, p. 1.

page 170

only *trading nation* *ibid.*

a managed forest Dargavel, 1995, p. 191.

paternalistic, secretive *ibid.*, p. 163.

page 171

bitterly resented Legg, in Frawley and Semple (eds), 1988, p. 227.

Hadn't the founding Doley, in Thwaites and Schaumberg (eds), 1993, p. 1.

This is not Routley and Routley, 1974, caption photograph 21.

Trees were being ripped Murray, 1997, pp. 63, 68.

page 172

I began painting Kelly, 1978, p. vii.

Jewish schoolchildren Schama, 1996, p. 6.

a shock Kelly, The People's Forest Collection, NLA TRC2845/63, 2:2:4.

The stream Jacobs, 1979, pp. 51, 337.

page 173

a feel for Carron, 2000, p. 17.

Are we justified Joseph, in Sharma *et al.* (eds), 1986, p. 466.

careful impact studies *ibid.*, p. 473.

a strong and valid Karunakaran, *ibid.*, p. 462.

page 174

Western technical advice Sankar, *ibid.*, p. 468.

The World Bank Saxena, 1994, p. 203; Doughty, 2000, p. 176.

'marginal' at best Doughty, 2000, pp. 138–139.

fabricate ... convenient Sankar, also quoting Vandana Shiva, in Sharma *et al.* (eds), 1986, pp. 469–470.
While Bob Hawke Hutton and Connors, 1999, p. 163; Mulligan and Hill, 2001, p. 256.
page 175
In Spain and Portugal Doughty, 2000, p. 1; Jenkin, in Thwaites and Schaumberg, 1993, p. 213.
miracle trees Doughty, 2000, p.169.
no universal answer Poore and Fries (1985), in Eldridge *et al.*, 1994, p. 3.
The Eucalypt Dilemma FAO, 1988, p. 4.
upset local values *ibid.*, p. 26

With the Giants
page 178
the philosophical and Kiernan, 1976, in Hutton and Connors, 1999, p. 161.
Heaven grant that Beattie, *ibid.*, p. 76.
page 179
with a love Law, in Gee, 2001, p. 215.
I saw a hillside Geoff Law's quotes come from an author interview unless otherwise specified.
Looks like a Law, in Gee, 2001, p. 215.
page 180
small players Marr, *ibid.*, p. 174.
one of the state's Bonyhady, 23.6.2001.
from his direct Senator Bob Brown's quotes come from an author interview unless otherwise specified.
filled with wonder D'entrecasteaux, in Brown, 2001, OBC.
the reigning eucalypt Hall and Brooker, 1978, p. 53.
page 181
as old as Solness, 1999, p, 159.
already in youthful Mueller, in Griffiths, 2001, p. 20.
dark and gloomy Walker, in Gee, 2001.
Some even took Keeling, on Headspace.
page 182
Having been shown Richardson, in Solness, 2000, p. 88.
what was right Richardson, in Hutton and Connors, 1999, p. 237.
I saw what Bob Hawke, in Brown, 2001, p. 37.
It was only ANM Law, 1986, p. 15.
page 183
One of the richest *ibid.*
page 184
venerable veteran Borschmann, 1999, p. 69.
how sorry they Bonyhady, 23.6.2001.
best hardwood Les Murray, conversation with author, 2002.

page 185
Bloody telephone poles Murray, 1997, pp. 63, 61.
Fourteen trees Brown, 2001, p. 9.
Why continue Law, 1986, p. 18.
page 186
The feeling expressed Law, in Solness, 1999, p. 88.
page 187
Law could think Hutton and Connors, 1999, p. 187.
a survey Kirkpatrick *et al.*, 1988, p. 79.
fortunately, reservation *ibid.*, p. 109.
was something that Law, in Gee, 2001, p. 216.
Trident Tree stood Solness, 1999, p. 88.
page 188
a single nursery Rolls, 1990, p. 7.
Hawke planted some Woodford, 2001, p. 1.
plenty of scope Cocks, in Beale and Fray, 1990, p. 37.
between 12 and 15 TWS, 2000, p. 2.
page 189
cultural icons Solness, 1999, pp. 7–9.
For years people Law, *ibid.*, p. 88.
page 190
like a rocket Peter Solness, conversation with author, 2002.
too tall to fit Solness, 1999, p. 158.
as William Anderson Anderson, 1776, in Reed (ed.), 1969, p. 177.
page 191
half a thousand Bonyhady, 2000, p. 253.
conceding that he Mueller to Gunn, 12.6.1867.
Then New South Brown, 2001, p. 49.
page 192
no trees Marr, in Gee, 2001, p. 313.
page 193
'vandalism' meted TWS Forest Chronology, online @ www.wilderness.org.au
page 194
They discovered TWS, 2002.
Guinness Book of Records TWS, media release.
page 195
a lasting present Bellamy, in TWS, media release, 21.12.1999.
a wedge-tailed eagle's TWS, 2001.
page 196
30 million members TWS, 2000, p. 11.
the Burnie wharf Burnie Port Corporation, 2001, p. 3.
Very tall trees Forestry Tasmania, 2000.
page 197
A vast and Ellis, 27.1.2001.

They take down This description of the clearfelling process comes from Brown, 2001, p. 43.

page 198

the 1500–2000 TWS, 2000, p. 8.

Once the timber TWS Tas, conversation with author, 2002.

which fed environmentalists' Ellis, 27.1.2001.

page 199

a hundred dollars *ibid.*

overseeing the largest Law, conversation with author, 2002.

the one thing Flanagan, on Earthbeat.

more intensive management Forestry Tasmania, 'Regional Forest Agreement' 1997.

page 200

the tall eucalypts Law, on Earthbeat.

70 per cent Brown, 2001, p. 36; a poll conducted by the Wilderness Society in Tasmania showing 78 per cent of respondents opposed to old-growth logging and clearfell was released on September 11, 2001: online @ www.wilderness.com.au

premium financial returns CSIRO, media release 1999/29.

page 201

most valuable use Australian Geographic, 1996, p. 1229.

'One Tree Project' *One Tree* catalogue, 2001.

The eucalyptus oil Abbott, online @ www.fgb.com.au

page 202

simple tasks Shiel, 1985, pp. 234–235.

only 10 per cent TWS, 2000, p. 2.

one of the highest ACF, 2001, p. 3.

we European settlers Foster, in Duffy (ed.), 1997, p. 192.

Drusilla Modjeska Modjeska, 2000, p. 3.

page 203

A single sugar Rolls, 1990, p. 11.

ten gums grew Woodford, 2001, p. 1.

'Tasmania Together' Tasmania Together, 2002.

page 204

Our greatest need Foster, in Solness, 1999, p. 136.

page 205

elegant and spare Gascoigne, in Macdonald, 1998, p. 37.

The weathered grey Gascoigne, in Edwards, 1997, p. 7.

Melbourne Museum Yen *et al.*, 2002 (in press).

hundreds of such Brown, 2001, p. 31.

There is considerable Yen *et al.*, 2002 (in press), pp. 1, 2.

page 207

temporary protection order Montgomery, 26.6.2002.

no softening *Sydney Morning Herald*, 22.7.2002.

The Ancient Kingdom of Fire

page 209

a natural laboratory www.ea.gov.au/heritage/awh/worldheritage/sites/blue

page 210

in heat Foster, 1999, p. 207.

fires were burning RFS, 2002, p. 1.

Lightning, which starts Rolls, 1984, p. 250.

'Cold' lightning hort.ifas.ufl.edu/gt/lightning/lightning.html

page 211

some people suggest David Morrisson, coversation with author, 2002; Lyndsay Holme, conversation with author, 2002.

Most have bark Pyne, 1992, pp. 27–29.

peak drop *ibid.*, p. 34.

three centimetres McDonald, 2001, p. 70.

shreds of hanging Pyne, 1992, p. 34.

carried ten, twenty Gill, and Cheney, in Gill *et al.* (eds), 1981, pp. 88, 152.

page 212

They have been Beale, 2002.

fireweeds Pyne, 1992, p. 21.

are cunning David Foster, conversation with author, 2001.

brigade in Wingello Foster, 1999, p. 209.

page 213

says Lyndsay Holme Lyndsay Holme's quotes come from an author interview unless otherwise specified.

page 214

fire services watched *Daily Telegraph*, 3.1.2002.

it was kind *SMH*, 02.01.02.

page 216

In terms of Koperberg, in *SMH*, 2.1.2002.

It's a weird Koperberg, in *SMH*, 28.12.2001.

really frightening Koperberg, in *Daily Telegraph*, 29.12.2001.

page 217

people told stories *SMH*, 5–6.1.2002; 9.1.2002; *Illawarra Mercury*, 31.12.2001.

It was the key Beale, 2002.

long, monumental Geoff Luscombe's quotes come from an author interview unless otherwise specified.

page 220

The Sad Destruction *Daily Telegraph*, 12.1.2002.

universal aesthetic James (ed.), 1994, vol. i, p. iii.

page 221

91 different kinds www.ea.gov.au/heritage/awh/worldheritage/sites/blue/

primarily for their James (ed.), 1994, vol. i, p. x.

Almost two dozen *ibid.*, p. 105.

65 different sorts NSWDATA, *ibid.*, vol. ii, p. 87.

most potentially conflagrant *ibid.*, vol. i, p. 64.
essentially similar James (ed.), 1994, vol. i, p. 37.
page 222
the next geological White, 1994, p. 54.
There were humans James (ed.), 1994, vol. i, p. 38.
firestick farming Jones, in Pyne, 1992, p. xii.
sufficiently long Ashton, in Gill *et al.* (eds), 1981, p. 362.
Even in the worst Pyne, 1992, p. 33.
page 223
After the flames Gascoigne, in Macdonald, 1998, p. 63.
in the afternoon Cook, in Rolls, 1984, p. 248.
The Continent of Smoke Flannery, 1998, p. 217.
Governor Phillip arrived Phillip, 1788, in Pyne, 1992, p. 183.
in 1790 Flannery, 1999, p. 15.
a grass fire Pyne, 1992, p. 193.
everywhere on fire *ibid.*
page 224
In the northern *ibid.*, p. 180.
the mountains have Evans, 1814, in *SMH*, 31.12.2001.
fire, grass, kangaroos Mitchell, 1848, in Rolls, 1984, p. 249.
page 225
in the town Strutt, in Smith (ed.), 1990, p. 130.
across Bass Strait Pyne, 1992, pp. 221–223.
enterprising aeroplane owners Griffiths, 2001, p. 131.
blackened 15 per cent Pyne, 1992, p. 406.
page 226
H. A. Lindsay's novel Lindsay, *ibid.*, p. 253.
complete fire protection *ibid.*, p. 269.
a fire through Lane-Poole, *ibid.*, p. 267.
immutable geographic Foley, *ibid.*, p. 325.
1981 before evidence Kershaw, Clark, Gill and D'Costa, in Bradstock *et al.*, 2002, p. 3.
Black Friday *SMH*, 28.12.1994.
rewrote its Bushfires *SMH*, 5–6.1.2002.
page 227
We've known about Phil Cheney's quotes come from an author interview unless otherwise specified.
page 228
The 1994 fires CSIRO Media Release 97/227.
page 229
a benefit to cost CSIRO Media Release 2002/02.
page 230
polite explanations *SMH*, 7.1.2002.

page 231

Heavens above Koperberg, in *Daily Telegraph*, 1.1.2002.

Even the praise *SMH*, 21.1.2002.

As Geoff Luscombe *SMH*, 12.1.2002.

Phil Koperberg made Beale, 2002.

page 232

If people kept David Foster, conversation with author, 2001.

The thing that Koperberg, in Beale, 2002.

The Land Through the Leaves

page 235

cliffy and barren Banks, in Flannery, 1998, p. 219.

page 236

a hundred new Laurence and Han, 1999.

page 237

one of the last Glover's *Mt Wellington and Hobart Town* … was sold to the Tasmanian Art Gallery and Museum for $1.5m by Christies in November 2001. See Art Foundation of Tasmania, 2001.

page 238

There wasn't a day Kelly, 1995, The People's Forest Collection, NLA TRC2845/63, 2:2:8.

botany took another Hill and Johnson, 1995, pp. 185–504.

Eucalyptus papuana Brooker and Kleinig, 1999, p. 24.

Murray Bail's novel Barbara Mobbs, email to author, 2002.

page 239

14 million hectares IUFRO, 2000, online @ www.ffp.csiro.au

DNA, which suggest James Holman, conversation with author, 2002.